More Praise for *George Buttrick's Guide to*

"One can read George Buttrick's lectures on preachin[g] erudition, one can read with deep enjoyment of their wit, or one [can read with] amazement over their enduring wisdom about the theology and craft of preaching. But for whatever reason, anyone who loves good preaching, especially those who strive to be faithful in the pulpit, should read this book. The day of the 'pulpit prince' may be over, but George Buttrick's humble yet brilliant stewarding of the Word will always be in season."

—**Thomas G. Long**, Bandy Professor Emeritus of Preaching, Candler School of Theology, Emory University, Atlanta, GA

"Some of the greatest preachers of the past are in danger of being forgotten—which is why I'm so grateful whenever a publisher invests in reminding us of homiletical geniuses of former times. George Buttrick certainly deserves that accolade, and today's preachers' will certainly grow in wisdom and stature if they read, ponder, and inwardly digest Buttrick's legacy."

—**Mark Galli**, former editor in chief, *Christianity Today*

"With the advent of twenty-first-century tools for sermon preparation, one may wonder what a pulpit giant of the last century has to offer. It turns out that George Buttrick has some of the finest insights on sermon mechanics I've ever known. His phrases glow. His pastoral heart shines. His indisputably wise insights on the craft of preaching are a gift to readers who inhabit both pulpit and pew."

—**Peter W. Marty**, editor/publisher, *The Christian Century*

"We need good preaching now more than ever, and Buttrick is the master trailblazer. His warnings about illustrations alone make the book indispensable."

—**Donna Schaper**, senior minister, Judson Memorial Church, New York, NY

"Very early in these magnificent lectures, one sentence in particular leapt out at me—'the Event of Christ eventuates in a certain style of life, but preaching doesn't tell people what to do, still less what not to do.' What if preachers could have learned this indispensable lesson when George Buttrick first voiced it decades ago? Perhaps it is not too late. We can still hear his eloquent proclamation through these pages, encouraging preachers to choreograph their words artfully, as an event of Christ's encounter in the midst of worldly struggles. We can still learn from the beauty of passionate preaching that transformed living comes not from reducing biblical texts to moral lessons but from focus on the wondrous Gospel of God."

—**Paul Scott Wilson**, professor emeritus of homiletics, Emmanuel College, University of Toronto, Toronto, Canada

"Buttrick would often say, 'Just as there is beauty in a bare tree, there is beauty in a bare sentence, unadorned with adjectives.' So I say it straight and unadorned: read Buttrick! These lectures are a gift to the church and a tribute to the power of preaching."

—**Thomas R. McKibbens**, retired American Baptist minister

"As one who had the privilege of experiencing George Arthur Buttrick teaching preaching and pastoral theology in a seminary classroom, I have returned repeatedly to notes taken in Buttrick's course in order to benefit from his lessons and to gain inspiration. Studying with Buttrick was a transforming experience. I wish that every minister and seminarian could encounter insight and wisdom such as was characteristic of Buttrick's instruction. And now, Charles Davidson has brought Buttrick's famous sublime profundity to new life in this re-presentation of Buttrick's lectures. I enthusiastically recommend this volume to pastors, students, and laity alike, to all who care about the preaching of the Gospel."

—**Marion L. Soards**, professor of New Testament studies, Louisville Presbyterian Theological Seminary, Louisville, KY

"To read this gem is to experience the theological passion, intellectual sophistication, rhetorical precision, and spiritual boldness of George Buttrick, a 'preacher of preachers' in the twentieth century. But more than this, to read these lectures is to encounter the Gospel afresh and meet the crucified and risen Christ as if for the first time. Readers will turn away from these pages with the reassurance that Jesus Christ is real and declare with the apostle Paul, 'I am not ashamed of the gospel.'"

—**Luke A. Powery**, dean, Duke University Chapel, associate professor of homiletics, Duke Divinity School, Duke University, Durham, NC

"I picked up this book expecting a nostalgic trip into the history of preaching. Instead, I am struck by the contemporaneity of these lectures as Buttrick crisply, even epigrammatically, speaks of the why and how of preaching. Beyond learning this master preacher's step-by-step guide to preparing a sermon, preachers today will resonate with his concerns for the authority of preaching, for a comprehensive understanding of the gospel that embraces the social world, and for the accommodation of popular religion to the dominant culture. While today's preacher may supplement Buttrick's perspectives with more postmodern and systemic frames, this book adds a vibrant voice to the current literature of preaching."

—**Ronald J. Allen**, professor of preaching and Gospels and Letters, emeritus, Christian Theological Seminary, Indianapolis, IN

"Especially in this time when, in his own words, 'our earth is filled with death and we (some) propose that God is dead,' these wisdom teachings from George Buttrick offer guidance and hope for every preacher who seeks to offer a timely word to the waiting congregation. Every preacher needs this text. Through these lectures Buttrick offers a guide on the who, what, when, where, why, and how of preaching in a way that makes his wisdom available to every fledgling and every seasoned preacher. His teachings are biblical, deeply theological, and overwhelmingly practical such that they not only invite the reader to absorb his words but encourage movement into a life and witness that proclaim the Gospel of Jesus Christ."

—**Gennifer B. Brooks**, Ernest and Bernice Styberg Professor of Preaching, Garrett-Evangelical Theological Seminary, Evanston, IL

"Whether in his East Side Manhattan congregation or in the Memorial Church at Harvard or in the Union Seminary Chapel pulpit often occupied by Reinhold Niebuhr and Paul Tillich, George Buttrick always seemed to be reaching for the right word of witness to a word of God high and above his own capacity to reach it. He never seemed to forget that his preaching derived from one 'high and lifted up' but present to us people. As I listened to him, I often felt that Isaiah 6 was happening again."

—**Donald W. Shriver**, president emeritus, Union Theological Seminary, New York, NY

"Reading this book was like experiencing a homecoming to my preaching vocation. Buttrick's wisdom called me home, yet again, to the truth that preaching is not a single skill to be honed but a practice that emerges from the whole of ministry— richly steeped in the study of scripture, broadly conversant with a range of other literature, deeply connected to the sorrows and hopes of one's people, prophetically aligned with those who bear the burdens of poverty and injustice, attentively adaptive to a changing context, and faithfully partnered to the living God in prayer. I am refreshed and inspired by these words to go deeper into the life of my calling."

—**Kimberleigh E. Wells**, pastor, New Hope Presbyterian Church, Asheville, NC

"Forty years after his death, *George Buttrick's Guide to Preaching the Gospel* is arriving just in time. Everybody who claims to be a preacher or who dares to listen to preachers will discover in these pages that the mind and the spirit must unite if the church is to offer a powerful proclamation of good news."

—**William B. Lawrence**, professor emeritus of American church history, former dean, Perkins School of Theology, Southern Methodist University, Dallas, TX

"George Buttrick opened a Chautauqua lecture with these words: 'We are living in a dark age as far as the church is concerned.' The very word *salvation*, he continued, turns off many people today, bringing images of a preacher thundering condemnation from the pulpit. Preaching remains a ministry to a world that needs it, a continual witness to what was central to Buttrick himself: By faith God's love will find a channel through us."

—**J. A. Ross Mackenzie,** retired director, religion department, Chautauqua Institution; former professor of church history, Union Presbyterian Seminary, Richmond, VA

"In living and traveling across the United States since 1965, I have beheld numerous testimonies from Christian laity and clergy regarding the life-shaping impact of George Buttrick's profound preaching. As a skeptical academic confessed to me about hearing Buttrick at Harvard Memorial Chapel: 'In his presence, my unbelief was rendered impossible. His preaching was a miraculous antidote.'"

—**Dean K. Thompson**, president emeritus, professor of ministry emeritus, Louisville Presbyterian Theological Seminary, Louisville, KY

"Buttrick is sometimes called 'a preacher's preacher,' but when I found him finding me, it was as a doubter's preacher. When reading these lectures, I hear that croaky voice all over again and can but thank God for all he meant and still means to me."

—**Wallace M. Alston, Jr.**, minister (retired), Presbyterian Church (USA)

"This book is chock-full of wise insights about preaching from a man who was a master at it, but none is more important than this: good preaching flows from the identity and integrity of the preacher."

—**Russ Moxley**, honorary fellow, Center for Creative Leadership, Greensboro, NC

"We are four decades beyond the death of George Buttrick, a time when the memory fades and the luster of a life can diminish. It is said that the epilogue of one's life, those stories beyond one's death, will continue to echo with vibrant power for a generation or two before slipping out of consciousness in any remarkable way. But there are some whose light shined so steadily that their life is held in common memory and we can continue to celebrate the wonder of that life. George Buttrick is someone who needs to be cherished and studied, and this book is a striking work that helps those in modern times to remember and experience the depth of pastoral commitment and scholarship that is remarkable for its lasting effect."

—**Keith D. Herron**, United Church of Christ minister; adjunct professor, Central Baptist Theological Seminary; former moderator, Cooperative Baptist Fellowship

"This is a book I have been yearning for but never hoped to see, the lectures on preaching from the last decade of the life of George Buttrick, one of the greatest preachers and pastor-theologians of the twentieth century. I remember my heart racing as I heard these lectures, then racing home to talk about them. It raced again as I read these pages. It is impossible to overestimate his formative impact on my life as a preacher and pastor. There are a thousand sermon prompts in this book, and ten thousand exquisite metaphors of the Gospel. Buttrick's preaching was a Christocentric, new-form exegetical preaching that went beyond the expository and life-situation preaching of the twentieth century and anticipated the next."

—**H. Stephen Shoemaker**, pastor, Grace Baptist Church, Statesville, NC

"George A. Buttrick has influenced me for thirty years through the *Interpreter's Bible* and his book on the parables. I have consulted him in the preaching task all these years without really knowing the person. This book has opened my eyes to the vibrant life and spirit of a great preacher whom I thought I understood but did not. His guidelines for preaching the Gospel are bracing and timely."

—**J. Donald Waring**, rector, Grace Church, New York, NY

"This book opens a timely conversation with George Buttrick about preaching for a new generation. Insights? Yes. And also questions: What kind of discipline lends itself to creative 'pertinence'? Can a high Christology inspire social responsibility? Are we truly serious about preaching without a sense of humor? And, ultimately, what have we genuinely experienced of the Gospel we preach?"

—**Tim Phillips**, lead pastor, Seattle First Baptist Church, Seattle, WA

George Buttrick's
Guide to Preaching
the Gospel

Books by George Arthur Buttrick

The Beatitudes. Nashville: Abingdon Press, 1968.

Biblical Thought and the Secular University. Baton Rouge: Louisiana State University Press, 1960.

Christ and History. New York: Abingdon Press, 1963.

Christ and Man's Dilemma. Nashville: Abingdon-Cokesbury Press, 1946.

The Christian Fact and Modern Doubt. New York: Charles Scribner's Sons, 1934.

Faith and Education. New York: Abingdon–Cokesbury Press, 1952.

God, Pain, and Evil. Nashville: Abingdon Press, 1966.

The Interpreter's Bible. General Editor. 12 vols. New York: Abingdon–Cokesbury Press, 1951–1957.

The Interpreter's Dictionary of the Bible. Editor. 4 vols. New York: Abingdon Press, 1962; *Supplementary Volume*, 1976.

Jesus Came Preaching. New York: Charles Scribner's Sons, 1931.

The Parables of Jesus. New York: Harper & Brothers, 1928.

The Power of Prayer Today. Waco, TX: Word Books, 1970.

Prayer. New York: Abingdon Press, 1942.

Sermons Preached in a University Church. Nashville: Abingdon Press, 1959.

So We Believe, So We Pray. New York: Abingdon–Cokesbury Press, 1951.

George Buttrick's Guide to Preaching the Gospel

Edited by Charles N. Davidson Jr.

Abingdon Press
Nashville

GEORGE BUTTRICK'S GUIDE TO PREACHING THE GOSPEL

Copyright © 2020 by Abingdon Press

All rights reserved.

No part of this work may be reproduced or transmitted in any form or by any means, electronic or mechanical, including photocopying and recording, or by any information storage or retrieval system, except as may be expressly permitted by the 1976 Copyright Act or in writing from the publisher. Requests for permission can be addressed to Permissions, The United Methodist Publishing House, 2222 Rosa L. Parks Boulevard, Nashville, TN 37228-1306, or emailed to permissions@umpublishing.org.

Since the author is deceased, the editor and publisher made a good faith effort to identify any material that might still be held in copyright by another publisher. If a direct quotation was missed and exceeds five hundred words, and is still managed for permissions, the copyright holder should contact permissions@abingdonpress.com.

ISBN: 978-1-7910-0174-2
Library of Congress Control Number: 2020935474

Original manuscripts for chapters one through eighteen in this book are archived, as follows: George Arthur Buttrick Papers, Harvard University Archives, chapters one and two ("Lecture Series, 2 of 4," HUG FP 90.45, Box 5, manuscripts) and chapters three through eighteen ("Manuscript on Sermons," HUG FP 90.45, Box 2).

Scripture quotations unless noted otherwise are from the Common English Bible. Copyright © 2011 by the Common English Bible. All rights reserved. Used by permission. www.CommonEnglishBible.com.

Scripture quotations noted NRSV are taken from the *New Revised Standard Version of the Bible*, copyright 1989, Division of Christian Education of the National Council of the Churches of Christ in the United States of America. Used by permission. All rights reserved.

Scripture quotations marked RSV are from the Revised Standard Version of the Bible, copyright © 1946, 1952, and 1971 National Council of the Churches of Christ in the United States of America. Used by permission. All rights reserved worldwide. http://nrsvbibles.org/

Scripture quotations marked (KJV) are from The Authorized (King James) Version. Rights in the Authorized Version in the United Kingdom are vested in the Crown. Reproduced by permission of the Crown's patentee, Cambridge University Press.

20 21 22 23 24 25 26 27 28 29--10 9 8 7 6 5 4 3 2 1
MANUFACTURED IN THE UNITED STATES OF AMERICA

For all of George Arthur Buttrick's students—past, present, and future—for whom the preaching of the Gospel of Jesus Christ remains their supreme calling.

Contents

xiii Foreword by Will Willimon

xvii Editor's Preface

xxiii Editor's Introduction: Glimpses into the Life and World of One of America's Greatest Twentieth-Century Preachers

PART ONE: REASSESSMENT

3   1. We Preach the Gospel (I)

13   2. We Preach the Gospel (II)

25   3. The Power of Preaching

37   4. The New Preaching

PART TWO: PRACTICALITIES

49   5. Background Preparation

59   6. Foreground Preparation: Text and Context

67   7. Foreground Preparation: Gathering Material

77   8. Foreground Preparation: The Sermon Outline

87   9. Sermon Illustrations

99   10. The Delivery of the Sermon

PART THREE: PREACHING IN THIS TIME

- *111* 11. Preaching and Pastoral Care
- *121* 12. Preaching the Whole Gospel (Or the Nonsense Gap)
- *133* 13. Preaching to a Skeptical Time
- *143* 14. Preaching to a Dehumanized World
- *155* 15. Preaching to a Revolutionary Age (I): The Background of the Task
- *167* 16. Preaching to a Revolutionary Age (II): The Road and the Message
- *179* 17. Preaching to an Age Under Judgment: The Cross
- *193* 18. Preaching to a Death-Filled World: Resurrection

- *209* Chronology of the Life of George Arthur Buttrick
- *213* Index

Foreword

My father-in-law served Methodist churches throughout South Carolina for fifty years. During his last year of active ministry, he journeyed across the state to the Furman Pastor's School to fulfill a lifetime goal—to hear the great George Buttrick. Like many pastors around the country, Buttrick had been a partner in Mr. Parker's ministry. Though he had never met him, he owed much to Buttrick.

I was a fledgling pastor, fresh out of divinity school, intimidated by the realization that of all people, God had called me to preach. All I had to arm me for the task was Buttrick's *Jesus Came Preaching*, given to me by an older, wiser preacher who said, "Here, you'll need this."

I remember Mr. Parker's late-night telephone call reporting on the Pastor's School. "Buttrick came on stage by himself, walking with a cane. He walked up to the microphone, looked out at us, took his time, then said in his beautiful bass voice, 'God Almighty had only one son... and he made him a preacher.' Five hundred preachers left that lecture, thanking God they had been called to preach."

For decades George Buttrick served as America's Prince of Preachers, a preacher's preacher par excellence. Through the good work of Charles Davidson, we at last have the book that demonstrates what all us preachers owe to Buttrick, as well as what he has to contribute as a guide to a new generation of preachers.

This book also provides an inside look at American mainline, Protestant Christianity at the middle of the twentieth century through the lens of one of its greatest leaders. The first thing that struck me in reading this *Guide* is the confidence and self-assurance in Buttrick's teaching and thoughts on homiletics. Buttrick sounds like a preacher who is accustomed to speaking before large, thriving congregations. He strides into the pulpit of Memorial Church, Harvard, unintimidated by the academics who are baffled at why Harvard, of all places, has a church at its center. While working for much of his life in Manhattan, his strong voice is not muted at all by the cacophony coming from the city.

I was moving from high school to college during Buttrick's heyday, so for me, Buttrick's copious references to Camus and the existentialists, Barth, Broadway plays, Tillich, and psychologists and sociologists are a reminder of the path of my own intellectual development as well as some of the most important influences on my own preaching. Buttrick obviously read and digested all the important public intellectuals of the day who our professors were forcing us college students to read. It is almost unimaginable in this day and time for a preacher to be so widely read and so unashamed to display such erudition in the pulpit. Buttrick clearly had high expectations for his congregation.

Overall, one is impressed by the strength of Buttrick's convictions, his self-assurance that the Gospel of Jesus Christ is stronger and more intellectually compelling than any of the Gospel's competitors. You can imagine how encouraging it was for a new preacher, fresh from the barricades of the antiwar movement, to encounter a preacher who saw the pulpit as a place to go head-to-head with the powers that be. In confronting racial injustice in America, Buttrick said that preachers must preach what Christ tells them to preach, "at whatever risk of loss in membership." Buttrick's view of the American church, mid-century, is that it is a sleeping giant with vast untapped potential. He attempts to stir the church to action by telling it that the church has the greatest chance of being "an inclusive fellowship" because it's the only group in town where we, in spite of our human differences, "can kneel together and pray, '*Our* father.'"

What a master of language. His pulpit speech is elegant but still strong, visceral, every word chosen with care and deep respect for speech. After narrating a sad story about lonely Rupert Brooke setting sail with no one to bid him farewell, Buttrick muses, "Our human voyage is a still lonelier

Foreword

affair. The ship of this strange planet—should we say of the cosmos?—plunges on its way with no apparent port of departure, for nobody knows how or where or why our human life began; and no apparent port of arrival, for every passenger is buried in the deep. We are on a lonely voyage."

How long has it been since you've heard that sort of lofty rhetoric from the pulpit? Perhaps you will say that Buttrick sounds dated and his exalted pulpit presence and speech wouldn't be tolerated today. Perhaps. Maybe you don't hear preaching like Buttrick's because we contemporary homiliticians are not as adept in the language, too shaky and uncertain in the pulpit, inadequately backed by a theology worth telling. Perhaps we have sold our congregations short, something Buttrick never does.

You'll see, in these pages, how Buttrick's sophisticated language was enlisted for rough and tumble interaction with the pressing social issues of the day. He spoke up for racial justice when few prominent white preachers would. As a student antiwar activist, I remember someone giving me a sermon by Buttrick, which was a blistering attack on the Vietnam War. "There's a preacher somewhere up North who talks like this?" I marveled.

Here's Buttrick duking it out with one of his favorite sparring partners, political conservatives: "Those who would have the American church 'stay out of politics' are quickest to deplore the fact that the church in Russia did not oppose the Lenin revolution, and that the church in Germany did not oppose Hitler. Both churches were more concerned about ritual and theology than about the sorrows of the poor. Then what about the failure of the American church to speak with clear voice about war, racism, and poverty? Actually, the conservatives are quite ready to hear *their* politics and *their* economics from the preacher's lips.... So the millionaire backers of Billy Graham raised no serious objection when the evangelist invited President Nixon to make a political speech in a Knoxville revival meeting."

When Buttrick talked with preachers, pastors heard him as a fellow-worker who, though he had preached in America's most prestigious pulpits, knew firsthand what it's like to summon the courage and to hone the gifts necessary to speak up for God on a regular basis.

Listen to Buttrick joshing his fellow preachers by gently mocking, "The *pudding-bowl sermon* begins and ends well, but sags in the middle.

The *igloo sermon* begins and ends badly, but climbs in the middle. The *begin-with-an-explosion sermon* is like fireworks: a brilliant flash soon lost in darkness. The *airfield-runway sermon* is a stay-there level flatness: the plane takes off, but the runway never."

This master of apropos illustrations warns, "An illustration should be interesting, but not too interesting. If it is not interesting, it doesn't illustrate; if it is too interesting, it distracts." You'll enjoy watching this well-read master of sermon illustration show us how it's done.

As you read Buttrick's sermons, lectures, and writing as presented here, you will undoubtedly ask, as a companion once inquired, "George, how have you managed to get so much done?"

Buttrick paused for a moment and answered, "Jesus Christ is more real to me than I am to myself."

That's it. He was a master wordsmith and elegant orator and had a brilliant, well-stocked mind, but perhaps the most enduring gift Buttrick can give us is to show that preaching is meant to be christological, the risen Christ really speaking to Christ's people through a real preacher. The living Christ shines throughout Buttrick's work and helps explain his pulpit confidence and theological conviction. His words, eloquent as they are, are not his. As Buttrick's companion commented, "He didn't just run on his own steam."

We preachers, attempting to bring the same Gospel to speech in a very different time from Buttrick's could have no more sagacious, encouraging guide through our present preaching challenges than George Buttrick.

Will Willimon

Editor's Preface

In 1986, I was visiting New York City. With some time to spare, I walked down to Madison Avenue Presbyterian Church, where George Buttrick had held forth for twenty-eight years before going to Harvard as preacher to the university. I wanted to stand for a few moments beneath the pulpit from which he had preached to the folk who lived in the poor ethnic neighborhoods surrounding the church, which was the vast majority of the congregants, as well as to the privileged few who lived well-heeled on Park Avenue.

But before I entered the sanctuary, I stood alone gazing up at the portrait of Dr. Buttrick hanging on the wall above the vestibule door when an elderly woman, leaning on her cane, came hobbling up to me. The scant words that tumbled from her mouth were these:

"Did you know Dr. Buttrick?" she asked.

"Yes, ma'am, I did. Did you happen to know him too?"

"Yes, I did," she said.

"Well, what did you think of him, if I may ask?"

"He was *profound*," she said.

And she turned and hobbled away and left me standing there as though I'd come solely to hear her say that one single word *profound*, and then I was free to go.

Over the course of three decades and counting, I've heard that same word applied to George Buttrick at least a dozen times. So I decided that I must do far more than simply remember him myself and therefore must pass on to you and to generations to come something of what I'd learned from him and about him. Better yet, to pass on to you, coming directly from him, a gift of great value. So that is the reason for these lectures on preaching from the final decade and a half of his life as he had given them in the classroom and at speaking engagements around the country, even as he was constantly in the process of revising them.

It's now *your chance* to sit at his feet. *Your chance* to "hear" this masterful preacher whom many other twentieth-century preachers across America called the "preacher's preacher." *Your chance* to encounter one whose voice, words, and summons to faith were so distinctly irresistible that many of us, blessedly graced to hear him ourselves, simply could not let go of him. Or, truthfully, in some mystical sense, he could not let go of us. As he preferred to say of himself, having been possessed of Christ, in the words of Saint Paul, "Woe is me if I preach not."

My first encounter with George Buttrick was as a college student in 1965, when he showed up one evening to give a lecture. Until that point I had never heard of him. His lecture was remarkable not only for what he said to us and how he said it but also for the fact that, for reasons still incomprehensible, he packed the place out. Every seat taken. The staircases and window sills of the forum hall, filled. Standing room only. And at the conclusion, a standing ovation. For a *preacher*? From an unlikely lot of largely areligious, at least *apparently* areligious, college kids who for the most part had deserted attending voluntary chapel services because there were plenty of other things on their minds besides God and Jesus and some traveling preacher they'd never heard of? How come so many showed up at 8 p.m. to hear him? Well, I'll never know.

Yet, this is how he closed out his lecture:

> Ships take their bearings not from flickering shore lights or from passing vessels but from the stars. No ship has any right to turn the ocean lanes into a shambles. Meanwhile every ship hearing an individual SOS must go at once to the point of need. Thus another parable. "Set your affection on things above"![1] We read that word, and take it for an amiable piety, whereas it is the only salvation. Without that word the strange paradox of our human life has neither cleansing nor hope. The answer is not on the horizontal

---

1. Col 3:2 (KJV).

Editor's Preface

line: it is on the vertical line. You say that we may again and again misread the "mind of the Spirit"? Not again and again; not if we pray in loneliness and with our friends. Sometimes we may fail, but not if we are faithful. But, of course, we "have this treasure in earthen vessels, that the glory may be of God lest any man should boast." Meanwhile he has the vessel in his hands![2]

༺ ༺ ༺

Welcome to these pages containing the final version of George Buttrick's lectures on the teaching of preaching to those called of Christ to proclaim the Gospel. Dr. Buttrick had them virtually publication ready, yet for reasons beyond his control they were not published before his death. It is an honor for me to have had the privilege of editing them and adding an introduction, thanks to permissions granted by George Buttrick's son, the late David Buttrick, and family descendants who retain publication rights to the Buttrick papers.

The reader should note that the footnotes and annotations to George Buttrick's chapters are mine. That task would normally have belonged to Agnes Buttrick had the lectures been published during her lifetime. Since not, the privilege has fallen to me along with responsibility for any omissions and errors.

Enormous gratitude is due Abingdon Press's Paul Franklyn, associate publisher, and Katherine Johnston, production editor, for their extensive work in guiding this project and bringing it to fruition. Abingdon was George Buttrick's publisher for many years, and he wished that it be so for these lectures. I am also immensely grateful to the Louisville Institute of Louisville, Kentucky, which funded the research for this book with a pastoral study grant, as part of a larger project still in the works, a biography of George Arthur Buttrick (1892–1980). Not least, I offer my sincere thanks for the kindness of the dedicated staff of the Harvard University

---

2. "Faith, Individual, and Community," a lecture given to the faculty and student body of Hampden-Sydney College in Virginia, Tuesday, March 23, 1965, 8 p.m. (George Arthur Buttrick Papers, Harvard University Archives, "Lectures bound together in binder," HUG FP 90.45, Box 5, manuscripts), 9. Hereafter, Harvard archival documents cited by call number only.

Archives, without whose invaluable assistance I would not have been able to examine the entirety of the Buttrick papers.

There are many other persons, all of whom I would name if space provided, who accompanied me through this journey in one way or another. Some were listening partners in conversation, some critical readers, and still others, including numerous individuals who contributed content by sharing their knowledge and stories of Buttrick, and even class notes, having been his students and graduate assistants as well as friends and companions in the last months of his life. Yet there is one person I shall name specifically, the late Dr. James H. Smylie, professor of church history at Union Presbyterian Seminary in Virginia, who in 1974 guided me through my first deep probing into the life and ministry of George Buttrick, for which I shall remain ever so thankful.

Special thanks, too, to members of the Buttrick and Gardner families, including grandchildren and great-grandchildren, nieces and nephews, who shared rich and abundant memories and memorabilia of George and Agnes Buttrick and their relatives. I especially want to name my dear wife, Georganne Spruce, who has been a steadfast partner throughout, including during the three months of daily reading and photographing of documents at Harvard, and for her applying her discerning eye to the manuscript with all the good sense and considerable skill of a retired English teacher who cherishes the written word, and who is a fine author in her own right.

As a footnote, yet an important one, George Buttrick had a natural and genuine gift for relating to persons of all walks of life and, not least, to children. I have heard some of those recollections of his sitting on the floor with little ones and telling them stories as he entered their worlds of fantasy and innocent delight. He even drew pictures for them. (His artistry with his ink pen was exquisite, visible in the meticulous and beautifully hand-scripted notebooks he kept from his days in high school and college, for they could well now be museum pieces.) One woman sent me an original drawing of penciled figures that he drew for her when she was but a little girl living with her parents on the mission field in India, and Buttrick was the visiting preacher. Her mother saved the paper for her

Editor's Preface

daughter and for posterity. The Buttrick archive also contains a page with drawings of animal "friends" that accompanied the bedtime stories that George told his three sons. It seems that he had more than taken to heart the very words of Jesus who said, "Let the children come to me, and do not hinder them; for to such belongs the kingdom of heaven."[3]

So now, but one question remains. What will you, dear reader, make of these gems from the dedicated life of scholarship and preaching and teaching ministry of George Buttrick, who through the years had an extraordinary devotion to training pastors in the art and craft and importance of their calling? His words are profoundly pertinent to the time in which we currently live. Will you, like the children of whom Jesus speaks, allow George Buttrick to suffer you unto Christ as well? There is no hindrance here. The doors are open. George will gladly shepherd you the Way in.

Charles N. Davidson Jr.
Asheville, North Carolina

---

3. Matt 19:14 (RSV).

EDITOR'S INTRODUCTION

Glimpses into the Life and World of One of America's Greatest Twentieth-Century Preachers

Charles N. Davidson Jr.

I—The Belly of a Whale Called Home

George Arthur Buttrick, the thirty-nine-year-old senior minister of Manhattan's Madison Avenue Presbyterian Church, standing trim in his five-foot-nine frame, is glancing with his head slightly bent toward his audience at the Yale University Divinity School, his face bearing the look of his customary solemn reserve. His British accent, "rich and full, has that baritone register ideal for a public speaker, but with an occasional tremolo, just perceptible as though the human pathos or reverent awe enshrined in the soul was escaping from its shrine and finding wings in speech."[1] He begins:

---

1. George T. Wood, "Studies of the American Pulpit: Rev. George Arthur Buttrick," *The Homiletic Review* 92, no. 6 (Dec. 1926): 435–36. To hear the voice of George Buttrick preaching and lecturing, go to Princeton Theological Seminary Library's digital collections at http://diglib.ptsem.edu and search for "George Buttrick."

Editor's Introduction

> In New York City church buildings are dwarfed by skyscrapers. Here and there a church has been swallowed in an office structure and lives in a commercial stomach, a tenant on sufferance, somewhat as Jonah lived in the whale. That fact may be portent.[2]

Unlike the stained-glass windows adorning many a steepled edifice, "our preacher," the guest lecturer on this occasion, does not paint a rose-colored picture. Neither does his image of "dwarfed" and "swallowed" church buildings augur well for Christians gathered for the worship of God beneath colossal strongholds of capitalism towering over them. There's even the hint of apocalyptic foreboding.

> Probably the pulpit has never seemed a strong tower; but in our age, with its journals, its "talkies," and its radios all dictating opinion and reporting the gossip of the world, preaching appears to many eyes to have shrunk to a futility.[3]

The topic for the first of Buttrick's eight lectures during the week promises to be of particular interest to those waiting and wondering, like Jonah: "Is There Room for the Preacher Today?"

By no means is Buttrick confining his remarks to city-dwellers like himself, who at eleven o'clock on a Sunday morning in midtown Manhattan may be sitting in a pew or speaking from the chancel of a Greek, Romanesque, or Victorian sanctuary along Fifth, Park, or Madison Avenue. Any "shelter of the Most High" that casts a "shadow of the Almighty" across the pavement could conceivably be a "tenant on sufferance" just about anywhere on earth.[4]

---

2. George A. Buttrick, *Jesus Came Preaching: Christian Preaching in the New Age* (New York: Charles Scribner's Sons, 1931), 3. The book comprises Buttrick's Lyman Beecher Lectures delivered at Yale Divinity School, Monday through Friday the week of April 12, 1931. "Chapters I, IV, VI, and VIII were given, in an early and different form, at Gettysburg Seminary also, in the spring of 1930" (*Jesus Came Preaching*, ix).

3. Buttrick, *Jesus Came Preaching*, 3–4.

4. Ps 91:1-2 (NRSV): "You who live in the shelter of the Most High, who abide in the shadow of the Almighty, will say to the Lord, 'My refuge and my fortress; my God, in whom I trust.'"

Editor's Introduction

So, how is this archetypal tenant's presence in the city to be characterized? And what if the said "leaseholder" happens to be not only the congregation itself but notably the person lodged in the pulpit?

> Does the preacher now impress us as a "legate of the skies"? To many he is a pathetic figure, an anachronism, a stage-joke—an inoffensive little man jostled by the crowd, and wearing the expression of a startled rabbit. With one hand he holds a circular hat on a bewildered head and with the other desperately clutches an umbrella. The crowd pushes him from the sidewalk; the traffic shoots him back into the crowd. Some curse him; a few laugh; most are unaware of his existence.[5]

You might say that this whimsical caricature does not bear a flattering resemblance to the "man of the cloth" presently giving the distinguished Lyman Beecher Lectures on the campus of this exalted Ivy League university—irrespective of the fact that he's speaking before an assembly of esteemed alumni, students, faculty, and clergy colleagues, some of whom, substantially older and dowdier than he, may fit the picture.

II—Servant of the Poor Man from Nazareth

The fact is that Buttrick's spiritual discernment, his penetrating mind and unimpeachable moral fiber—his "cloth"—stemmed from humble beginnings.

The son of an itinerant English Primitive Methodist minister from Durham and an Anglican Scots mother from Aberdeen, George was born and reared in his early years in Seaham Harbour of Northumberland, "a wretched little seaport town" ninety miles south of the Scottish border. "It was a village of poor people, radically poor."[6] The working-class "Harbour" flats stood a steep drop below the upper-crust cliffs of "Seaham" where the

---

5. Buttrick, *Jesus Came Preaching*, 4.

6. Davidson/David G. Buttrick oral history interview, March 24, 2016 (8). "Wretched little seaport town" was George Buttrick's own description of Seaham Harbour, according to his son David, who had visited the town to see it for himself. All oral history interviews will hereafter be cited as "interview."

big money was.[7] Firsthand knowledge of the poverty and destitution of the folk who lived on that *lower berth* were what gave George his lifetime love for the poor and his keen knack for knowing just how to relate to them.

Madison Avenue Presbyterian's membership during the years of the Great Depression consisted of 800 families on "home relief" with no income, 1,200 families of "low, low income," and "200 families on Park Avenue," said David, the youngest of the three Buttrick sons.[8] It was "a poor person's church, and that was the attraction that got my father."[9] "The staff went up and down Park Avenue to get money for the other families."[10] "Father loved calling on the poor families on Madison Avenue. He had a way with them."[11]

Buttrick was meticulously methodical and industrious, working sixteen-hour days routinely, beginning with mornings in the office studiously absorbed in reading, thought, and preparation, which encompassed translating Hebrew and Greek texts into English. He constructed his entire sermon outline in minuscule handwriting bled of blue and red ink on a single legal-size sheet of paper divided neatly and orderly into multiple compartments crowded with notes, references, asterisks, checkmarks, and ruled lines crisscrossing the page. Like a hawk perched in a treetop, he could zero in on every aspect of the task that lay at hand. If for some incongruous reason God had been so inclined that Buttrick, a lifelong pacifist, become an army general planning troop movements, locations, and battlements, then not a single soldier would have failed to know exactly where to be, exactly what to do, and exactly in what order and what time to do it.

---

7. Davidson/David G. Buttrick interview, October 16, 2014 (35) and March 24, 2016 (8).

8. Davidson/David G. Buttrick interview, October 14, 2014 (17). George Arthur Buttrick and Agnes Gardner Buttrick's three sons: John Arthur Buttrick, economist and professor (1919–2007), George Robert Buttrick, minister and pastor (1923–2007), David Gardner Buttrick, minister and professor (1927–2017).

9. Davidson/David G. Buttrick interview, March 24, 2016 (7).

10. Davidson/David G. Buttrick interview, October 14, 2014 (17).

11. Davidson/David G. Buttrick interview, October 14, 2014 (21).

Editor's Introduction

"Faithlessness in the week's work will show like a blight when Sunday comes—for it is a blight. But faithfulness is its own strong faith. It breeds its own convictions. In short, we are required to live a disciplined life,"[12] which for Buttrick included afternoons and often evenings ringing doorbells.

"Father made over 1,000 calls a year."[13] He once dictated a letter to the rector of the Church of the Epiphany in Washington, DC, confessing a venial sin that few pastors would ever find any need to pardon.

> As my wife told you over the phone, I work at the rate of some thirty appointments, big and little, each week, and have not missed an appointment for twelve or fifteen years. Probably I needed this sickness for the "mortification of the flesh," but I am chagrined that the mortification should have involved my failing you. Please forgive me.[14]

Yet there was one thing that was far less forgiving or forgivable. It was the fact that the ethnic diversity of the church's surrounding neighborhoods had fallen deeper into the economic doldrums of the 1930s. Recalling those boyhood years himself, David Buttrick reflected,

> New York at that time was an immigrant city, and blocks would fill up according to the nationality. One family would come over. They invite the others, and they all get in the same block—those brownstone slums that are now filled with stockbrokers.[15] Sixty-eighth Street, that's where Hungarians lived. Seventy-first where I was, was Czechoslovakian but they let me play stick ball in the streets with them.[16]

Stick ball or no stick ball, scavenging for daily crumbs and leftovers on the margins of America's affluence was not to be confused with the

---

12. Buttrick, *Jesus Came Preaching*, 185.

13. Davidson/David G. Buttrick interview, October 16, 2014 (3). Buttrick worked nine months of the year at the church and spent the summer months of June, July, and August preparing lectures and writing books at the family home on Lake Charlevoix in Michigan, with periodic travel for lecturing and preaching.

14. Letter to the Rev. Charles D. Kean, March 9, 1954 (Washington, DC, General Engagements, HUG FP 90.8/1, Box 30).

15. Davidson/David G. Buttrick interview, October 14, 2014 (17).

16. Davidson/David G. Buttrick interview, March 3, 2016 (8).

Editor's Introduction

"margins" of speculation that had wildly bid up stock prices on Wall Street till their fatal day of collapse on Black Tuesday, October 29, 1929.

Buttrick deemed it imperative for anyone who was a servant of the poor man from Nazareth to speak up, and, if need be, brazenly so on behalf of the jobless, and even for the sake of the ones lucky enough to have a job.

> Industry... is so monotonous in some of its processes that one wonders if it can breed any but monotonous folk—the light within their brains blown out. It denies to workers even the small privilege of ballot to help determine the conditions of their toil. It compels them to live under the menace of unemployment so that today there are millions out of work in this Republic—a calamity directly affecting not less than one-fourth of the population of the richest nation in all history. Its gains are so unequally distributed that there are (without any exaggeration of language) the most glaring disparities of wealth and poverty, such that, if we had eyes to see, the residential area of any great city would appear as the flush on the cheek of a consumptive. To this impasse has the profit-motive in industry brought us! Should the preacher speak? One wonders, at times, if it is not too late. One hears the travailing multitudes saying to the Church, "Sleep on now and take your rest."[17] One hears an ominous rumbling, sees the gathering gloom, and fears the temple-veil of our social order may be rent in twain. Pray God it is not too late![18]

That would ordinarily be enough to open the ears of any divinity school audience in case it had fallen asleep. But, if not, then this:

> What is it to be a Christian? To accept the "cup of salvation"? To cultivate the walled garden of the soul? Yes. But that is not all: to be Christian is to take up one's own cross. Not merely one's burden; we are conscripted to carry burdens: there is no escaping them. But we volunteer to carry crosses.[19] Crosses are other people's burdens—the shame of our city streets, the oppressions of industry, the loneliness of the immigrant, the guilt of the imprisoned, the pangs of the unemployed and the sorrows of war.[20]

---

17. Buttrick, *Jesus Came Preaching*, 101. With reference to "Sleep on now and take your rest," Buttrick inserted a footnote here, reading, "Matthew 26:45 and parallel passages."

18. Buttrick, *Jesus Came Preaching*, 100–101.

19. Buttrick's paraphrase of ch. 19 (the R. R. Smith publisher's edition) of "The Mark of the Disciple," in W. M. Clow, *The Cross in Christian Experience* (New York: Hodder and Stoughton, 1911; preface, 1908).

20. Buttrick, *Jesus Came Preaching*, 108.

And one more thing about being Christian.

> Certainly the Church, at whatever risk of loss in membership, must be made an inclusive fellowship. The compassing of that end, even if no direct mention were ever made of social needs, would be in itself an allaying of social bitterness glorious to behold. There is no other inclusive fellowship. A labor union or an employer's association is not inclusive: each in its own camp caters to those who make common cause in economic theory. A fraternal order is not inclusive: its ritual is secret. A luncheon club is not inclusive: its mind is notoriously standardized. A school is not inclusive: it sets limits of age. Most churches are not inclusive: they minister, perhaps of necessity, to a group—university, suburban, or artisan. But of all institutions the Church alone has chance to become inclusive, for only the Church builds on the common denominator of human life—on the sense of God. City churches especially have a great gift to bestow if they so order their life that, in a sacred place beyond the bitterness of class and racial strife, men can kneel together to pray "*Our* Father."[21]

"Racism offended Father."[22] "He met every two or three weeks in a restaurant on 125th Street with black pastors. It continued through his entire twenty-eight years in New York City."[23] "He never let go of that one. He said that in his 'wretched little seaport town' of Seaham Harbour, if a black face showed up, they were honored as part of the Queen's empire."[24]

And, if part of the queen's realm, then why not part of Christ's for reasons not attributable to perishable empires, yet having everything to do with an imperishable "kingdom not from this world"[25] impinging upon this one.

III—Traveling outside the Bounds

Not far from his first boyhood home in the heart of John Wesley country, George Buttrick received the degree of bachelor of arts with honors

---

21. Buttrick, *Jesus Came Preaching*, 105–6.
22. Davidson/David G. Buttrick interview, October 14, 2014 (21).
23. Davidson/David G. Buttrick interview, March 24, 2016 (7).
24. Davidson/David G. Buttrick interview, October 14, 2014 (21).
25. John 18:36 (NRSV).

in philosophy from the "poor kid's college, namely Manchester."[26] But prior to the end of his course of studies, he abruptly changed direction. His father, Tom, had avowed that George *would* become something other than a preacher, such as a doctor or lawyer.[27] So he "forbade the choice" of ministry for his son.[28]

Is there not a discordant voice somewhere within every would-be disciple, a voice of noblest intent that invariably sounds just like the voice of home?

"Home was irksome; its freedom carried restraints," George noted more than a decade later, as if speaking with subconscious projection of himself upon the parable of the prodigal about which he was preaching. "The boy craved a freedom without restraints. The loving rule of his father fretted him. Life beckoned. There were entrancing worlds beyond the disciplines of home. Home would not be home to a boy of alien will. The boy must first find himself."[29]

Just so, the boy began to hear an intensifying whisper from deeper within.

> It is doubtful if any man ever did choose Christ except as Christ had first chosen him. For myself, I did not choose Christ, but tried to avoid Him. I tried not to be a preacher: I could see the glory in Christ, but was impatient with the pettiness of the church and had not then eyes to see beyond the pettiness. I never wished to make much money (I always had sense enough to see that would be a nuisance), but hoped to have enough: an honorable life in the British Civil Service, perhaps, with some liberty to write, and (on the side) reverence for Christ as a private devotion. But He chose me for a preacher—not an easy life if a man would be even half-honest. Here I am,

---

26. Davidson/David G. Buttrick interview, October 14, 2014 (2). David said that Manchester was known throughout as "the poor kid's college." His major professor was the philosopher Samuel Alexander (1859–1938), who wrote the widely acclaimed book *Space, Time, and Deity*.

27. Davidson/David G. Buttrick interview, October 15, 2014 (5).

28. From an unsigned Buttrick family memoir furnished by David Buttrick, depicting George Buttrick's life during his years, 1921–1927, as minister of Old First Presbyterian Church, Buffalo, New York (hereafter cited as "Buffalo memoir").

29. George A. Buttrick, *The Parables of Jesus* (New York: Harper & Brothers Publishers, 1928), 189–90.

Editor's Introduction

trying to speak for Him, understanding what Paul meant when he said: "Woe is me if I preach not."[30]

George's turn to the study of theology resulted in a coil-like tautness between himself and his father, and for some years to come. Yet the tension did not lack for the mutually desired reconciliation that in due time released them both from the breach that had become their bind. His mother, Jessie, "a little woman with wit and a splendid sense of humor," no doubt had more than just a "little" to do with the outcome. Without a victory laurel to place as crown upon the head of either of the two male combatants, her presence at least provided a calming effect upon the "eloquent if somewhat stubborn man" to whom she was married.[31]

Traveling outside the bounds of Primitive Methodism, George found a new spiritual home among the English Congregationalists. The fact that he was already receiving his university education at Manchester's Lancaster Independent Theological College, founded in the nineteenth century for the training of Non-conformist Congregational ministers, played no small part in his decision to become sufficiently nonconforming himself. Which is to say: to obtain "eyes to see" beyond any "pettiness of the church" for the sake of welcoming the yoke of Christ upon his own shoulders. "The sword of the spirit is moved only by its hand of flesh," he said.[32] That same spirit that lifted George's hand to the plow.

While digging around to unearth the meanings of classic philosophical treatises, like those of Kant and Hume on one side of the plow, and on the other side ancient biblical texts that are the "pearls of great price" buried among the rest of Christly treasures a preacher might discover, Buttrick joined the Albion Congregational Church of Hull. And there the speed of his plow gathered considerable momentum. For there he met the

---

30. George A. Buttrick, "The Heart of the Matter," sermon preached at MAPC, Feb. 27, 1949 (HUG FP 90.42, Sermons, Box 11, M.A. 1550, 2–3). "Woe is unto me, if I preach not" (1 Cor 9:16, AKJV).

31. Buffalo memoir. David Buttrick remembered visits from his grandparents and confirmed the conflict between his father and grandfather over George's choice of vocation.

32. Buttrick, *Jesus Came Preaching*, 19.

xxxi

bright, lovely young Agnes Gardner, who eventually would become his wife. Her father, John Gardner, was minister of the church.

In April 1912, "Mr. Buttrick was received into Church Fellowship at the April Communion."[33] In September, when the Rev. Gardner sailed off for a preaching tour in America, never to return again to England except to visit, the young George, now *student* minister, assumed the Albion pulpit. The local Congregational association magazine noted the date: "Mr. G. Buttrick preached in the morning on September 15th."[34] And thus began the pilgrimage that by 1927 had led across the sea and into the "whale's belly" of New York City, following brief pastorates in Congregational churches of Quincy, Illinois, and Rutland, Vermont, and then a Presbyterian one at Old First Church of Buffalo, New York.[35]

IV—Shell-Shocked

War is no respecter of persons when it comes to the victims of its deadly pestilence. To one degree or another it takes a toll on just about everybody by the time the troops come marching home from places like Tannenberg, Jutland, Gallipoli, Verdun, and the Somme. The Great War "to end all wars"[36] was no breezy exception.

George's father, a staunch pacifist and conscientious objector, had refused to pay taxes that supported the earlier Second Boer War, when the British invaded the Republic of Transvaal in South Africa with some four hundred thousand troops.[37] That salvo was a first employing the

---

33. *The Congregational Magazine*, May 1912, "a publication of the regional association of Congregational churches around Hull," as stated in historical notes by John Buttrick, George and Agnes Buttrick's oldest son, and shared by his brother, David Buttrick.

34. *The Congregational Magazine*, October 1912.

35. First Union Congregational Church of Quincy, IL, 1915–1918; the Congregational Church of Rutland, VT, 1919–1921; and Old First Presbyterian of Buffalo, NY, 1921–1927.

36. A refrain from World War I, derived from and paraphrasing H. G. Wells, *The War That Will End War* (London: Frank & Cecil Palmer, 1914).

37. Second Boer War, October 11, 1899–May 31, 1902. In a letter dated December 3, 1974, to Benjamin E. Shove of Camillus, NY, George Buttrick wrote, "I have opposed four wars during my long life. My wife's father and my father (both English preachers) refused to

Editor's Introduction

widespread use of concentration camps as part of a scorched-earth policy that ravaged and destroyed just about everything by way of daily sustenance for an entire population. The ensuing controversy rattled the pulpits and pews of the Primitive Methodist churches.[38]

Tom Buttrick was among the minority of his fellow PMs accused of lowering the flag of the British empire. His not-quite-yet preadolescent son George retained an indelible memory of the day government officials arrived at the house to confiscate the family clocks in reprisal for Tom's adherence to what he believed was Christ's clear conscience about the nonuse of the sword.[39] From that moment on, in at least one respect that his father hadn't forbidden, George Buttrick was destined to follow in Tom Buttrick's footsteps.

A fledgling YMCA chaplain's assistant assigned to an ambulance unit of a British army regiment fighting in the European theater of the "Great War" was all but guaranteed to receive a surefire gate ticket to the killing fields of hell. "In Britain they use conscientious objectors on the front lines hauling people away from the battle."[40] The human carnage was mind-shattering. Ten shell-shocked days of the ghastly unmentionable had come close to shattering George's life as well.[41]

Down through the years the topic of the First War remained largely off-limits to those who inquired of Dr. Buttrick about it. Even family apparently knew it best not to ask too many probing questions, like the kind that children ask: How did it go? What did you see? Were you ever scared?

---

pay taxes to wage the Boer War. Our sons and now our grandson have taken the same stance" (HUG FP 90.9/2, Box 13).

38. See references to the Second Boer War in Michael Hughes, "British Methodists and the First World War," *Methodist History*, 41, no. 1 (October 2002): 317–18. http://archives.gcah.org/bitstream/handle/10516/6554/MH-2002-October-Hughes.pdf?sequence=1&isAllowed=y.

39. Interview granted Charles Davidson by George and Agnes Buttrick, April 1–2, 1974 (hereafter cited as "George Buttrick Interview"). The interview was in conjunction with Davidson's ThM thesis, "George Arthur Buttrick: The Christocentric Preacher and Interpreter of History" (Union Theological Seminary, Richmond, VA, May 1974).

40. Davidson/David G. Buttrick interview, October 14, 2014 (14).

41. George Buttrick Interview. Ten days was the extent of his deployment. See Charles N. Davidson Jr., "George Arthur Buttrick: Christocentric Preacher and Pacifist," *Journal of Presbyterian History* 53, no. 2 (Summer 1975): 144.

Editor's Introduction

Did you witness any people getting killed? What was it like carrying off cots of men bleeding to death? Did you lead the troops in prayer? Did you hold a soldier's hand as he took his last breath? Did you ever cry yourself?[42]

He didn't even share so much as where he was located, though "probably France. Maybe he made it to the Maginot Line, who knows? And survived."[43]

Years later, in conversation, having let his guard down ever so slightly, and in more detail than his pacifist sons were able to share, he confided in his secretary. She wrote in her diary, "He said in the first war he had a throat affliction which caused the Doctor to say 'You'll never preach.' It was a pretty hard pill to swallow—but out of it he learned that God's will is sovereign—and first thing he knew after that he was preaching."[44]

The cause of the affliction? Unspecified. The likely cause? Poisonous gas.

His doctor recommended that upon discharge he travel to the United States to be with the Gardner family for his convalescence, or, as the increasingly feeble George said in his old age while looking back and reminiscing, "I chased a woman across the ocean."[45]

Foolishly or not, just before setting sail on the SS *St. Paul* from Liverpool to Ellis Island, arriving dockside July 11, 1915, he sat for his honors philosophy exams at Victoria University for four grueling days, writing in longhand a battery of sixteen hours' worth of essays that demanded anything but short-minded answers to complicated questions.

Consider a few of the eighteen topical requirements he checkmarked as having satisfactorily explored:

1. "Does the recognition of the gradual development of moral ideals invalidate the belief in an absolute moral standard?" (Parenthetically, war complicates the answer.)

---

42. George Buttrick revealed only cursory, general details during his interview with Charles Davidson, April 1–2, 1974.

43. Davidson/David G. Buttrick interview, March 24, 2016 (21).

44. *Elizabeth Stouffer Diaries: 1932–2007*, inclusive (Schlesinger Library, Radcliffe Institute, Harvard University), Sunday, March 4, 1945.

45. George Buttrick Interview. Agnes Gardner, the daughter of John Gardner, who became Buttrick's wife.

Editor's Introduction

2. "In what sense, if any, can an action be really disinterested?" (Does the question mean in war, too?)

3. "Against what, precisely, is the 'Refutation of Idealism' directed, and how far is it successful?" (With explicit reference to Immanuel Kant, please.) (Oh, some say war solidifies the refutation, and that pacifism takes the bullet.)

4. "'There must be some third thing, which on the one side is homogeneous with the category, and with the phenomenon on the other, and so makes the application of the former to the latter possible.' Discuss this." (Now, for a budding preacher and theologian, could Christ have anything to do with the third thing? One thinks immediately of the *Homoousios* clause in the Nicene Creed. Is the "Son of one substance with the Father"? And if so, how is the Son also of one substance with the ones who wrote the creed?)

5. "Discuss the presuppositions involved in Mill's method of formulating the inductive methods by means of letter-symbols. What is the bearing of this question on the general theory of induction?" (This question bears absolutely no meaning whatsoever to those inducted into uniform, and even less meaning to those who will never make it back home.)[46]

This "No Man's Land" in "The Flanders Fields" where "the poppies blow, Between the crosses row on row"[47]—what think we of them now?

The deck of the SS *St. Paul* afforded some welcomed days and nights of restful contemplation beneath the sun and stars of God's glorious heavens. These were interspersed with a few sullen moments of rumination over those knotty conundrums that philosophers ponder and soldiers curse upon God's blood-stained earth—awaiting to be absumed in *that unfathomable Mystery*.

---

46. The parenthetical comments following each exam question are those of the editor-narrator.

47. "In Flanders Fields," a poem by Lt. Col. John McCrae commemorating those who died in the trenches along the "Western Front."

Editor's Introduction

V—What to Say? What to Do?

A "lonely voyage" is not everyone's cup of tea, but it comes with both the first-class and second-class ship's fare. It's the one imponderable nuisance in which neither time nor space discriminate. And while some palliatives help to ease the passage from "life before" to "life after," there is simply no substitute for a living faith.

> Rupert Brooke, taking ship from Liverpool to New York, felt suddenly lonely, for he seemed the only passenger without friends on the dock to wave him good-by. So he ran back down the gangplank, picked out an urchin, and asked, "What's your name?" "Bill," said the boy. "Well, Bill, you are my friend and here is sixpence. Wave to me when the ship goes." The boy waved a handkerchief in a very grubby hand. Our human voyage is a still lonelier affair. The ship of this strange planet—should we say of the cosmos?—plunges on its way with no apparent port of departure, for nobody knows how or where or why our human life began; and no apparent port of arrival, for every passenger is buried in the deep. We are on a lonely voyage. When we confront that fact, biblical faith begins.[48]

Buttrick said, furthermore, "There is no dock and no 'Bill' on the dock. So we try to build our securities (that is what the bank calls them) in the ship itself. It is a mammoth affair, and we can easily pretend that it is bastioned in rock. But it is not: it is a ship with no visible coast astern or ahead, an infinite sky above and an infinite sea beneath, the vessel's prow cutting the waters on an unstayed course—if there is a course."[49]

But there must be a course, some plottable, chartable course. Right? Or, are those existentialists *on course* when they say "an authentic life confronts apparent nothingness"? And are we one of those "passengers who say, 'This world only: there is only life on shipboard'"?[50]

If, in 1915, you had been a blue-collar worker employed as one of the *twenty-one thousand* on a mass-production assembly line in Mr. Ford's

---

48. George A. Buttrick, "Lonely Voyage," *Sermons Preached in a University Church* (Nashville: Abingdon Press, 1959), 13. For the story about Rupert Brooke he cites Edward Marsh, *Rupert Brooke: A Memoir* (New York John Lane Co., 1918), 95.

49. Buttrick, "Lonely Voyage," 14.

50. Buttrick, "Lonely Voyage," 14.

Editor's Introduction

Model-T "Tin Lizzie" Highland Park Plant for the recently declared five-dollar daily wage for an eight-hour shift, bolting fenders to their frames and ratcheting screws into their sockets, would you have considered yourself to be living "an authentic life"? Would you have appraised yourself as one who "confronts apparent nothingness" so long as you could put bread on the table and clothes on your back and send your kids to school?

On the other hand—if, by the end of October 1929, when there is sudden "hell to pay" for those white-collar stockbrokers who place orders of automotive securities for trade in the "pit" on Wall Street, you are still one of Mr. Ford's line workers, now at his River Rouge Plant, and still putting bread on your table and clothes on your back and sending money to your kids to send their kids to school, and still bolting fenders to frames, still ratcheting screws into sockets, yet you are now *but one* of *one hundred thousand* coworkers, *what then?*

When the company's group photo of factory employees is taken, and you stand back and look at it, and it's simply a sea—a wide, deep, massive sea of faces—but you can hardly pick out a single one of them, much less your own, would you be among those "passengers who say, 'This world only: there is only life on shipboard'"? Would you yet profess it to be an "authentic life confronting apparent nothingness"? And what about two years hence, after the bottom has fallen out of the stock market *and the ship*, and you have lost your job and your hope?[51]

"Our preacher," by now into his fifth Yale lecture of 1931, "Preaching Christ to the Individual of To-Day," turns the spotlight squarely upon the male preachers to whom he is preaching, as if to ask them, *How are you addressing those questions?*

> The preacher may be appraised, as may any other man, by this simple but final test: "Does he see faces or things?" There are business men who see only things—sales-resistance, charts, profits; there are other business men who see faces—the faces of those who work for them, and the faces of those who have no work. There are statesmen who see only things—battleships, voting booths, newspaper-headlines; and there are other statesmen who see faces—faces of the poor, faces of little children and myriad faces slain in

---

51. For details pertaining to the aforementioned realities on the Ford assembly lines, see, among other sources, http://www.mtfca.com/books/15_factory.htm.

war. There are would-be preachers who see only things—church buildings, card-indices, year-book figures; and there are other preachers, ordained by a tenderness beyond the hand of man, who see faces—faces wistful and sin-scarred, lonely and brave. Jesus saw nothing on earth but faces; nothing in heaven but faces; nothing in hell but faces. Always He swung the conversation back to the human. If men discussed the prospect of harvest, He would say: "See the fields of face white already unto harvest."[52] If men were absorbed in the little quest for things, he summoned them to a nobler crusade: "Come ye after me, and I will make you fishers of men."[53] He lays His hands on all our institutions—the church, the factory, the prison, and the school—and asks: "What is its human issue?"[54]

Unfortunately, "There are ministers who decry 'the futility of ringing doorbells.'"[55]

But: "To mediate the Presence—that is at once the preacher's burden, his sovereign gift, his sufficient credential, his enduring joy: 'It was kind of you to come that you might bring us God. Oh, sir, do give us God.'[56] In that task also Christ shall not fail. 'Light shall shine out of darkness, the light of the knowledge of the glory of God in the face of Jesus Christ.'"[57]

VI—A "Thousand Stars" and "One Sun"

No Buttrick lecture on preaching is complete without posing one paramount question: "Is Christ Still the Preacher's Authority?"[58] Each generation must answer that question anew for itself. "The night of pagan cults

---

52. "John 4:35, freely rendered" (Buttrick's footnote).

53. Matt 4:19 (cf. AKJV).

54. Buttrick, *Jesus Came Preaching*, 120–21.

55. Buttrick, *Jesus Came Preaching*, 118. A phrase pertaining to Harry Emerson Fosdick, explained in Buttrick's lecture in this book, chapter 11, "Preaching and Pastoral Care."

56. "An incident related in *When Faiths Flash Out*, chap. I, by David Baines-Griffiths (Revell.)" (Buttrick's footnote to the story of George Borrow who "wandered into the fields of Wales and fell into conversation with a group of gypsies.") See Buttrick, *Jesus Came Preaching*, 140.

57. Buttrick, *Jesus Came Preaching*, 141. Cf. 2 Cor 4:6 (AKJV).

58. Buttrick, *Jesus Came Preaching*. The title of his second Beecher lecture.

had a thousand stars; the day of the apostles' Gospel had but one Sun. He was Alpha and Omega."[59] "But our age has scant respect for tradition," says the lecturer.[60]

> In music the masters are ignored, their rhythms beaten into a tattoo, their haunting sequences abducted and made drunk. In art likewise a new fashion prevails, whether good or bad few know, for few can comprehend. In morals the upheaval is so vast that it seems at times as if all the roads were gone, all the bridges down, all the floods let loose. In religion the revolt has swept beyond the outer earthworks to the very citadel, so that it is not now a question of dogma (as of some literally infallible scripture) but of the reality of God. Even in science doubts are raised concerning the validity of science, and confession now is made that laws and categories deemed rock-ribbed in objectivity may be in large measure the impalpable artifices of our mind.
>
> The authority of Jesus has not escaped the onset. He would not wish to escape. He covets no refuge but the wide heaven of truth. Someone has called Him a "lonely Figure unassailed." Lonely He is, but no longer unassailed. Nor is His chief battle with the old foes. The new doubt has been raised in the house of His friends. Not the doubt of His existence: that flimsy ghost of skepticism has been laid: a record too resolute and an influence too personal have slain it. This doubt rather: "How can we be sure of anything He said and did?" Can words addressed to Capernaum in Aramaic sound anything but faint and far when addressed in translation to Los Angeles or New York?[61]

They're *their* questions, for sure—*their* questions in "the house of His friends." This assemblage of "tenants on sufferance" has come from near and far to hear him, the "preacher's preacher," preach for the sake of *their* tenancy in pulpits spread across the land.

Yet one hard, stubborn, persistent reality remains. They, too, live in the same arenas, as depicted. They, too, have identical qualms and hesitations stuck in their throats like barbed fishhooks, the sort that Buttrick pulled from the mouths of the trout he caught in the Jordan River during

---

59. Buttrick, *Jesus Came Preaching*, 29.

60. Buttrick, *Jesus Came Preaching*, 30.

61. Buttrick, *Jesus Came Preaching*, 30–32. Buttrick is lampooning some of the banalities and extremes of "higher criticism."

Editor's Introduction

his summers in Michigan. They *must fish* for answers as though their next meal depends upon it, because *someone else's does too*.

So they fish. They fish their way through all the biblical commentaries they have on their shelves, just as Buttrick checked them off one-by-one on his sermon worksheets. They examine the Driver, Plummer, and Briggs International Critical Commentary on St. Luke.[62] They ponder every pertinent jot and tittle in the *Hebrew and English Lexicon of the Old Testament* "with an appendix containing the biblical Aramaic."[63] They stare with a blank face at one or two of the Dead Sea Scrolls. They reread their red-letter edition of all four Gospels in the King James English for the fortieth time. They plumb John Wesley's *Notes on the Bible* and John Calvin's *Institutes*. They wade through the works of Irenaeus, Eusebius, and Origen (*Against Celsus* on "the miracles of Jesus"), who said, contrasting Jesus's works of wonder and his moral life to the trickeries of sorcerers, "How could anyone fail to believe that according to God's promise he was God who had appeared in a human body for the benefit of the race?"[64]

Yet, if they're still consumed by doubt, they can always "go modern" and devour the pages of Albert Schweitzer's *The Quest of the Historical Jesus*[65] in the original German by borrowing a copy from a friend in case they don't already "own" one. And, even then, they are still left asking the question: "How can we be sure of anything He"—Christ—"said and did?"

> Schweitzer: "He comes to us as One unknown, without a name, as of old, by the lake-side, He came to those men who knew Him not. He speaks to us the same word: 'Follow thou me!' and sets us to the tasks which He has to fulfil for our time. He commands. And to those who obey Him, whether they be wise or simple, He will reveal Himself in the toils, the conflicts, the

---

62. Alfred Plummer, et al, *A Critical and Exegetical Commentary on the Gospel of S. Luke* (Edinburgh: T & T Clark, 1896).

63. Francis Brown, et al., ed., *A Hebrew and English Lexicon of the Old Testament* (Oxford: Clarendon Press, 1907).

64. J. Stevenson, ed., *A New Eusebius* (London: SPCK, 1957, 1968), 224.

65. Albert Schweitzer, *The Quest of the Historical Jesus* (London: Adam & Charles Black, 1910). First German edition, "Von Reimarus zu Wrede," 1906.

Editor's Introduction

suffering which they shall pass through in His fellowship, and, as an ineffable mystery, they shall learn in their own experience Who He is."[66]

As if to lock the question of "How can we be sure of anything He"—Christ—"said and did?" in a steel vault and throw away the key, the inimitable Buttrick concluded, "*To trace an origin is not to resolve a mystery.*"[67]

It's a gamble, isn't it? Sometimes a *high*-stakes gamble if you're going to "stake" your life upon it. Especially when, as "He" said: "Very truly, I tell you, whoever receives one whom I send receives me; and whoever receives me receives him who sent me."[68]

Will the *"Very truly, I tell you"* wash? Will it wash in Emerson, Sever, and Wigglesworth Halls on the Harvard Yard? Or from behind the bars of Alcatraz overlooking the waters of San Francisco Bay? Or in the ghettos of Camden, Passaic, and Jersey City? Or in the Mississippi Delta flats or cotton field shanties of Alabama?

In Alabama, between 1880 and 1900, somewhere in the vicinity of 700,000 to 1.1 million bales of cotton were harvested.[69] That was a lot of cotton to mess with for those "tenants on sufferance," which for them technically meant that "after the lease has expired your service is still required," bendin' over and pickin' in the scorchin' hot sun.

And, worse.

Letterhead: The Tuskegee Normal and Industrial Institute (Founded by Booker T. Washington) for the Training of Colored Young Men and Women

Date: February 21, 1921

To: Mrs. M. B. Owen, Director of Archives and History, Montgomery, Alabama

Dear Madam: In compliance with your request of January 27th, for certain information regarding lynchings in Alabama, we are sending you herewith a complete record of the lynchings in Alabama from 1871 to 1920. We hope

---

66. Schweitzer, *The Quest of the Historical Jesus*, 401.
67. Buttrick, *Jesus Came Preaching*, 130. Italics added.
68. John 13:20 (NRSV).
69. C. Dale Monks, "Modern Cotton Production in Alabama," Encyclopedia of Alabama, April 12, 2011, http://www.encyclopediaofalabama.org/article/h-1588.

this will be of service to you, and are very glad to comply with your request. Total Lynchings: 273.

Yours very truly, R. R. Moton, Principal[70]

Summary: Two hundred seventy-three names (that is, persons); color of skin (a few white, very few); charges brought against; locations; listed in chronological order lynching by lynching. Mostly for murder and rape (the vast, vast majority), "alleged" arson, burglary, "attempted" robbery, political activity, barn burning, incest, miscegenation, "attempted" rape, elopement with a white girl, mistaken for another, refusing to give evidence, for giving evidence, poisoning mules, for giving evidence against "White Caps.," assault, sheltering a murderer, race prejudice (of an unknown colored man), for making unruly remarks, charge not reported, insulting a woman, being an outlaw, being a desperado, refusing to give witness, and to prevent giving witness.[71]

Buttrick had asked the right question: "Can words addressed to Capernaum in Aramaic sound anything but faint and far when addressed in translation to" *white churches in Alabama*, and beyond? For in Capernaum, "They were astounded at his teaching, because he spoke with authority," and on the Sabbath.[72] About what? The same thing he *did* in Nazareth: "The Spirit of the Lord is upon me to bring good news to the poor. He has sent me to proclaim release to the captives and recovery of sight to the blind, to let the oppressed go free, to proclaim the year of the Lord's favor" (Luke 4:18-19 NRSV).

On April 14, 1936, Buttrick gave the Founder's Day Address at the Hampton Institute in Hampton, Virginia, a historically black university, formerly Hampton Normal and Agricultural Institute, which was founded in 1868 to educate "freedmen."

His address began, "There has been found in recent years a tablet from the parapet that ran between the inner court and the outer portico of the Jewish Temple in the time of Jesus. The Greek transcription has this

---

70. Photo image of the letter and list, "Record of Lynchings from 1871 to 1920, Compiled for the Alabama Department of Archives and History by the Tuskegee Normal and Industrial Institute," Alabama Department of Archives and History, http://digital.archives.alabama.gov/cdm/ref/collection/voices/id/2516.

71. "Record of Lynchings from 1871 to 1920."

72. Luke 4:31-32 (NRSV).

warning: 'No stranger is to enter within the balustrade and embankment round the sacred place. Whoever is caught will be answerable for his death which will ensue.'"[73]

His theme was "we are members one of another."[74] That is, by the authority that was given by Jesus to Paul: "We, who are many, are one body in Christ" (Rom 12:5 NRSV).

Buttrick interpreted,

> The Jew did not regard the Gentile as being as closely bound to him as the ear is to the eye; the Gentile was a "dog." The Greek did not think of the Egyptian as his fellow-member in one body: all strangers were "barbarians." No master felt himself linked with his slave as the left hand is to the right: the slave was a slave. But a new faith said, "For by one Spirit are we all baptized into one body, whether Jews or Gentiles, whether bond or free."[75] Paul was two thousand years before his time.

Which meant that much of the world to which Buttrick's Yale audience of preachers had been preaching was two thousand years behind Paul *and Jesus*, or at least in the all too many cases and places where *Jesus was still being lynched*. Which just shows how dangerous it is to accept Jesus as one's personal "authority" if you're the one preaching against the lynching or the ones Jesus died for "on the tree" to set free.

"Apostolic preaching had but one word—Christ," Buttrick said. "Apostolic preaching linked to that Word one overmastering adjective: 'Christ *crucified*.'"[76] "In that zeal Christian preaching arose. It captured art and empire, philosophy and sacred ritual, and laid them at His feet as 'gold and frankincense and myrrh.' Can we so preach? Must we not so preach? Is He still our credential and our sovereign power? It is the pivotal issue."[77] "We are just now concerned with the fact that the first Christian preaching

---

73. George A. Buttrick, Founder's Day Address, Hampton Institute (HUG FP 90.42, Box 17, Sermons and Addresses).

74. Buttrick, Founder's Day Address, 1. Scripture: Rom 12:5.

75. Buttrick, Founder's Day Address, 1–2.

76. Buttrick, *Jesus Came Preaching*, 195.

77. Buttrick, *Jesus Came Preaching*, 33

had for its cloud by day and its fire by night Christ—Him crucified and Him risen."[78]

"Christian preaching in our day has that one Word from which all other words derive their life. The cults of our day have in their night a thousand stars: our Gospel has but one Sun."[79]

VII—Christ and the Calendar

Between 1923 and 1946, George Buttrick traveled back and forth across the entire United States and all over metropolitan New York City by taxi and subway, as well as by train up and down the northeast corridor from Baltimore to Boston, for a total of 794 separate outside engagements.[80] These included a National Preaching Mission tour in 1927 and another in 1936, alongside invitational lectureships, commencement addresses, baccalaureate services, and convocations at a multitude of colleges, universities, seminaries, ministers' conferences, and denominational assemblies, on a wide variety of texts and topics, and, not to be forgotten, sermons in outbound places like the little church down the road from his lakeside summer getaway, where he expounded upon the topic of "Culling Apples."[81]

A few instances: "We Need to Pray" (Second Presbyterian Church, Amsterdam, New York).[82] "That Was I Worth to God" (Broad Street Church, Columbus, Ohio).[83] "Secret Discipleship" (the University of Chicago).[84] "The Firebringer" (Rice Institute, Houston, Texas).[85] A series: "Christ and

---

78. Buttrick, *Jesus Came Preaching*, 29–30.

79. Buttrick, *Jesus Came Preaching*, 54.

80. Buttrick Speaking Registry, 1923–1946, including dates, places, and topics (HUG FP 90.42F, Box 1, Scrapbooks, Guest Books, Sermon Registers, Travel Diary, Testimonial Books, ca. 1920–1976).

81. June 1, 1938, East Jordan, Michigan.

82. Feb. 28, 1932.

83. Feb. 25, 1935.

84. Apr. 28, 1946.

85. Jun. 5, 1932.

the Changing World": (1) "The Conflict of Loyalties," (2) "Christ and the Causes of War," (3) "Christ and the Realm of Toil," (4) "The Church and the New Order," (5) "Prayer and the Changing World" (Grinnell College, Grinnell, Iowa, "The Gates Lectures").[86] And, the topic not announced (Home for the Incurables, New York City).[87]

Meanwhile he continued to preach on Sundays from Madison Avenue's pulpit, sometimes for both the morning and evening services, sharing the latter and the Wednesday night service with other ministers on staff. Additionally, he taught communicants' classes and offered adult education courses on books of the Bible to foster biblical literacy.

Sunday evenings he frequently featured a "book review sermon" about some timely tome of theology, such as Harry Emerson Fosdick's *The Man from Nazareth as His Contemporaries Saw Him*,[88] or a popular work of fiction deserving more than a lick and a promise. "The best novels every year, he would preach on them, and go from the novel to the Gospel."[89]

As with any busy pastor, a myriad of meetings congealed the ink on Buttrick's calendar. Lunch and dinner engagements, committees on end without end, official monthly gatherings of the boards of trustees and elders, in which the big fish and little fish swam together in sporadically stormy waters when the space between them was less than serene. And finally, though all too seldom, a welcomed evening at the symphony with Agnes. She, too, who kept a vigorous schedule in addition to tending to their three children, was involved with commitments to the congregational women's groups, teaching in the church school, and "building up resources for the poor" as she worked tirelessly along with the ever-faithful layperson who operated the church's social service agency, caring for the indigent.[90] And besides all that, being a historian in her own right

---

86. Feb. 11–13, 1936.

87. Feb. 17, 1942.

88. Harry Emerson Fosdick, *The Man from Nazareth as His Followers Saw Him* (New York: Harper & Brothers, 1949). Book review sermon, March 26, 1950 (HUG FP 90.42 Sermons, Box 12).

89. Davidson/David G. Buttrick interview, October 14, 2014 (23).

90. From various interviews with David Buttrick. Ethel King directed the church's social service agency.

Editor's Introduction

with a degree in classics, she spent hours upon hours in the library closely checking the exact citations for all the footnotes of her George's thirteen published books.

One typical week on George's calendar for March 1943 looked like the following:[91]

Sunday, March 7: Yale University (yet again) at the 11 a.m. morning worship, followed by an address at Smith College at 5 p.m.

Monday, March 8: back to the study in the morning with a presbytery meeting all afternoon.

Shrove Tuesday, March 9: the morning in his study again, the trustees at 1:00 p.m., somebody named Smith at the Grier School at 3:00, teaching his class at UTS at 4:10, and at 8:00 attending the church's Men's Club.

Ash Wednesday, March 10: the morning in his study again, with the afternoon blank (or beating the pavement and knocking on doors) until 5:45 and a prayer meeting, then the Lenten School at 8:15 followed by a 9:45 p.m. conference with Mrs. R.

Thursday, March 11: the morning in the study again, the afternoon (likely knocking on doors once more) followed by a 5:30 meeting about the upcoming Saturday wedding, and capping off the day at 8:00 p.m. with a gathering of the Mother's Club.

Friday, March 12: the morning open (in his study presumably), afternoon open (beating the pavement again?) until 4:30 and a "Tea" on the heels of a 4:00 meeting with someone called "Peacock" (every church has one), and lastly the evening unscheduled, which likely meant he was at home reading a book.

Saturday, March 13: the wedding at 10:30 in the morning (New Yorkers like to get on early with their day), and a 2:00 funeral for someone whose name as written in his diary is indecipherable, though most assuredly still known to God.

Sunday, March 14: The "B & G" (Boys and Girls) service at 9:20, the "H.S." (High Schoolers) service at 9:50, the main service at 11:00, then at 1:15 the

---

91. HUG FP 90.4, Box 1, appointment books.

xlvi

train to Louisville, Kentucky, for the upcoming week's Mullins Lectures at the Southern Baptist Theological Seminary.

For the sake of "All's Well That Ends Well," the closing paragraph of the fifth and final lecture in that series went as follows (he's speaking to preachers at the height of World War II):

> The work of preaching is not easy; for the times are hard and may well become harder to the point of outright danger. In the fairest weather preaching is not easy: it is an unremitting labor. Sometimes we cannot see results, but we are not asked to succeed: we are asked only to be faithful to the task. George Tyrrell wrote to Baron von Hugel: "What a relief if one could conscientiously wash one's hands of the whole concern! But then there is that strange Man upon His cross who drives one back again and again!" *Drives* one back: Nay, He *wins* us back again and again, and we know that there is no joy to compare with the joy of being His messengers.[92]

On the train, in a hotel, sitting at an airport, or at home in his easy chair, Buttrick was forever reading. He was a voracious consumer of books, and blessed with a steel-trap memory. He kept lists of them at the back of a number of years of his pocket diaries.

Toward the end of his life in his mid-eighties, a former student and then personal assistant carried on many a delightful and elucidating conversation with him. Curious about "GAB's" (George's acronym for himself) capacity to recall people, dates, conversations, passages from books he'd read, line after line of poetry he could recite, and all without keeping notes or records of anything much that crossed his mind, his companion and friend provided an explanation: "More than once he looked at me and would grin, really grin and say, 'I have a mind like a vice.'"[93]

His son David confirmed it to be so. "He was unbelievable. He could read faster than I, and I'm a fast reader. Boop, turn the page. Boop, turn it

---

92. Lecture 5, the Mullins Lectures on Preaching, the Southern Baptist Theological Seminary, Louisville, KY, March 15–19, 1943 (Manuscripts and Related Materials, ca. 1930–1979, HUG FP 90.45, Box 4). See George Tyrrell letter to Baron F. von Hugel, *The Hibbert Journal*, vol. 8, 1919–1910, 238. Referenced in George A. Buttrick, *Christ and Man's Dilemma* (Nashville: Abingdon-Cokesbury Press, 1946), 203, 217n45.

93. Oral history interview with Dr. Marion L. (Marty) Soards, professor of New Testament Studies at Louisville Presbyterian Theological Seminary, Louisville, KY, Oct. 10, 2017 (23).

again. I mean, that fast. And yet giving quotes out of it. Give him a phrase, and he'd tell you more, right off of almost sight reading."[94]

George's companion posed for George yet another apropos question, regarding a life of such extraordinary achievement.

> I asked him, I said, "How have you managed to get so much done?" It just was a simple question like that. He paused for a second and said—I'll never forget the answer. He said, "Jesus Christ is more real to me than I am to myself." That was his answer. It was a kind of mysticism of a sort, that I never perceived about him before that moment. He didn't just run on his own steam. He really had a concept of Christ and Christ living, and Christ being with him, and living in him and through him. He really was very much a Christological thinker at that level. That made a huge impression on me. I'll never forget that line. It wasn't what I was expecting, so it just hit me like a ton of bricks.[95]

"Jesus Christ is more real to me than I am to myself."

VIII—"Christ or Chaos"

From the very outset and until the end of his days, Buttrick insisted that "Jesus is the minister's Gospel, his burden, his joy, his passion, his duty."[96] For that reason he pressed his listeners toward a decision by asking, "What will you do with Christ?"[97] It was *the* quintessential question that must move from the periphery to front and center stage of the preacher's vision when preparing to preach.

The need to answer that question in a new time and new place, perhaps even in a new way, does not obviate the question. For Buttrick, the Christian preacher has no divinely sanctioned liberty to remove the "King of hearts" from the preacher's deck of cards, for in doing so the Gospel can't remain Christ's Gospel by enthroning some lesser authority

---

94. Davidson/David G. Buttrick interview, Oct. 14, 1014 (23–24).

95. Davidson/Marty Soards interview, Oct. 10, 2017 (8).

96. George A. Buttrick, "What Will You Do with Jesus?" *Record of Christian Work* 44, no. 12 (December 1925): 893.

97. Buttrick, "What Will You Do with Jesus?" 896.

Editor's Introduction

than Christ in the pulpit. This would be dealing a depleted hand to many a defeated person, absent any *consummate* "good news" to grasp hold to.

Consider that many other hands of cards are dealt in such a way that the jacks of spades and diamonds are squarely pitted against the twos and threes of hearts and clubs. Without the presence of the "King of hearts," how can "the least of these" finally overcome all the jacks of the world who parade forth wielding their mighty swords? That is to say, how shall they overcome *unless* having first taken up "the whole armor of God" and "girded [their] loins with truth," "put on the breastplate of righteousness" and "shod [their] feet with the equipment of the gospel of peace," taking upon themselves "the helmet of salvation and the sword of the Spirit, which is the word of God" and which is *Christ Jesus*?[98]

World War II, as all wars do, shuffled many a "stacked" deck of cards, and plenty of wild cards besides, confounding Christians and churches on all sides of the conflict. The result was that churches, and factions within, found themselves playing their hands against one another, as happened in both Germany and the United States. During 1939 and 1940, Buttrick played his own hand as president of the Federal Council of Churches of Christ in America by taking the provocative pacifist position that sided with the noninterventionists. He did so much to the chagrin and fluster of many of his friends, including his good colleague at Union Theological Seminary, Reinhold Niebuhr.[99]

In his presidential address to the Federal Council, "The Witness of the Church Today," Buttrick pled for reconciliation with would-be enemies, not in any sense to justify the sins of Japan and Germany but to prevent the cataclysm of yet another Great War like the one he had all too recently witnessed himself.[100] As for Japan,

---

98. Eph 6:13-17 (RSV).

99. See Davidson, "George Arthur Buttrick: Christocentric Preacher and Pacifist," 143–67.

100. George A. Buttrick, "The Witness of the Church Today," *Biennial Report, Federal Council of Church in America*, 1940, 49.

Appeasement, which means to pacify by concessions, is a shallow word: it moves from man to man. Reconciliation, which means to make friendly again, is a profound word: it moves from God to man, and from man back to God. By sale of war materials we still appease Japan. Those who condone the policy argue that otherwise Japan might attack us. In brief, we are to make Japan a strong military power lest she should act like a strong military power. It is logic so illogical that some of us cannot follow it. Reconciliation, not appeasement, would have said to Japan three years ago: "We wish to live in righteous peace with you and with every nation. We will trade with you now in average bulk, and in goods not easily translated into implements of war. We confess our national sins. We pledge help to cancel inequalities and to assure your brighter future. But we will not help you in aggression. We would rather compensate our merchants for loss of your trade, preferring poverty to a profitable collusion in crime."[101]

As for Germany, and in witness to Christ,

Appeasement meets the occasions of war, while reconciliation grapples the *causes* of war. How many people are content to simplify issues that are far from simple! "Stop Hitler!" We stopped him under another name twenty years ago. Here is one of the appalling dilemmas of our time: Germany, like every land, yearns for peace; but by stooping to stop Hitler, as in some ways we must, we unite Germany in his support. Here is a worse dilemma: we use his weapons to stop him, leaving him free to say (or some other dictator after him), "The doctrine and weapons were right. Next time I will not blunder." Let others advocate defense and preparedness. These advocates themselves know, if they are wise, that the Church has a deeper task. For, except the mind of Christ be honored, no civilization is worth defending. And what danger is ours, while our thoughts are filled with guns, that we may forget Christ! Let others talk of military victory or defeat. They are incurably sanguine of the fruits of armed victory."[102]

Indeed, what civilization collectively cares in the least about Christ when it is convinced that guns more than anything else will save it? Worse still, civilizations have corrupted the name of Christ, as did Hitler's Nazi regime, by coopting him to their devilish ends by non-Christlike deeds of killing that only crucify Christ once again. Many skeptics, like cynics of

---
101. Buttrick, "The Witness of the Church Today," 50.
102. Buttrick, "The Witness of the Church Today," 50.

Editor's Introduction

old, keep asking the disparagers' question: Of what count is Christ to us anyway?

> The historians of His day either deemed Him not worth mention or had never heard of Him. He devised no statecraft, led no army, framed no set philosophy or ethic, sang no song—except a song in the soul of mankind. His cradle was a borrowed manger; His death-bed a felon's cross. A century after His death, the best religious mind (as we might have called it), referred to Him as "the deceiver," "that man," "the hung." But his disciples said that He rose from the dead, and they believed it. The faith in which in His lifetime they had been dull scholars became in His death their overmastering passion. They "turned the world upside down" with the Gospel that God is redeemingly made known in Jesus. Nothing could be much more amazing—except, perhaps, the fact that millions have taken them at their word. Rome, thinking to trample on Him and finding in Him no resistance, stumbled over Him to her doom. He is the astonishment of our human history. George Bernard Shaw writes to a fellow-author: "How do you explain that you, George Moore, and I are now occupying ourselves with Jesus? Why should we discuss Him, as though He were somehow crucial 'for us and our salvation?'"[103]

Just so and because so, with war's end and Germany's defeat followed by Japan's capitulation after Hiroshima and Nagasaki, George Buttrick put his pen yet again to pad and paper, occupying himself with the same Gospel of the very same Jesus. Of *Christ and Man's Dilemma*,[104] he said, "That book got me into trouble."[105]

> When the atomic bomb fell, I began to write, and wrote for thirty days at the rate of almost two thousand words a day until the book was finished. "Christ or Chaos" is no longer a hysterical or histrionic plea. It never was, though to the casual it may have seemed. Now it is a sober choice: Christ or chaos. Our ignorance, badness, and mortality have brought us to the edge of chaos; and we have no power, even though we are pricked with eternity,

---

103. George A. Buttrick, *The Christian Faith and Modern Doubt* (New York: Charles Scribner's Sons, 1934), 123–24. For the Shaw quotation, see Frank Harris, *Stories of Jesus the Christ* (New York: Pearson's Library, 1919), 3.

104. George A. Buttrick, *Christ and Man's Dilemma* (Nashville: Abingdon-Cokesbury Press, 1946).

105. George Buttrick interview.

Editor's Introduction

to choose Christ—unless He chooses us. So this book pleads for the real Christ—not for Christ as a vague ideal, for that would be no match for our selfishness; not for Christ as a name for our good intentions for they are less than straws in our modern tempest; but for Christ as the Incarnate God.

If that "theology" should bring the reader to a stop, I ask only that he give the book a chance. It has come from travail, and from a surety that "there is none other name under heaven whereby we must be saved."[106]

The intractable issue is that we humans are sinners, yet we cannot extricate ourselves from sin. Reinhold Niebuhr framed it thusly: "The individual, and more particularly society, are regarded as too involved in the sins of the earth to be capable of salvation in any moral sense."[107] Buttrick, who had been significantly moved by reading Niebuhr's *Moral Man and Immoral Society* in 1932, once again would be profoundly affected by Niebuhr's *Faith and History* in 1949, prompting him to say not only that the latter was "a very important and formative book for me," but also, "I think [Niebuhr] probably the best theologian of the century."[108] This he emphasized despite their public disagreements over war-making and specifically pacifism, even though those differences persisted until Niebuhr's death in 1971 during the peak of the Vietnam war. Buttrick then added,

> In my last conversation with him, he deplored Vietnam [and] called it a "prodigious, guilty blunder." But he also said he felt we would have to keep a military presence in Southeast Asia and in Bangkok. Reinie believed in politics as the science of the possible. He didn't like the balance of power theory, but he believed we must proceed on it and then proceed beyond it.[109]

The ecclesiastical debate would continue. Yet added to the agenda was a new form of pacifism, namely "nuclear pacifism," even as Buttrick, still as staunchly pacifist as ever, retained his decades-long involvement with

---

106. Buttrick, *Christ and Man's Dilemma*, 8.

107. Reinhold Niebuhr, *Moral Man and Immoral Society* (New York: Charles Scribner's Sons, 1932), 70.

108. George Buttrick interview.

109. George Buttrick interview.

Editor's Introduction

the International Fellowship of Reconciliation and the Presbyterian Peace Fellowship.[110]

In chronological age, these two theological giants, Niebuhr and Buttrick, were but three months apart; in anthropological realism, on virtually the same page; and in conscientious conviction about what Christ and his teachings required of them in response to war, light-years asunder. In that respect, they reflected the deep divisions that befell Christian churches and their leaders at home and abroad. Niebuhr had relinquished his former pacifism while Buttrick doggedly stuck to his own. Yet they agreed on their biblical theology of human pride and sin, and the degree to which a fallen world can descend with a vengeance into the depths of wretched depravity. Only God's prevenient and redemptive grace can save the day, and this only *within history* to the extent that from *beyond history* God's kingdom is revealed to eyes that for the moment are blind to God's mysterious ways.

For Buttrick this meant trusting that Christ lives at the beginning, the center, and the end of history, and that what we see in Christ is clue to the fact that "history is the Dialogue between God and man in the language of event, and of the [Christ] Event. God began the conversation, God continues it, and God alone can determine when the Conversation shall end."[111]

In 1942, just as Germany was conquering most of Europe, Buttrick published his most widely read book, entitled *Prayer*. The outgrowth of numerous lectures he had given across the country since 1938, it was a concerted effort to probe some of the deepest matters of faith related to the deepest matters of human need.[112] Therein he also confronted "the killing shadow of the *false totalitarianism* of the scientific theory of the world" and its concomitant bedevilment, natural law, as "contradictory and incongruous" with petitionary prayer.[113] With his own christological

---

110. International Fellowship of Reconciliation (http://www.ifor.org/#mission); the Presbyterian Peace Fellowship (https://www.presbypeacefellowship.org).

111. George A. Buttrick, *Christ and History* (New York: Abingdon Press, 1963), 96–97.

112. George A. Buttrick, *Prayer* (New York: Abingdon Press, 1942).

113. Buttrick, *Prayer*, 84.

scalpel in hand, he dissected "some defective theories of prayer" and problematic aspects of human psychology and personality in light of his theology of prayer. He also worked through various forms that prayer can take, both private and public, with a final chapter on "Prayer and the New World." When all was said and done, and being a man of deep prayer himself, he concluded by saying,

> A certain pastor, who lives where simple faith is shadowed by dark persecution, was asked to tell the secret of his calm endurance. "When the house is dark," he answered, "I do not try to sweep away darkness with a broom: I light a candle." Prayer is more than a lighted candle: it is the contagion of health. It is the pulse of Life.[114]

As with the efficacy of prayers prayed to a loving God, so it is with Buttrick's capitalization of the word *Gospel*, whether referring to the books called Gospels or to the subject of those books, the One who *is* Gospel. Both prayer and Gospel come together as gift of the same Spirit speaking always in the *present tense*.

And so, in late 1951 and into early 1952, Buttrick set off on an extensive world-wide preaching tour, carrying his Gospel manuscripts in hand and the words of the living Christ in his heart and in his mouth.[115]

IX—"Signs of Another World"

"What is the parable?" Buttrick once asked in an Easter sermon.

> Imagine a man who has never left New York City. His neighbors tell him that beyond these streets there are mountains, grassy plains, and oceans. He might deny, but he would always fitfully believe. For at the street corner there is a man with a flower-cart, and flowers do not grow on sidewalks. From Riverside Drive he can see the Hudson, and must ask whence its mighty flow. Besides, the Narrows could be joined with an ocean, and Central Park Meadow could be the token of vast prairies. That man would always be stumbling on signs to disturb his conviction that all there is is New York. So you and I live in the city called mortal life. There are always

---

114. Buttrick, *Prayer*, 303.

115. Buttrick was commissioned as the Joseph Cook Lecturer by the Board of Foreign Missions of the Presbyterian Church USA, to the Philippines, Japan, Hong Kong, Thailand, Indonesia, India, Pakistan, the Near East, and parts of Europe.

Editor's Introduction

signs of another world. There are flashes of conscience and stirrings of pity, and always in the hour of crisis the overmastering impulse to pray. You and I move to and fro in the city called mortality always wondering about mountains and oceans that eyes cannot see.[116]

That said, Buttrick's calendar, when opened to Wednesday, April 7th of the week before Holy Week, 1954, reveals a presaging hour.[117]

The day contains its usual menu of appointments one-after-another, beginning with a 10 a.m. interment service, followed by a 1 p.m. meeting of Sigma Chi (the "circle" of thirty to forty distinguished New York clergy and religious academics who have met together monthly since the year 1865, its members delivering formal papers on a broad range of topics covering the entire gamut of human inventiveness "well up to the standard in timeliness, appropriateness, and intellectual and spiritual quality" that one would expect of theological nobility listening to one another's replies),[118] then 3:00 and 3:30 appointments with individuals, a 4:30 tea, and the 8 p.m. Lenten School. But sandwiched in the space between 3:30 and 4:30 an inked-in arrow with the curvature of a half-moon points to the bottom of the page and the time marked as 3:45. Beside it, the name of "President Pusey."[119]

> I never dreamed of it. When a representative from Harvard showed up in my study one day and said, "George, you've preached to a full church for about twenty-eight years now. I've come to ask you to preach to an empty church in a skeptical and pluralistic society."[120]

---

116. George A. Buttrick, "Great Christian Affirmations: I Believe in the Life Everlasting," an Easter sermon preached at Madison Avenue Presbyterian Church, April 5, 1947, *The Madison Avenue Presbyterian Church News* ("Notes for George's Books," HUG FP 90.45, Box 2).

117. Buttrick appointment book for 1954 (HUG FP 90.4, Box 2).

118. Henry E. Cobb and Frank Mason North, *A History of Sigma Chi Read at Its Seventieth Anniversary*, December, 18, 1935, p. 8 ("Buttrick Articles 3 of 4," HUGB B869.572, Box 1).

119. Buttrick appointment book for 1954 (HUG FP 90.4, Box 2).

120. Roy Stauffer's interview with George Buttrick, ca. May 1972, in preparation for a student paper entitled "George Arthur Buttrick: His Life, His Thought, and His Preaching," submitted to Dr. Herman Norton for a course on the History of American Preaching, May 10, 1970, p. 8 ("Vanderbilt Divinity School 1971–72," HUG FP 90.15, Box 7). Buttrick had critiqued the content of the interview with insertions, deletions, and corrections from his own pen.

Editor's Introduction

> I tried to fight this thing. I told the Lord there wasn't any sense in such a move. At my time of life, it wasn't possible or probable for me to learn a new style of preaching.[121]

For two months his struggle persisted. Then, at 2:00 one morning, George awoke and said to Agnes, "You know, there isn't much percentage in arguing with God, is there?" To which she replied that his question meant they were headed for Harvard.[122]

The "flashes of conscience and stirrings of pity" accompanied by the "overmastering impulse to pray" might well have been those of any preacher who dared to stand to preach in a "Memorial Church." Especially one on an Ivy League campus that for all practical purposes had buried the classic creeds of Christendom, remembered mostly for being stodgy Puritan ones, beneath the tombstones of an early eighteenth-century Massachusetts Bay Colony cemetery.

The Memorial Church that sat at the center of Harvard Yard was not at the center of most Harvard "thinking." Attendance for the 11 o'clock worship when George Buttrick arrived to preach his first sermon on Sunday, January 2nd, 1955, was sparse by standards that routinely pertained to this sixty-two-year-old cleric. Three hundred persons, which was "three times the size of a normal Harvard recess Sunday congregation,"[123] were present that day in a sanctuary that seated 1,200. President Nathan Pusey, however, was abundantly clear about one thing: he would be seated confidently and visibly wherever he needed to be to convince the unpersuadable that he meant what he said when he sought to signal a new age for Christianity under the "Crimson" shield bearing the Latin motto

---

121. Roy Stauffer's interview with Buttrick, 9.

122. Roy Stauffer's interview with Buttrick, 9.

123. *Divinings: Religion at Harvard; From Its Origins in New England Ecclesiastical History to the 175th Anniversary of the Harvard Divinity School, 1636–1992*, vol. 2, in George H. Williams, *The "Augustan Age": Religion in the University, the Foundations of a Learned Ministry and the Development of the Divinity School*, ed. Rodney L. Petersen (Göttingen, Germany: Vandenhoeck & Ruprecht with the Boston Theological Institute, Newton, MA, 2014), 373 (hereafter cited as *Divinings*).

Editor's Introduction

VERITAS—TRUTH that dated at least as far back as the Overseers meeting of January 6, 1644.[124]

The atheists and skeptics for the most part had remained home. Likely they were reading the likes of Albert Camus, August Comte, Sigmund Freud, the *Boston Globe*, and the *New York Times*, after walking the dog. Some of the curious, especially the biblical scholars, would have noticed the morning *Times* article headlined "Data on 'Lost' Hittite Culture Dug Up," which read in part,

> Evidence that the "lost" Hittite civilization survived at least until the time of Christ has been dug up this year in southeastern Turkey. Scholars have long been baffled by the disappearance of Hittite architecture, sculpture and religion after the Hittite city-states were crushed by the Assyrians at the end of the eighth century B.C. Through this crossroads kingdom, athwart some of the principal caravan routes from the East, the Persian cult of Mithras is believed to have gained access to the Roman Empire. Roman soldiers stationed in Commagene helped carry the worship of Mithras to every part of the empire, including Londinium (ancient London), where a Mithraic temple was recently uncovered. The Mithras cult, a monotheistic faith promising eternal life, was Christianity's principal competitor until the fourth century after Christ." This summer an unusual eight-foot stele (slab of stone) with a Greek inscription was found near Antiochus' tomb. It warns, "Those who come in ignorance to desecrate this place must fly away; those who come to plunder will suffer dire consequences." A similar malediction on impious intruders was found at the entrance to the tomb of Mithradates."[125]

That would have been the perfect setup for George Buttrick: What are the cultic competitors to Christianity *now*? Where are their vaunted shrines located? To what gods do they bow down? Are any of them parked in modern guise along the crisscrossing pathways of Harvard Yard? Are any of them amply fortified against the vandalisms of permanent desecration and plunder? *The gods of Angst? The cherubs of Progress? The deities of Nationalism? The divinities of War?* What about the temples of science and

---

124. "History," Harvard University, https://www.harvard.edu/about-harvard/harvard-glance/history.

125. *New York Times*, Sunday, January 2, 1955, 2.

Editor's Introduction

humanism, hallowed by the attributes of a closed system, that elevate the "Human Ape" to the highest pinnacle in the universe reserved for God—the God who much prefers to offer self-revelation in the low places?

For six years, week after week, Buttrick held forth with brilliance and erudition in the midst of a standing-room only congregation, speaking in his "gravelly," "crackling," and "raspy" voice,[126] contending for the Christian faith on decidedly secular ground. He had done so having come to Harvard with no more than a "poor kid's" British bachelor's degree as his certified academic pedigree. Never mind that he also had come forearmed with honorary doctorates from Hamilton, Middlebury, and Albright Colleges, Yale University, Miami University of Ohio, Princeton University, and Columbia University, with seven more waiting in the wings, of which the crowning one would be from Harvard itself.

Plus, by then he had already devoted considerable mental perspiration to the massive amount of work and scholarship involved with his general editorship of the twelve-volume *Interpreter's Bible*, first conceived in 1946, and which by 1985 would sell 2,641,716 volumes worldwide.[127]

Nonetheless, in order that he be sufficiently consecrated for the responsibility of teaching Crimson undergraduates as well as graduate divinity students, Harvard had first to confer upon him the minimal credential required of a don of the university. For that, an *Artium Magistrum*, commonly known as the master's degree, was bestowed without prerequisite.

Yet—had *Christ* not summoned and equipped George Buttrick to preach, then what? Beyond his own extensive knowledge of history, literature, theology, philosophy, art, and ancient languages, what would he have had to say worth saying that hadn't already been said, or could just as easily have been said by someone else at Harvard? And what, too, to be said by way of obeisance to all of the Yard's sovereign disciplines?

> Our humanisms will probably cling for a time to their empty hopes. There is much about them to win our gratitude. They sometimes serve man's need, at least on the surface level, more instantly and with less parade than a

---

126. *Divinings*, 383.

127. George A. Buttrick, gen. ed., *The Interpreter's Bible*, 12 vols. (New York: Abingdon Press, 1951–1957).

half-recalcitrant church. But they shy away from the fact that "something has gone wrong," which fact the church within the churches still confronts. They think that nothing has gone wrong which science, governmental reform, and the new economics cannot cure. We need all three agencies, but not in a blind hope. The humanists are by and large a noble company. I live among them with a "lively sense of favors," and feel more at home than in the "little churchinesses" of many a church. But I know—as who does not in his realistic moments?—that they are painting over with white paint the flaw in the marble in the hope that thus the architecture of our life will become pure, the noble habitation of noble men, who nevertheless are not noble, until and unless....[128]

I shall not forget the day when, in morning prayers at Harvard, a professor said to the surprise of the Harvard mind that we had better keep the word "devil": otherwise the battle that we know, should we succeed in evaporating it by our theories, would carry away with it the tang and verity of our whole life![129]

And—for the sake of such verity, to keep the living *Christ* in the conversation:

> There is this to be said for Christian faith: its hopes are substantial hopes, and it never romanticizes about death. It says bluntly in proper terror: "The last *enemy* to be destroyed is death."[130] In the onset of the terror it finds God, or, rather, is found of God. It says that the enemy has been overcome in Jesus Christ, in whom our best hopes, such as the hope that personality has a value worth keeping, are validated. He "hath brought life and immortality to light through the gospel."[131] That faith is worth examination, if only because it has bred the kind of character that has "stopped the mouths of lions."[132] Education, confronting destiny, must choose between a dull stoicism that sees nothing beyond death, or a romanticism which whistles in the dark a broken tune about the immortality of influence, *or an outright Christian faith.*[133]

---

128. George A. Buttrick, *God, Pain, and Evil* (New York: Abingdon Press, 1966), 59–60.

129. Buttrick, *God, Pain, and Evil*, 66.

130. 1 Cor 15:26 (RSV).

131. 2 Tim 1:10 (AKJV).

132. Heb 11:33 (RSV).

133. George A. Buttrick, *Faith and Education* (New York: Abingdon-Cokesbury, 1952), 33. Emphasis added.

By George Buttrick's reckoning, the preaching of the *Word made flesh in Christ* must ever remain *outright*.

A member of the Harvard class of 1959 summed it up in a letter to the editor of *Harvard Magazine*:

> If Memorial Church...is a supreme example of the Protestant meeting house, then a supreme preacher is needed to animate the structure, and that Buttrick surely was. In the history of the building has anyone else been able to fill it with worshippers Sunday after Sunday, year in and year out? The very sound of Buttrick's voice was extraordinary, a pattern of inflections so unique and captivating that merely to exchange a few pleasantries with him over the phone was a memorable experience. To this vocal gift he added theological insight, immense literary knowledge, a matchless rhetorical style, and an honest faith in God. Hearing George Buttrick preach gave me a lifelong belief in the power of rhetoric to do good in human affairs. It also made me a Christian.[134]

X—Home

While during the last two decades of his life he continued to be invited as a guest preacher and lecturer in churches, colleges, universities, and seminaries throughout America, Buttrick also received extended opportunities to teach what he referred to as "the new preaching." Upon retiring from Harvard in 1960 as the Preacher to the University and Plummer Professor of Christian Morals, he was named for a one-year appointment to the Harry Emerson Fosdick Visiting Professorship established by John D. Rockefeller, III, at Buttrick's old haunt, Union Theological Seminary.[135]

Immediately thereafter, Garrett Biblical Seminary of Evanston, Illinois, called him to teach overcrowded and wait-listed classes as professor of homiletics, from which he retired in 1969.[136] Then for the fall and winter terms of 1969–1970 he conducted courses on the "Principles of

---

134. *Divinings*, 384. The writer of the letter was John R. McDermott, *Harvard Magazine*, 85, no. 3 (January–February 1983): 23.

135. See Buttrick's inaugural address, "What Is Truth?" *Union Seminary Quarterly Review*, Dec. 16, 1960, Special Issue, 106.

136. Now named Garrett-Evangelical Theological Seminary.

Editor's Introduction

Preaching" and "New Testament Thought and the Mind of Today" at Davidson College in North Carolina, followed by a short-term stint in the practical theology department of Vanderbilt University's Divinity School. Agnes and he then moved in the fall of 1971 to Louisville, Kentucky, where until human frailty overtook him in 1979, he taught courses in homiletics and pastoral theology at both the Presbyterian and Southern Baptist Theological Seminaries.

In 1968, a doctoral candidate at New Orleans Baptist Theological Seminary had written to Buttrick in conjunction with preparing to write a thesis on the subject of "A Critical Examination of the Preaching of George Arthur Buttrick." At some prior point the student had heard the master homiletician lecture in person and had become inspired by his words. Buttrick replied with his opening signature sentence, minor variations of which his secretaries over the years, and lately his wife, knew by heart.

> I write in reply to your kind inquiry of January 31. You have chosen a poor subject for your dissertation. There is little of my sermonic material in print. Have you seen my book, *Sermons Preached in a University Church*?[137] As for the lectures in Homiletics which you heard, they are almost continuously in process of rewriting, the reason being that preaching itself is now in rapid transition. At a guess it will become more existential and more a process of dialogue.
>
> Last summer, at the Ministers' conference in Princeton Seminary, I gave a series of lectures on "What is the Preacher's Message Today?" These dealt with new accents in the "Old, Old Story." "Preaching to a Dehumanized Age—to a Revolutionary Age—to an Anxious Age—to a Death-filled Age, etc." These lectures have not yet been published. I may work on them for publication this summer and possibly introduce them by an extended discussion of the "New Homiletics."[138]

---

137. George A. Buttrick, *Sermons Preached in a University Church* (New York-Nashville: Abingdon Press, 1959).

138. Those lectures, as planned, written, and left publication-ready by George Buttrick for Abingdon Press in the early 1970s, went unpublished during his lifetime due to portions that were to be contributed by his son, David Buttrick, who was too immersed in his own life of teaching and scholarship to complete his additional chapters. This book brings George Buttrick's original intention to fruition with publication of the final iteration of his lectures

As for my use of the Bible: I have always been an expository preacher and am convinced that the new preaching must be rooted in Scripture, but in a new way: e.g. in the pericope rather than in the isolated verse. I myself am in process of writing out what I am sure must be a new approach. As I said above, you have chosen a very poor subject. Yet, believe me, I am most grateful for your confidence.[139]

Until his very last days in the pulpit and the classroom, George Buttrick, as always, began his mornings in the study doing his homework. He devoted afternoons and evenings to meet with students in small groups for discussing whatever was on their minds, as well as in one-on-one sessions for further private critique of the written sermons they had presented in class for fellow student response and comment.

Preaching was ever on Buttrick's heart, in his thoughts, on his lips, and circulating as the life-stream in his blood. He was in fact a "preacher's preacher." Any who were fortunate enough to hear him, or to have had him as teacher, knew not only how profoundly he had spoken to them, but also how certainly and compellingly God had spoken through him.

> Preaching today can no longer be rationally argumentative or unconvincingly "eloquent." It must be dialogue with the congregation as silent partner; and there could well be opportunities for later give-and-take. Preaching must address itself to questions people are asking, not to giving neat answers to questions nobody is asking—which is to say that preaching must answer a prior utterance by the congregation and, in that sense, be dialogue. But, and this is the important item, real preaching comes of a prior dialogue between God and the preacher—a far more important dialogue than that between man and man.[140]

---

on "the new preaching," available now to an entirely new generation of readers, including clergy, theological faculties, and laity. For a brief overview of the "New Homiletic," see William H. Willimon and Richard Lischer, eds., *Concise Encyclopedia of Preaching* (Louisville, KY: Westminster-John Knox Press, 1995), 226–27. Also, O. C. Edwards Jr., *A History of Preaching* (Nashville: Abingdon Press, 2004), chs. 28–32.

139. Letter to Paul W. Stevens dated Feb. 7, 1968 ("Stevens, Paul W. and Dissertation on GAB," HUG FP 90.8/1, Box 27).

140. Letter to the Reverend James Miller Harvey, the Episcopal Church of the Resurrection, Philadelphia, June 26, 1965 ("H—General Letters" HUG FP 90.9/2, Box 5).

Editor's Introduction

George Buttrick's last weeks on God's good earth were spent hospitalized in Louisville. His longtime cardiologist, Dr. Donald Moseley,[141] once made the observation that George "had the most remarkable capacity to recover of any patient I've ever had." When asked, "Why do you think that is?" he replied, "He can think of all the reasons he needs to get better for everyone else."[142]

Agnes, who had suffered a fall and was recovering in rehab and at home during the time that George lay in hospital, sent handwritten love notes to him each day, conveyed by one of their sons since she was unable to make but a few brief visits herself. In one of her notes, midway through George's final tribulation (there had been earlier ones: close relatives killed in World War II, a serious automobile accident, a heart attack, and hip replacement), she wrote with cherishing endearment,

> Dearest G.—so here we are again, but things look so well with you that I am happier by the minute and definitely glad you've just had visitors—in fact jealous—& already I've been trying to get permission & now I hear that you are making phenomenal progress. Things seem going better than our first ideas—Holy mercy—hurrah. Well, we are going to be able to say "hello" & "hello" again. Love. Love. Love.—Ness—The wife![143]

Among the last heartfelt sentiments expressed in her final love note, like others over the sixty-four years of their marriage that had begun as a love story, for certain, amid the saying of prayers and singing of hymns in the Albion Congregational Church of Hull, England, she said to her dearest George as plainly and sincerely as any words she'd ever handwritten or spoken with her lips, now with her feeble fingertips slowly pushing the pen: *"Well, tomorrow is a celebration and points to the 'glory-be' end of your*

---

141. Donald H. Mosley, MD, https://www.legacy.com/obituaries/louisville/obituary.aspx?pid=190661890.

142. Davidson/Soards interview. The conversation was between Dr. Mosley and Dr. Marion Soards, Buttrick's former student.

143. "Notes to George Buttrick from Agnes Buttrick during his hospital stay," HUG FP 90.34, Box 3.

Editor's Introduction

trouble. *Sunday next week may be peacefully the 'glory-be.' You are coming home! a great celebration.*"[144]

There were always four homes for George. First, his heart's home with his beloved Agnes. Second, his "home" preaching the Gospel of Jesus Christ from the pulpit. Third, his fondly remembered home with his parents and sisters in Seaham Harbor.

And the fourth, for that "*great celebration*"?

Once, when giving the benediction concluding his commencement address to a sanctuary full of graduating seminary students and their families, who were about to set forth upon the road of their life's calling, he put it like this:

"Brave journeying to you until you reach home, your *real* home."[145]

---

144. "Notes to George Buttrick from Agnes Buttrick during his hospital stay," HUG FP 90.34, Box 3.

145. Benediction on the occasion of the commencement exercises at Union Theological Seminary, Richmond, VA (now Union Presbyterian Seminary), May 12, 1974. The title of his address was "The Minister's Search for Self-Identity." A recording is available in the library of Union Presbyterian Seminary. During the ceremony the editor of this book received the degree of master of theology, his honors thesis entitled "George Arthur Buttrick: The Christocentric Preacher and Interpreter of History."

Part One
REASSESSMENT

CHAPTER ONE

We Preach the Gospel (I)

To the question, "What do we preach?," the average preacher would answer without hesitation, "The Gospel." But do we understand? Are we a-tiptoe with joy? The word *Gospel* (good spiel) means glad tidings! Now any good news is by nature an event, not what has been merely thought but a happening. So somebody coming into your home might exclaim, "The most wonderful thing has happened!" Glad tidings provoke exclamation. What *has* happened? God, the uncreated, unimaginable in purpose and power, "for us and for our salvation came down and became truly human."[1] That happening boggles the preacher's mind, shakes her heart, and taxes all wonder. She proclaims that Event: Christ living, dying, raised from the dead, and present in Spirit.

We now note the strangeness of any event. If it occurs in the order of nature, an earthquake or a spring flower, it can be gathered into a sequence the scientist too hastily calls "cause and effect," blotting out its particularity under an abstraction named "universal law," as in, "All earthquakes are due to the cooling of earth's interior fires." But an observation regarding nature does not apply in history. What happens to us as human beings, including an earthquake, has another face. For us a happening is *invasive*. It "takes place": our place. It is *disruptive*. It "comes to pass": our door. It is *ecstatic* in that word's original meaning: it requires us to stand

---

1. From the contemporary version of the Nicene Creed, formulated after the time of Buttrick's writing.

3

Chapter One

outside ourselves to ask, "What now shall I do?" Any event is thus crucial. The Christ Event, God's visitation in the flesh, is the crux of history, the happening that rules all happenings.

I

We pause to say what preaching is not, for negative statements, despite a book named *Positive Thinking*,[2] have an initial bite while positive statements are ill-defined. The Decalogue is for witness. So preaching is not a moralism. Preaching leads on to an ethic, for the Event of Christ *eventuates* in a certain style of life, but preaching doesn't tell people what to do, still less what not to do. Many a preacher falls into this moralistic trap, as in a notice recently seen outside a certain church: "Don't procrastinate: the early bird gets the first worm." That preacher was peddling advice, but hardly on the level even of *Aesop's Fables*. Why not instead quote George Bernard Shaw: "They killed Him on a stick, but he seems to have gotten hold of the right end of it"?[3] Then the very notice board would have proclaimed the Gospel.

Again, preaching is not selling peace of mind. The Gospel is the only comfort, but it is not passport to money-making or to what is now called "an attractive personality." Perhaps Christ himself had no so-called peace of mind.[4] People such as us were too brutal toward him. But he had the

---

2. Norman Vincent Peale, *The Power of Positive Thinking* (New York: Prentice-Hall, Inc., 1952).

3. "We have always had a curious feeling that though we crucified Christ on a stick, he somehow managed to get hold of the right end of it, and that if we were better men we might try his plan." George Bernard Shaw, "Preface on the Prospects of Christianity," in *Androcles and the Lion* (New York: Brentano's, 1916), xiii.

4. Buttrick consistently criticized the "peace of mind" and "positive thinking" nostrums of Dale Carnegie (*How to Win Friends and Influence People*, 1936) and Norman Vincent Peale (*Power of Positive Thinking*). Buttrick wrote, "Another impressive form of sidestepping is seen in our modern cult of 'peace of mind.' It would have us believe that there is no evil that we ourselves cannot overcome by a prayer-formula and 'confidence.' 'Positive thinking' can guarantee both an attractive personality and business success. This world is a world in which we can always 'win friends and influence people,' if only we keep telling ourselves that 'every day in every way we are getting better and better.' When we set Jesus alongside this cheap evasion it dwindles into selfishness." George A. Buttrick, *God, Pain, and Evil* (Nashville: Abingdon Press, 1966), 137–38.

peace of God. He bequeathed it to us in his last will and testament: "My peace I give [bequeath] to you."[5] Peace in the New Testament meaning is first the mending of the vertical line between God and humanity by the grace of God, and only then it becomes the fastening on that upright of the horizontal line between persons and persons.

Once again, preaching is not the discussion of religion. That vague word opens the door to any religion. Karl Barth proposed that our faith is the death of all religion. He meant that religion as popularly understood is the human attempt to reach God—by laws kept, rituals fulfilled, disciplines obeyed, or ethical regimens fulfilled. But no one on her own can reach God. So, William Blake shows a man at the foot of a ladder that disappears in the sky. If the man tries to climb he will fall soon from dizziness, so he stands there crying, "I want! I want!"[6]

But he does not need to climb because God "for us and for our salvation came down and became truly human." So preaching is not a discussion of some religion. There are other caveats: it is not argument or an excursion into rationality. But these negatives are enough to serve our present purpose.

II

Next we note that the Event is a fourfold Event, a many-splendored thing.[7] The preacher proclaims *the life of Christ* not as biography but as newly understood in resurrection light. We need not try to dodge problems raised by honest biblical scholarship, such as those uncovered by form criticism or by the fact of redaction, or by what is now called "demythologizing." Here is my own conviction: these overlays can themselves be an opening for the Holy Spirit and themselves point to a hard core

---

5. John 14:27 (RSV).

6. William Blake, "I Want! I Want!", engraving, The Fitzwilliam Museum, Cambridge, UK, May 17, 1793. https://www.fitzwilliamprints.com/image/1094684/blake-william-i-want-i-want-by-william-blake.

7. The fourfold Event: chapter 1, the life of Christ, the death of Christ; chapter 2, the resurrection of Christ, the living (Holy Spirit) of Christ.

of actuality. There is a staunch record that we here call the life of Christ. Mark's Gospel gives a rough-and-ready chronology. Note some facets of the picture.

We see Christ sharing and bearing our humanness. To speak thus is not to deny deeps in him that go far deeper than our glib word *divine*, but it is to maintain that if he were not genuinely human he would have nothing to say to us. He was not an angel come slumming. He was not a marionet let down from the sky. The proposal sometimes heard that he knew all along that he was the Son of God makes his temptation a mock encounter and turns even his cross into phony dramatics. He hungered for food. He hungered for friendship. When he cut his finger the blood was like our blood. The Apostle's Creed blazons that fact: "was crucified, dead, and buried." He was "in all things tempted as we are,"[8] yet with no break in his obedience to the will of God.

He confronted our choices. He did not lead a pastoral life in a simple culture, despite many a pulpit. He spoke Aramaic, knew some colloquial Greek (spoken then from Spain to northern India), probably learned Hebrew in the synagogue school, and picked up tags of Latin from the Roman garrison. There were Greek academies and Greek gymnasia in Galilee, with instances even in Jerusalem. Just over the Nazareth hill he saw caravans moving from Damascus to Tyre and Sidon. He was cosmopolitan. He lived in our crisscross of decision. Should he join the Zealot underground or collaborate with Rome along with the Sadducees or go monastic with the Essenes or parade a disciplined piety with the Pharisees? These groups have their present-day successors. He refused all these roads. The cosmopolitan Christ! So what becomes of our uptight proposal that "he taught spiritual truths to individuals"? He was not a little holy man peddling platitudes to hermits. He lived our human life.

Yet he is our judgment, for his human words strike to the marrow of our bones. He does more than quicken our conscience, for our conscience of itself can't be trusted: it is like a ship's compass thrown out of "true" by

---

8. Heb 4:15 (GAB). Buttrick's initials (GAB) following a biblical citation indicate that the English translation from the Greek or Hebrew text is Buttrick's.

the ship's cargo. Christ "cleanses us from an evil conscience,"[9] and thus and then confronts us. He says, "Be pure in thought and deed"[10]—as if we could of ourselves! He says, "Love your enemies"[11]—though we rush to hate and kill them. He says, "Do good by stealth"[12] though we want to get credit for the little good we do. We speak of his sinlessness: who are we to know? What we mean is that in every crux of our life he is our judgment. He was so searching in word and act that his friends begged him to leave them, "for I am a sinful man,"[13] yet knew that if he did leave them they would have neither sun by day nor moon by night.

But judgment was held in a deeper love. Otherwise the judgment would leave us naked and lost. A story tells of a sculptor who fashioned in clay the perfect statue, and then feared that the night frost might break the clay. So he wrapped his bedclothes round the statue, and in the morning was himself found dead from cold.[14] We are anything but perfect, but Christ wrapped his life round us, and so died. The New Testament has a new word for this passionate goodwill—not *eros*, the fine fire of sexual love, for *eros* without this new love becomes erotic; and not *philia*, the solace of home love and friendship love, for *philia* without this new love

---

9. Heb 10:22 (GAB).

10. Paraphrase in consequence of the Sermon on the Mount and Beatitudes: "You, therefore, must be perfect, as your heavenly Father is perfect" (Matt 5:48, RSV).

11. Luke 6:27 (KJV).

12. Alexander Pope's paraphrase of Matt 6:3-4, "When you give alms, do not let your left hand know what your right hand is doing, so that your alms may be in secret" (RSV). Thus, Pope: "Do good by stealth, and blush to find it Fame," in "Epilogue to the Satires in Two Dialogues (1738), Dialogue I," in *Alexander Pope: Selected Poetry & Prose*, ed. William K. Wimsatt, 2nd ed. (New York: Holt, Rinehart, and Winston, 1951), 363, l. 136.

13. Luke 5:8 (RSV), spoken by Peter to Jesus.

14. The story of French artist Gabriel Briand's sculpture of the god "Mercury drawing a thorn out of his heel," for which Briand received posthumously the Medal of Honor from the Paris Salon in 1868. "One night the cold was so bitter that he heaped upon his bed all the clothes he possessed. He suddenly remembered his masterpiece, which he had just finished, and dreading lest the damp clay should be frozen, he stripped himself and put all his clothing and best 'covering around the figure.' The next day, the sculptor was found lying on his bed frozen to death." W. H. Crossland, "XXXIII: The Royal Holloway College," *Transactions*, vol. 3, New Series (London: The Royal Institute of British Architects, 1887), 146.

becomes philistine; but *agape*, an abstract mold word at first, but now by Christ himself a very wellspring.

So, the preacher preaches the life of Christ, yet not as stated biography. Had that been all, Christ might have dwindled to a paragraph in some ancient history book. We are moved not by love alone but by love willing to suffer and die, rather than be anything else but love. Besides, there would be little promise or power in signalizing a past event. So, we turn to the next item in the Gospel, *the death of Christ*.

III

One chord in a symphony may haunt the memory. A friend says of one such chord in the Beethoven "Fourth,"[15] "Since that is so, everything is all right." Such a chord in the Gospel symphony is an agony of discord, the cross. The New Testament links it again and again with pain and evil, with sin and death. Now why? This stress is the preacher's burden because our culture thinks it is overcoming evil and blinks at the word death. *What is sin*? Not a breach of the moral code, though that breach is usually involved. Bad people break the code from below it, while good people break the law from above it (in the name of a higher law), as Jesus broke the Sabbath code, which (incidentally) was bastioned deeper than the statutes of our common law. In any event, guilt doesn't run between a person and a code but between a person and God. Sin is the human attempt to be one's own god. Our world is populated with atomized "godlets." If they join forces in a greedy corporation or a national power structure, there is still infighting for personal control. Any newspaper provides evidence. In some instances, the newspaper is itself evidence, its headlines a "come-on" and its ads defying decency. Who can measure the havoc of our sins? Reinhold Niebuhr has somewhere said that if there were no sin, the burden of pain and evil might be a tolerable load.

---

15. Ludwig van Beethoven's Fourth Symphony in Bb major, Op. 60, 1806. The "dissonant" F-chord that "may haunt the memory" occurs at circa 3:15 in the first movement, as striking contrast to the allegro vivace that follows. Thus, the cross as "an agony of discord" contrasted with what follows, the Easter resurrection.

Thus it was sin that raised the cross. The word *sin* is nowadays a nonconductor, but the fact remains. All kinds of sin converged on Calvary: the avarice of storekeepers, the trampling of empire, the pride of ecclesiastics, the treachery of friends, and the bloody unconcern of the crowd. Say rather that sinful people there converged. Add what we call "natural evil": the flies stung, and the sun struck like swords. Add pain: cramps overtook him as the blood ebbed. Add death: on a gallows on a city dump. This is the discord of all human music. Yet it is the dissonant chord, the "rest chord" before the Great Amen.[16]

How and why? Before that question the preacher stammers, but the stammer stumbles on truth. How could any person be brash and confident before the cross? One fact is starkly clear: we can't save ourselves. How would we even begin? We can't go back to erase even one small lie. History moves forward; there is no return ticket. If we could go back, we have no eraser. That lie is not now ours alone: it is in the stream of history, and not a million chemists could extract it. If we could go back, we would take ourselves with us! Nothing is shallower than our modern doctrines of self-help. What price "progress"? Evolution and "the stream of history" can't save us, despite the nobility of de Jardin.[17] He has not grappled with the enormity of our transgression. Slums, racism, and southeast Asia[18] are hardly exhibit A of an evolving saintliness. Only God can save us. Only God who created life can recreate it. But how? The preacher still stumbles, but she is on the highroad.

God's redemption of our life can't be distant, it can't be by "wave of hand" or "turn of eye" from some remote paradise.[19] God can't say to the angels, "I've always had trouble with that unruly little planet, but write off

---

16. See n15.

17. Pierre Teilhard de Chardin (1881–1955), French Jesuit and evolutionist, author of *The Phenomenon of Man* and *The Divine Milieu*, who espoused the eventual consummation of all cosmic life in the "omega point" of divine, christological unity.

18. The Vietnam War, 1955–1975, waged in North and South Vietnam, Cambodia, and Laos by French and American colonial powers and their South Korean, Australian, Thai, and other allies, against communist North Vietnamese adversaries and their Russian, Chinese, and North Korean allies.

19. "It is by no breath, Turn of eye, wave of hand, that salvation joins issue with death!" from Robert's Browning's "Saul," XVIII, *The Complete Works of Robert Browning*, Cambridge Edition (Boston: Houghton Mifflin Company, 1895), 184.

their debt in the celestial ledgers." No, for we are not angels, and cannot read the angelic records. We are earthborn, and we have turned the earth into bloody shambles. If we are to be saved, we must be saved here in the midst of history.

God must take our flesh, walk our streets, knock at our door, and be victim of our cruel pride. Is that statement a presumption? Yes, but how else can we see it, and what else can we say? God must knock at our door and say in our speech, "Your sins are forgiven." How else could we understand? How else could we accept pardon? How else could we respond in joy, saying, "This I believe"? "See the Christ stand!"[20]

God's redemption can't be trivial. Our sin in Vietnam, in any comfortable suburb or any uncomfortable ghetto, is not trivial. If God shrugged off our lifelong pride or the red swath of war with an, "Oh, forget it," God would not be God and we would not be persons. Our concern would be nobler than God's unconcern. How to phrase this mystery? There must be trouble in the abyss, vast trouble, if we are to be saved. The New Testament word translated in the older versions, "He is the propitiation of our sins," is a mistranslation: the word is "expiation." But that is no trivial word: in its Hebrew antecedent it goes back to the Old Testament "mercy seat" with all its agonies and cleansings. Doctrines of "propitiation" (the word is not there) that show God bartering Christ to the devil or Christ buying off God's justice (against God's love) are wrong, but they appeal to me more than some hopeless doctrine of self-help, or one that belittles Christ as mere "example." Sin and death are a fatal urgency. God is not trivial. There is a "Lamb slain from the foundation of the world."[21]

Again: God's redemption can't be local in either time or space, else it would be prisoner of the first century. Suppose Christ had blessed only that time: we would have been bereft, for sin comes down from generation to generation. In that sense and in a deeper sense it is "original sin." Freud bridles at such realism, and then unwittingly repeats it, for he tells us (what the Good Book told us long ago) that the sins of the fathers are

---

20. "O Saul, it shall be A Face like my face that receives thee: a Man like to me, Thou shalt love and be loved by, forever: a Hand like this hand Shall throw open the gates of new life to thee! See the Christ stand!" Browning, "Saul," 184, last line. See also Acts 7:55-56.

21. Rev 13:8 (KJV).

"visited on their children."[22] How far back? All the way back. "As in Adam all die"![23] Suppose Christ had blessed only that land: again we would have been bereft. No national bounds can imprison human guilt. "Total depravity" does not mean that any of us is totally depraved. If we were, we wouldn't know it. It means that the whole area of human life in every land is disfigured by mortal pride. Every corporate structure is pockmarked—the National Association of Manufacturers, the Teamsters' Union, the city government in every city, the science that in the pretense of neutral mind consents to the wicked prostitution of science, yes, and the church itself. Redemption can't be local: "He is the expiation for our sins, and not for ours only but also for the sins of the whole world."[24]

We now stand before the cross. It is not trivial: "My God, my God, why have you forsaken me?"[25] The cry of dereliction is a midnight of midnight: even rats forsake a derelict ship. The cross is *not distant*. It is set up outside every city wall. The Northwestern University Chapel has planted it eastward outside the chancel window, in the common earth, where the traffic moves unheeding. Amazingly a gallows has crossed an ocean, and while we weren't looking became the monstrous, wonderful focus of our worship. Nay, it has chosen to stand above our graves, and that is the final nasty anachronism (a gallows over the grave of someone you love?) unless, unless—the cross is not of one land or one generation. You can buy Christmas cards in the Orient, though there the babe has tiny upraised slits for eyes. You can find pictures of the cross in every generation. Thus, the preacher's Gospel: God has visited our planet and taken on his heart the drear midnight of our sins.

IV

The cross is not the final term in our faith. It is an essential term, for without it there is no redemption of "the fatal flaw" that disfigures human life. But had the cross been the whole story, history would have been

---

22. Exod 34:7; Num 14:18.
23. 1 Cor 15:22 (KJV).
24. 1 John 2:2 (RSV).
25. Ps 22:1 (GAB [NRSV]).

tragic. We would have had to say what some in our age of violence do say: "The best is at the mercy of the worst."[26] After Calvary, Easter! Yet the resurrection would have been a hollow triumph without the cross. Our clichés propose that only through "sacrifice" are we cleansed. Yes, but whose sacrifice? The sacrifice of a gangster daring death brings small cleansing. The sacrifice of the average church member, meaning you and me, is no huge asset. Only God's self-giving, in sharing of our life, can cleanse the whole family of humankind, provided that is not the end of the Story.

So the life and death of Christ give content and purchase to his resurrection, as the resurrection validates his life and death: "This is my beloved Son: hear him."[27] We must add that the resurrection would have been "locked in history" without his presence. The Holy Spirit gives the total Event its contemporary thrust. The Event is fourfold, yet indivisibly one Event. A friend wrote a book entitled *The Crucifixion in Our Street*.[28] It showed clotheslines strung from tenement to tenement across the road on New York's east side, the clothes props transecting the lines in a hundred signs of the cross. That friend knew the Gospel, so there was a sequel entitled *The Resurrection in Our Street*.[29] Both books came alive through the Holy Spirit of the present Lord. The Event is ongoing, dynamic, and instant. A sermon has those same marks. "Dynamic": the New Testament word is *dunamin*, dynamite! The explosive power of true preaching! But we anticipate. Our next glad task is to speak to the third and fourth terms in the one Event.

---

26. "See how much the estates, liberties, and lives, even of the best men, lie at the mercy of the worst, against whose false oaths, innocency itself is no fence," Matthew Henry, late minister of the Gospel in Chester, *An Exposition of the Old Testament in Four Volumes*, vol. 3 (Edinburgh: C. Wright & Co., for the Publisher J. Wood, 1758), 205.

27. Mark 9:7 (KJV).

28. George Stewart, *The Crucifixion in Our Street* (New York: George H. Doran Co., 1927).

29. George Stewart, *The Resurrection in Our Street* (Garden City, NY: Doubleday, Doran & Co., 1928).

CHAPTER TWO

We Preach the Gospel (II)

The third term in the Christ Event. Term? What a dull word! A sunrise from beyond time and space! Our faith is always "surprised by joy."[1] President Nixon described the moon journey as "the greatest event since the creation." He has been wrong before—and since. However, there are only three happenings: the creation, the incarnation, and the eschaton. That mid-Event illuminates the other two, for Christ is Alpha and Omega. If one event in the fourfold Event should be highlighted (it shouldn't), it would be the resurrection.

I

That light is now flung back on what Christ said. The Sermon on the Mount is an instance. That first group of teachings in Matthew's Gospel

---

1. The title of C. S. Lewis's autobiography, *Surprised by Joy: The Shape of My Early Life* (New York: Harcourt Brace, 1955). Buttrick indicated that it was he "who first urged that his [Lewis's] work be published in America. The publishers sent me 'Screwtape' to read, explaining that they were fearful if it would sell!" ("Letter to Professor Thomas Van Osdall, Ashland College, Ohio," Dec. 20, 1965, Buttrick Papers, Harvard Archives, HUG FP 90.8/1, Box 1). "They told me that another firm had examined the book and decided not to publish it: they feared that the American public would not understand the book's strange pattern. It had gone through a dozen editions in England in a few months. After a few pages I began to chuckle, and after a few more was carrying it round the house, saying, 'Listen to this!'" ("The Screwtape Letters," Sermon M.A. 1159, May 2, 1943/P.M., M.A.P.C., Buttrick Papers, Harvard Archives, FP 90.42, Box 8).

has sometimes been labeled a "Christian ethic." Is there any such? Our faith is faith, not a code of conduct. One scholar has described the Sermon as "unconditional demand." Yes, of course. But that is not its climate. The dark light of the cross and the blinding light of Easter Day both play on Christ's word, which is now made contemporary by the Holy Spirit. So, what we read is more than a lifestyle; it is the morning road under the morning brightness of the Risen Lord.

That light is flung back on his deeds. Consider his healing miracles. They were not ends in themselves, and they were more than the compulsions of his compassion. Sometimes he refused to heal. Sometimes he hid his healings. All whom he healed died at last. In the light of the resurrection we now understand: the healings were just what he called them: auguries of the kingdom in which there is neither pain nor death. The word of Christ, "The kingdom of God is come on you," is the sign: Easter Day is the countersign.

Focally that light is flung back on the cross. The cross otherwise is blank dismay. What has flung the shadow of the cross over our planet? A great joy. Now we know that God raised Christ from the dead. So we know also that God was in his dying. Doing what? Bearing the sins that slew him, yes, and bearing them away beyond sin and all destruction. There could have been no tremendous doctrines of atonement without the Resurrection.

II

We should not pretend that the various accounts of the resurrection can be reconciled. They can't—except in their own burning joy. One record seems intent to show us that he rose in the same flesh in which he died;[2] another indicates a new body by which he "entered, the door being shut."[3] One account locates his return in Jerusalem;[4] another, in Galilee.[5]

---

2. Luke 24:36-43.
3. Cf. John 20:19-29.
4. Luke 24:13-48, John 20:19-29.
5. Mark 16:7, Matt 28:7, John 21.

We worry about these seeming contradictions, while the Gospels themselves seem strangely unconcerned. When shall we understand that these four books, miniature yet mighty, go clean beyond literal and objective history, if there is or ever could be such boredom: they are faith-history. Not dreary factualism but heart-seized confession. Who could reconcile the versions of even human love? Only fools would try. The resurrection Gospel simply overwhelms every attempt at the telling. When shall we understand that "the letter kills, the Spirit makes alive"?[6] Of course, there are certain deeper accords.

The versions are all lowly. The word of the Risen Lord to the woman was not "All hail," despite the King James account, for that conceit was not in him. The Greek word is as homey as homemade bread. It is closest perhaps to our word *Hello* if spoken in a glad tenderness.[7] If we or anybody like us had been trying to concoct a fiction, would we have chosen that word as the first word of the resurrection? No, we would have gone Cecil DeMille, with ten thousand trumpets and ten thousand banners on the sunrise hills. We would have had Christ batter down the gates of Caiaphas and Pilate to confound those scurvy rascals forever. We would have shown him reclaiming his clothes from the soldiers who gambled for them. He would have put to flight the whole Roman army. But the Gospels are true to his lowliness. Thus they bear the signature of truth. Notice, and then notice again: he appeared only to those who loved him!

The versions agree that the first witnesses were taken by surprise. There is nothing in the record to justify Bultmann's phrase that they "came to believe" that.[8] Even the deathless Emmaus story says, "their eyes were opened"—*then*, suddenly, as they recognized what he had done in that last sad Supper. He met the witnesses in a sudden wonder. One account says, "they were afraid."[9]

---

6. 2 Cor 3:6 (GAB). "For the letter kills, but the spirit makes alive" (IG-ENT, 713). IG-ENT indicates the *Interlinear Greek–English New Testament* translation.

7. Gk. *chairete* (greetings), root: *chairó* (rejoice).

8. "All that historical criticism can establish is the fact that the first disciples came to believe in the resurrection." Rudolf Bultmann, *Kerygma and Myth*, ed. Hans Werner Bartsch, Torchbook ed. (New York: Harper & Row, 1961), 42.

9. Cf. Luke 24:37.

Of course. The blank wall of death became in that moment an open gate through which they saw worlds on worlds. They could no longer live in their closed world, for it was no longer closed. Of course. They were afraid in blinding rapture. How much people then believed in resurrection is a question. The Sadducees didn't: they foresaw only the dim bleak realm of Sheol. The Pharisees did. The common person groped on misty flats. One thing we do know: a crucified man was reckoned accursed. He, return? Would that be blessing? His friends were seized by wonder: their sun had "risen in the west." As to that, the various accounts agree.

There is another crucial agreement: all the records tell us that the resurrection was the act of God: "whom you slew, God raised."[10] Only God could set him free from the darkness of the tomb and brutal human blindness. We must not speak of the resurrection as if it were some kind of magic levitation. No, the Event of Easter Day revealed a plan that is "before the foundation of the world."[11] The purpose of creation was now an open secret in the Easter light. The Christ of time was beyond and above time: "Without him nothing was made":[12] such was history's origin. As for history's end, "the kingdom of the world has become the kingdom of our Lord and of his Christ, and he shall reign for ever and ever."[13] God is "dead"? No, God raised his Son from the dead. Of this the New Testament speaks in one voice. So why try to reconcile versions as if they were pedestrian science or little matching pieces of a crossword puzzle? That attempt approaches blasphemy. There is one brimming tide of joy. The various accounts are flashes in the waves as they break.

III

We should comment on modern skepticisms that affect the preaching of the Gospel. Nowadays people stick a finger in their eyes to prove they

---

10. Acts 5:30 (paraphrase), "The God of our fathers raised up Jesus, whom ye slew and hanged on a tree" (KJV).

11. Eph 1:4 (RSV).

12. John 1:3 (GAB).

13. Rev 11:15 (RSV).

can see. Only rarely does the New Testament defend faith in the resurrection. It *does* on occasion, for skepticism is nothing new. The mood of these rare reactions is, "Do you think we could lie about Jesus?" In our time, since we try to live by dull debate that resembles eating straw for breakfast, the doubts are rife. So we now air them.

Suppose the resurrection is not historic fact but only the mind's illusion? The word *historic* raises profound questions. When a person says of his neighbor, "He is staunch and true," is that judgment "historic"? As for the other word *illusion*, it leads into psychiatry. People suffering from illusions are subject to strange heights and glooms. They can't grapple with daily life because they live in an unreal world. Is this the picture of New Testament folk? They laid hands on an alien time and changed it, not to break it but by giving it a new glow and power. These folk with all their failures were "for real."

Suppose the resurrection stories are just that: a deliberate fiction? We can easily trace the origin of this misgiving. The modern person trusts only scientific eyes and ears, refusing mystery. Then what of the cosmos? How would any of us begin to make—anything? What of our own life, given the strange power to view ourselves in time—from a stance above time? The first disciples answered this charge of "concoction" with a certain indignation: "If Christ is not raised we are false witnesses of God,"[14] that is, worthy of the final damnation. They were not liars. They called Jesus "the Truth." They warned one another joyously to "speak the truth one to another in love."[15] Almost they were the core of truth telling in the ancient world. They died rather than traduce their Lord.

But, the skeptic continues, where is the substantial evidence? Strange word, that word *substantial*, like a brick hurled through a window. Is that the only way to prove somebody is outside the house? We have no recording of Christ's resurrection voice, no legal affidavit of his presence. Would these be "substantial"? They would be in Aramaic, a virtually dead dialect; and, besides, anybody could brand them forgery—with small fear of

---

14. 1 Cor 15:15 (GAB). Gk. *pseudomartyres* (false witnesses). Cf. Exod 20:16 (RSV), "You shall not bear false witness."

15. Eph 4:15 (GAB paraphrase).

rebuttal. Here are certain plain facts. *One*: the apostles were changed by the resurrection—from cowardice to courage, from dim understanding to piercing insight, and notably from selfishness to a new kind of love. *Two*: the New Testament was written, with a thousand references to Christ and not any of them *in memoriam*. The New Testament has been the light to the human pilgrimage. *Three*: the church rose, not to sing dirges round a grave but hallelujahs round a conquered grave—a church whose persistence despite its obvious defections is its own strange evidence. Are these items "substantial"? Yes and no. The trouble with them is not a lack of logic but a too-sharp challenge to the will.

As for all these doubts, don't we have our own evidence? One of the leaders of the God-is-dead movement said, "But Jesus gets me." Incidentally, Jesus didn't advise him to forget God. But our point is that, for that man, Jesus is not dead. Nor for "Jesus Superstar"![16] In that play the New Testament receives its usual drubbing from the contemporary stage: Jesus, the lowly Savior, is given a name he would have repudiated; and his picture is as thin as varnish. But Jesus, once more, is never reckoned "dead." Here is my own confession: I live by his presence. When I forget him, I don't live. I see all things from Nixon to nostrums to nagging doubts through my best imaginings of him, Christ, as he is thrust forward from a sunrise of mystery. He is more real to me than myself or any neighbor in the flesh. He will never bludgeon us into belief: our freedom is too precious to him. But we *may* believe, because he will never forsake us. Once more: he comes again only to those who love him; and "blest are those who have not seen" (under bondage to failing sight) and "yet have believed."[17] His first followers said of the skeptic and the resurrection, "Why do we go in jeopardy of our lives?" They meant, "Wouldn't we be fools to die for a fiction?" Maybe that willingness to suffer for Christ's sake is the evidence for which an alien world waits age on age.

Take note that we are already engaged with the fourth term of the one indivisible Christ Event. Why? Because we can't talk about him in

---

16. Andrew Lloyd Webber's and Tim Rice's *Jesus Christ Superstar*, the 1970 musical rock opera that debuted on New York City's Broadway in 1971.

17. John 20:29, "Blessed are those who have not seen and yet believe" (RSV).

loyalty except by the gift of his present Spirit. This doctrine, this life, is now neglected or abused rather than acknowledged in love. So a frank word about the abuse. There is nowadays a rush or rash of what might be labeled "Spiritism." Perhaps that is the price we must pay for the neglect. The trouble here is that those who prate about the Spirit unwittingly try to split the Christ Event into four terms so as to throw the other three into the discard. A certain woman evangelist (not of these parts) almost crooned about "sweet Jesus," not without undertones of sexuality. Said one hearer, "She is a marvelous witness to the Spirit." He might more wisely have said, "No, she wallows in him, and he is not that kind of sauna bath."

She forgets the other terms of the One Event, more especially his life and word. He spoke about segregation. For that word he was broken on the wall of human prejudice. He opposed national and racial segregation, as witness the parable of the good Samaritan; and the segregation of the rich from the poor, as in the parable of Dives and Lazarus; and the segregation of the godly community from the world, as in the parable of the two prodigals. What right has that evangelist to ignore the life and word of Christ? As a matter of fact, she comes close to ignoring his death. Oh yes, she sings,

> In the cross, in the cross
> Be my glory ever.[18]

But was she ready to be overborne by the sins, private and corporate, that slew him? Was she willing in that stark sense to be "baptized into his death"? Does she oppose at final risk the assault of greedy trade, rampant militarism, and a blind nationalistic pride? To preach an amputated Christ is blasphemy. Revivalism can become the enemy of evangelism.

There are other dangers in "Spiritism." As for "healing missions" in our time, they are valid. The church has neglected its healing ministry, and so has invited such plausibilities as Christian Science. So far, so good. But can you imagine Paul speaking at a healing mission, saying, "So I glory in my infirmities"?[19] They would reckon him some kind of nut. Can we offer

---

18. Frances J. Crosby, "Jesus, Keep Me Near the Cross," 1869.

19. 2 Cor 12:9, "Most gladly therefore will I rather glory in my infirmities, that the power of Christ may rest upon me" (KJV).

God an unbribed devotion except in "infirmities"? Is our faith only fair-weather faith? Jesus did not ask release from pain: he walked right into it. As for the ten lepers who were healed, nine forgot to thank him. It might have been better for them to have remained lepers: They would have been kept out of circulation. The whole issue should be rethought—under the total Event of Christ. We could instance also the modern cult of "speaking in tongues." That also has clear New Testament warrant. Paul spoke "in tongues." A college student of fine intelligence told me convincingly that he found great release in speaking in tongues. The question remained as to whether his hearers found release. What about Vietnam? What about the crosstown ghetto? No, these sharp questions do not outlaw glossolalia. Yet Paul refused to give it centrality. He warned that it could become bedlam. He said flatly that he would rather speak one word with his mind than a hundred words in "tongues." These caveats are sharp because the need for them is sharp.

V

Yet the fourth term in the one Event has been tragically ignored. Christ himself was anointed by the Spirit. Of his own preaching he said, "The Spirit of the Lord is come on me."[20] At Pentecost the Spirit possessed his followers. Charles Williams has rightly named his history of the church by the title, *The Descent of the Dove*.[21] The origin of the dove symbol is hard to trace. Maybe it goes back to the dove given as promise and pledge of the end of the great flood, and thus to the early covenant God made with Noah and the human race. There is no preaching except in the light and power of the Holy Spirit. There is no church without the indwelling Presence. Only so is the church "the body of Christ." This mighty truth we cannot compass. Who could grasp the sunrise? So all we can presently say within the limits of homiletics and the clock is to spotlight this and that gift of the Spirit without whom preaching is vanity.

---

20. Luke 4:18 (GAB), Isa 61:1.

21. Charles Williams, *The Descent of the Dove: A Short History of the Holy Spirit in the Church* (Grand Rapids: Eerdmans, 1972 [New York: Oxford University Press, 1939]).

Thus: the Spirit interprets and inspires the scripture from which we preach. Our sermon phrase (with Billy Graham it was almost a trademark), "the Bible says," has its dangers. The Bible is not a level tableland. Still less is it a compendium of "words to the wise." That job belongs to Ann Landers. The Bible says—many things: that the sky rests on pillars that rest on a flat earth. Does it? We can't squirm out of the question by pleading that such passages are metaphor: they are not. That belief was accepted cosmology in that era. The Bible says of one Israelitish war victory that the victors should kill all prisoners including women and keep the younger women for themselves for obvious purposes.[22] "The Bible says"! What is the answer? The Christ Event is the crown and fulfillment of the Bible story. He is Lord of the sabbath. He is Lord of the church. He is Lord of the scriptures. There is only one question to ask as we read the book. This question: How does this passage look under the eyes of the Spirit? The literalist blasphemes; he leaves the Spirit unemployed. The skeptic with his poor surface judgment about the "folly of believing in an ancient book" little knows: the book is under the living Presence. The preacher studies the sacred page, and it comes alive. The promise is fulfilled: "He will take what is mine and declare it to you."[23]

The Holy Spirit gives the preacher the instant, and therefore the timely, word: "in that very hour,"[24] while he works at a desk, while he preaches in the pulpit. That promise is not *carte blanche*, though many a preacher has so presumed on it. We can't lazily stab the book with a penpoint, recite the verses (verses are a disfigurement), and then expect the luminous truth to flow forth in liquid gold. The context (it counts!) tells of preachers being hailed before princes and ruler, as Paul was hailed before Agrippa.[25] Small fear that some preachers will suffer that fate! But the promise *is* true

---

22. Num 31:1-54, the war of Israelite revenge and vindication against the Midianites, led by Moses.

23. John 16:13-15, "When the Spirit of truth comes, he will guide you into all the truth.... He will glorify me, because he will take what is mine and declare it to you. All that the Father has is mine. For this reason I said that he [the Spirit of truth] will take [Gk. *lambanei*, receive] what is mine and declare it to you" (NRSV).

24. Luke 12:12 (RSV).

25. "Hailed before" as when called out, summoned, ordered to stop.

for the preacher who suffers and rejoices in the birth pangs of a sermon. One well-known homiletician writes about "the agony of preaching."[26] He refers primarily to confrontation with a blind and alien world. But he might have used the same phrase of the pain of preparation of any sermon, though a better title in any context would be "the agony and ecstasy of preaching." The Holy Spirit gives the faithful emissary the instant word (bright breakthrough in the familiar frustration), and the road map, and the whole preachment.

The Holy Spirit is the preacher's fortifier. You and I ask of the martyrs how they could be so brave. They too asked. If we were tied to a post in the sea at low tide, and if we knew we would slowly drown in the incoming tide, would we sing hymns? Two young girls did just that as martyrs in the Scots church.[27] They were girded by the Spirit's power. Many a preacher faces a slower death in our now polarized church. Wealthy people, who know little about the Book, tell the preacher to "stick to the Bible." Suppose he did—to the thunder of Amos or Christ's warning to the rich. These critics are not inhumane: they wouldn't starve a dog. But they would and do starve out a preacher, making an uncertain future for him and his family. But even then, the Spirit is the preacher's fortifier. Some preachers leave the church. Some are thrust out. Most stay in, saying with their Lord: "There are many things but you cannot bear them now."[28] Yet they speak the truth in love. Only by the Spirit's comfort and power can the preacher endure the nagging frustrations of the present church. In the Spirit he is well content.

The Holy Spirit unifies the church and thus clears a path for the preacher's word. The Spirit bridges the gap between preacher and people, yes, and between factions in the church, provided there are Pentecost groups who wait the Spirit's coming. Of course, the preacher too can "grieve the Spirit," and of course the church can rebel against the Spirit, but, granted this openness in prayer, the Spirit brings unity even in the

---

26. Source unknown.

27. Andrew Lang, "Scotland," *1911 Encyclopedia Britannica*, vol. 24, 452, public domain. The Wigtown martyrdom of young Margaret Wilson and older Margaret MacLauchlan. Commemorated in the painting *The Martyr of the Solway* (1871) by John Everett Millais.

28. John 16:12 (GAB), paraphrase.

dislocations of our time. The Spirit's will is ecumenical. In the book of Acts the day of Pentecost is obviously set over against the tower of Babel.[29] The tower builders were cursed by pride ("let us make us a name"), and therefore reciprocally with anxiety ("lest we be scattered abroad"), so their tower fell and confusion of tongues fell on them.[30] The Pentecost company waited on their Lord. Then the Spirit, like a rushing wind that blew away dead leaves, like a fire that purged away their dross. Then and thus they became one communion. There is such a group in every church. Every church waits their prayer, and the Spirit's coming.

The Holy Spirit is the preacher's justifier. Who is equal to the telling of the good news? No one. Who is good enough? No one. Who can proclaim God's mercy in Christ? Only the forgiven sinner. Thus, the preacher qualifies, provided not trying to live in easy presumption of pardon. Sometimes the preacher is lazy, sometimes is pursued by a carnal imagination, sometimes despairs, and sometimes is tripped by a cheap success, as empty as it is cheap. Yet despite grades that are just short of failure, if Christ were to ask, "Do you love me?" the preacher could answer in a glad and honest yes. All right: there is a legend of Nicodemus that he tried to carve a statue of his Lord, and botched the task, and fell on sleep in a sad heart; and that while he slept angels turned failure into a striking likeness. Thus the Spirit mends and completes our broken sermons and broken lives. Then in our incorrigible pride we are prone to say what Nicodemus said when he woke: "I carved better than I thought."[31] Then that pride is forgiven. A friend stands by us in the constant Judgment and pleads our case when we have no case. The "fruit of the Spirit" is precisely that kind of grace.

VI

These instances only wave at a great wonder. We are all asking about the new form of the church, and have no clear answer, for it is not given

---

29. Acts 2.

30. Gen 11:1-9 (RSV).

31. The Legend of Volto Santo (Holy Face), a wooden crucifix in Lucca, Italy. https://www.twopartsitaly.com/blog/2017/9/16/the-legend-of-the-volto-santo-holy-face.

humans to pinpoint coming events or the patterns of a new age. But Paul by the wisdom of the Spirit gave guidance to the church when it had no form, when, torn away from the synagogue and groping in an alien culture, it took new form. Obviously, we are in a crux in human story. All things change before our eyes. Beyond doubt the church must change, yet not unled. Another instance: the Spirit grants us wisdom in the crisscross of a tumultuous time. Let's take busing controversies as an instance.[32] Nobody could then accuse us of an easy question or an easy answer! What is education? Not "reading, writing, and 'rithmetic," but "learn of me." What's that mean? Children learning to live with other children of other races. All right: busing is a small price to pay for such joy and peace. Besides, we might thus learn open housing through open hearts, and thus end all busing.

So we should not neglect the great fourth term of the One Great Event. For though our mind is God's gift, and though the doors of a church should be high enough for us to take our heads inside, we cannot intellectualize our way in this ambiguous earth. Modern people trust their reason. But reason can rationalize, making "the worse appear the better reason," or it can become unhinged. The ambiguity rests on the preacher, for in the very fact of being a preacher he separates himself, despite his fervent wish, from unbelievers. So he is liable to the charge of false piety even though he is guiltless. How do we find our way? We don't because we can't. But we don't need to try. In prayer and trust we are led—of the Spirit, who is Christ living, dying, raised in power, and our present Lord.

---

32. Busing to facilitate integration of public schools following the Supreme Court's 1971 decision.

CHAPTER THREE

The Power of Preaching

Has preaching any power? Many a preacher wonders and fears. Her pipings seem lost in a hurricane. Her function seems to have been stolen by press, radio, and television. Perhaps she is a vestige, a relic, a curio. Her mood is an Elijah mood: "I, even I only, am left; and they seek my life, to take it away."[1] If that mood is right, if the preacher's day is done, she should not ask for an oxygen tent: she should die. She should not cumber the ground. Paul said, "I'm not ashamed of the gospel: it is God's own power for salvation to all who have faith in God."[2] But that is about the Gospel, not about sermons—unless the two are inevitably one. Are they? We now ask.

I

She should come to terms with the word *power*. Power is determined by what we wish to do. So we should keep asking, "Power for what?" A wrecking car has power to pull a disabled truck, but no power to plant a garden. A bomb has power to blast a city, but no power to perform an eye operation. A space capsule has power to reach the moon, but no power to mend a broken heart. Even crudely physical power would be null and void

---

1. 1 Kgs 19:10 (RSV).
2. Rom 1:16 (CEB).

without our human desire and ability. When we ask about the power of preaching, we face a sequence of questions, as follows: (a) Power for what? (b) Have we the wish and ability? and (c) If we lack the ability, whatever our desire, is there any real power back of us?

Power for what? What is the purpose of preaching? Not to persuade people to join the church, unless the church is a true door to a kingdom. Not to convert people (converted from what kind of life to what kind of life?), unless conversion makes a person a witness to a kingdom. Not to "heal" people (the healing can be hugged and advertised), unless the healing sets a person free to hail a kingdom. The purpose of preaching is to testify to a kingdom that was and is and is to be: "Jesus came preaching the gospel of God, and saying, 'The time is fulfilled, and the kingdom of God is at hand; repent, and believe in the gospel.'"[3] "At hand" does not mean "in your midst," for it wasn't, at least not in main intention; and it doesn't mean "within you," for the Gospel is not any such vague mysticism: it means in him, Christ, who had now "come upon them."[4] All right: preaching doesn't make the kingdom: it heralds the kingdom and testifies to it in joy.

So the purpose of preaching is to open mortal life to everlasting life incarnate in Christ. It isn't in noisy competition with a noisy world, whatever some preachers may believe. It doesn't try to entertain, though it is the only excitement. It doesn't blast judgmentally like a battleship, for Christ didn't come to destroy. It doesn't get sidetracked into saying, "Join the church: a hundred new members for Easter"; no, for Christ is Lord of the church. It is not diverted into saying, "Believe the Bible," for Christ is Lord of the Bible, which is inspired by his Spirit. Preaching is not "relevant" (a now almost sainted word) in the sense that it can be easily related to our raucous time: it is not "relevant." It is a "scandal," but it is related—by confrontation. It is pertinent. It is the only pertinence. The purpose of preaching is to say, "Do a roundabout-face, for the everlasting kingdom has come upon you in Christ."

---

3. Mark 1:14-15 (RSV).

4. Acts 1:8 (RSV), "You shall receive power when the Holy Spirit has come upon you."

II

Now to the question that seems a culmination but is actually immediate: *Who is back of the preacher?* If she has no power beyond herself, she is "dust to dust." If she is merely professional, however thorough and skillful her training, professionalism will slay her. If her sermons are sermonic, they will set people's teeth on edge. If her words are only words, they are already "gone with the wind." In my boyhood a favorite weapon was a bundle of newspaper at the end of a long string. I brought down the weapon on the soaking wet canvas of a vendor's truck and split the canvas. Immediately the vendor asked, "Who's back of you?" He might well ask! I had no bank account. The preacher is even more bereft. She herself is a sinner, and any holier-than-thou stance only compounds the sin. Her words are lost in a tumultuous world. She dies. She has no power, unless *unless* Christ, the incarnate kingdom, is with her and moves through her.

Thus we touch the most neglected doctrine in Christian thought: that of the Holy Spirit. The New Testament is the book of the Holy Spirit: the Old Testament also, though there the word is "Thy presence," whereas in the New the word is God in Christ. The church is the community of the Holy Spirit, and only so can it have authority. Why do the Epistles seem unconcerned with our agonized quest for the very words from the very lips of Christ? Why this apparent unconcern about "the historical Jesus"? Because Christ was with them in Spirit. The main question was not "What did he say?" (though that was an essential) but "What *is* he saying?" Their prayer was "that you may know the mind of the Spirit."[5]

Only by the Spirit can we account for either the persistence of the church or the persistence of the kingdom. The preacher now is prone to self-pity or at least the sense of frustration, for how to expect a hearing in this blind and blatant culture? But what of the preacher in the first

---

5. Buttrick wrote elsewhere, "The early church asked just one question in the crux of decision: 'What is the mind of the Spirit?' They consulted the Risen Christ. They could not ransack the past, much less read the future. They deeply wished to know what Christ asked of them then and there, and left past and future in his sovereign hands. No, they did not receive specifics in every instance or even in many instances, but they were given a clear direction, and light step by step as they traveled." George A. Buttrick, *God, Pain, and Evil* (New York: Abingdon Press, 1966), 112. See Rom 8:26-27, 1 Cor 2:10-16, and Phil 2:5.

century? The Empire might tomorrow lead the one preaching to martyrdom in the arena, the synagogue report her as subversive, the pagan temple with its thousand prostitutes seduce the congregation, the bustling marketplace surely ignore her except when threatening its profits, and the crowd, uncaring and dead of heart, treat her as less than a cipher. If you had proposed that a few slaves meeting for an hour in some cottage to hear about a crucified Messiah would outlast the pagan temple, you would have roused a hoarse laugh in any street in Corinth. Forget the catacombs (or any other era of "the underground church," as if one ever could): we have said enough to raise our question. Cultures change, empires rise and fall, and preaching itself takes color from an alien world. Then how does preaching persist? Not by the preacher's skill or by what we choose to call "personality." No, but because Christ in his present power stoops to be born of our weakness. The Lord God everlasting came into our planet through his Son who "came preaching," and who by his resurrection power carries the preacher's word through any cross and any grave.

So we need only enumerate the names for the Holy Spirit in the New Testament to know in joy the preacher's power. The Spirit is the preacher's *strengthener*: the true meaning of the name Comforter. The Spirit is the preacher's *interpreter*: light plays on the book to reveal its trenchant and compassionate truth. The Spirit is the preacher's *advocate*, pleading with God that pardon may fall on the preacher's pride and laziness. The Spirit is the preacher's *instant word*, giving "in that very hour what you ought to say,"[6] though not without the preacher's fidelity. The pagan emperor carpeted his tent with a rug woven all over with the sign of the cross: this to greet Saint Francis in a time when to tread on the cross was final blasphemy. The saint never looked at his feet. So the emperor roared, "You have trampled the cross!" Instantly the saint answered, "There were three crosses: I trod on the other two."[7] In "that very hour"!

---

6. Luke 12:12 (RSV). Greek δεῖ (it is binding), thus "what you *ought* to say." Buttrick wrote, "Giving to him 'in that very hour what he shall say.'"

7. See George Arthur Buttrick, *So We Believe So We Pray* (New York: Abingdon-Cokesbury Press, 1951), 64, citing Ernest Raymond, *In the Steps of St. Francis* (New York: H. C. Kinsey & Co., Inc. 1939), 223–25. The "emperor" was the Sultan of Egypt whom St. Francis of Assisi met during the fifth Crusade in an attempt to prevent war with the Muslims. As legend has

III

Now we ask: Is preaching the best means of heralding the kingdom? What are the substitutes? Discussion groups? They have their place provided some members really believe in Christ. Otherwise the group vainly hopes that by pooling ignorance it can flesh out wisdom. Milton did not go into a huddle with other poets to write the sonnet on his blindness. The preacher does not echo the group, still less the crowd. She truckles[8] as little as the stars. She begs your pardon as little as the tides. So the real joy of the group is that it may uncover a genuine preacher.

What else? Pageantry and drama? They have found their home in the church, and there they have been reborn. Modern worship explores them, though it is not always worship: Luther said something about "pernicious dramatics." Drama has an essential place. The trouble is that it demands long preparation in both authors and actors. So how can it replace the instancy of the word—and the Word? An advocate for the arts came to our church claiming that drama is the focal proclamation because it gives us chance to "live" the Gospel, not merely speak it. She meant "act," not "live." I sat there feeling leprous. When she invited the leper to speak, I beat upon a leprous breast, cried aloud "Unclean! Unclean!" and then proposed that her only fault was that she had preached. When she protested, I pursued her bloodthirstily: "You should have come with a drama." That's the issue: a drama is a splendid ally, but it is too slow to be more than an ally.

Then what of movies, radio, and television? Movies just now are pornographic in a wretched pharisaism posing as "realism." Radio is reiterated advertising with intervals of canned music, under control of big business in its steal of the middle air that Paul described as filled with invisible demonisms; he may have been right. As for television, it is mostly trivial pap

---

it, accompanied by Brother Illuminato (possibly a translator), Francis is reputed to have said to the Sultan, "Thieves were also crucified along with our Lord. We have the true Cross of our Lord and Savior Jesus Christ; we adore it and show it great devotion; if the holy Cross of the Lord has been given to us, the cross of the thieves has been left to you as your share. That is why I had no scruple in walking over the symbols of brigands," in Marion A. Habig, ed., *St. Francis of Assisi: Omnibus of Sources*, 3rd rev. ed. (Chicago: Franciscan Herald Press, 1973), 1614–15.

8. Acts in subservience.

for trivial minds, with every few minutes outright appeal to our greedy fears. Yes, preachers good, bad, and indifferent use all three media, and we should be grateful for the good in this employment. But McLuhan's astonishing trust in our electronic communication,[9] with Thor Hall as his sponsor,[10] is sadly misplaced. The "medium" is not the "message." How could it be? My F.M. machine,[11] much appreciated in certain stations, is still not Gospel: it is a piece of machinery. Furthermore, all these means offer canned speech, words at secondhand, language partly sundered from the person speaking and the person hearing. Voices do not wander off by themselves, except in *Alice in Wonderland* where the grin appeared without the cat.

There is no substitute for firsthand speech. No other means of communication is so instant, so multicolored in mood and modulation and meaning, so freighted with personhood. The doctor asks in present and personal word, "Where does it hurt?" The lawyer pleads her case in court where there can be give and take. The wise politician takes to the hustings. The teacher confronts her students, making clear that education enlists a number of learners, older and younger, engaged in the mind's adventure. Part of the trouble at the University in Berkeley was that thousands of students never saw a professor: they saw only a television screen.[12] They were not treated as persons. Thus, we strike a wellspring: only personal speech by personal presence can treat persons as persons.

IV

But what kind of speech from the pulpit? The preacher has power that puts to shame all other power, including nuclear power. Yet not without

---

9. Marshall McLuhan and Quentin Fiore, *The Medium Is the Message: An Inventory of Effects* (London: Penguin Books, 1967).

10. Thor Hall, *The Future Shape of Preaching* (Minneapolis: Fortress Press, 1971). See ch. 4, n23.

11. FM radio.

12. Various student protest movements occurred at the University of Berkeley in the 1960s pertaining to free speech, civil rights, women's rights, and the war in Vietnam.

discipline. So *not jumbled speech*. We have used a seminal phrase for the Gospel: "The most wonderful thing has happened." But shake those words in a hat, and proclaim them as they are blindly chosen: they would be nonsense, not Gospel. The sermon should be prepared and the words chosen. It is a journey: by route 154, to 20 and 75, to 85; otherwise the preacher may travel in circles. Many do. As for the words, there is no escape from the discipline of some form of writing.

Not dull speech. No, for pondered speech catches fire. In a De Morgan novel a worldly daughter gasps as she comes on her equally worldly mother reading the Bible. The mother answers, "But you see, my dear, it may really be true, and not just like being in church."[13] What a judgment on us that, though we have glad and golden tidings to proclaim, we should have prompted the proverb, "Dull as a sermon." The true preacher works at text and context. She broods to find how the ancient word, which under the Spirit's light is never old but always new, is laid on our time. She prays urgently over a sermon that has bogged down (yet not too urgently, for that sermon will leap from the bog). She prays laughingly as the sermon first glows and then breaks into flame. Why do we say, "that we may bless all those with whom we come in contact," when we could say, "faith in Christ is springing gladness, infectious courage," or better, "the servant-in-Christ is absurdly happy and always getting into trouble"? No dull words: even a dull mind is never dull in Christ.

No jargon words: not theological jargon, not psychological jargon, not any jargon at all. The words should be simple and clear. The rhythm of the sentence is more important, with more power to quicken the imagination, than any striving for the unusual in diction. When I asked a student about an evangelist's sermon, he answered, "He must be a nice guy." When I asked again, "But what about his sermon?" the reply was, "Gee, Doc, I didn't know what he was talking about." I pressed him for details.

---

13. William De Morgan, *Alice-for-Short: A Dichronism* (New York: Henry Holt & Co., 1907), 469. Buttrick quoted from memory. The printed sentence read, "'You see, my darling,' she said, 'it may be really true, and not only like Going to Church.'" On the book's frontispiece, the *New York Times Review* called it "The first great English novel that has appeared in the 20th century." *The Independent* said, "Every page is as interesting as the last, and would be read with pleasure even if torn out of the book and caught fluttering down the street."

Chapter Three

"Washed in the blood of the Lamb," was one item that left him baffled. I know what it means: I was raised in a Methodist parsonage; and besides, I've read Vachel Lindsay's tremendous poem, "General William Booth Enters into Heaven,"[14] where the phrase is a sweeping refrain. But in colleges such words run off like water from a roof; they do not sink in like rain on a garden. No jargon!

Not argumentative speech, since nobody likes to be worsted in an argument. The preacher is bound to win an argument if only because the person in the pew is silent. To win the argument and lose the listener is a poor exchange. The true preacher wins her congregation by using *their* arguments, though even so she might be foolish to enter the area of debate. Notice how Jesus preached. The Samaritan woman testified, "Come, see a man who told me all that I ever did. Can this be the Christ?"[15] How did he preach? "You can't serve God and cash."[16] How? Speaking to people under the yoke of the law, he said, "Take my yoke upon you, and learn of me."[17] No need for stress or strife: "For I am gentle and lowly in heart, and you will find rest."[18] Then, since human nature is thus-and-so under God's creation: "My yoke fits"!

We shall return, like General MacArthur, to this matter of words, which are more important than any beach in the Philippines.[19] We should not say, "Deeds, not words," for words are deeds—deeds of the lips as much as woodcarving is a deed of the hands. No other weapon is so potent. A bomb may destroy the enemy: it can't change him into a friend; it only raises up enemy children in a worse hate. Of course, words can themselves be poison. The Epistle of James, aware of words' superlative power,

---

14. Vachel Lindsay, "General William Booth Enters into Heaven," *Poetry: A Magazine of Verse* 1, no. 4 (Jan 1913): 101–3.

15. John 4:29 (RSV).

16. Matt 6:24 (GAB paraphrase of "You cannot serve God and mammon").

17. Matt 11:29 (KJV).

18. Matt 11:29 (RSV).

19. General Douglas MacArthur, commander of Philippine and US armies during World War II, due to Japanese occupation of the Philippine islands was forced to escape to Australia where he declared, "I shall return," which he did, leading an expedition to retake the islands, and saying as he landed, "People of the Philippines, I have returned!"

declares that they can set on fire the whole circle of our life on earth.[20] He was prophetic! Gamaliel Bradford's book on some discredited figures in American history—titled *Damaged Souls*—tells us that they all had fatal power with words.[21] But we are speaking about words under the Spirit. Such words are God-indwelt words. They are God-empowered words. There is no weapon to match them: "Now you are clean through the word that I speak to you,"[22] said our Lord. Why do we forget? Why are we slipshod? Why do we not preach with "great joy" and fear and trembling?

V

So we return to the preacher under the Spirit. She cannot defeat the present Christ, who has overcome both wickedness and death, but she can temporarily stop Christ who then says again that he can "do [no] mighty works there, because of unbelief."[23] God can then send the Spirit in quest of a worthier voice—outside the church if the church fails him. God may then use humanist courage because God cannot use our timid and hastily prepared platitudes. That is to say, the preacher's freedom is still the preacher's to use or misuse. Her very eyelids are a sacrament of freedom: she can lower that tiny window shade and shut out suns, stars, the faces of friends, and the sight of the ghetto; or open her eyes and heart to the truth in Christ, truth meaning the mystery unveiled, God enfleshed in Christ.

In Herbert Farmer's *The Servant of the Word*, there is a fine passage in which he asks why a newspaper should be called, for instance, the *Chicago Daily News*. Obviously, it is not itself the news. Paper and printer's ink are not the war in Vietnam or a tidal wave in Japan or some political gimmick from Washington. The paper only *reports* the news. But—here is the nub of the matter—without the newspaper or some other medium the news would not be known. So the message and the human means become one:

---

20. Jas 3:6-10.

21. Gamaliel Bradford, *Damaged Souls* (Boston: Houghton Mifflin Co., 1923).

22. John 15:3 (GAB): "You have already been cleansed by the word that I have spoken to you" (NRSV).

23. Matt 13:58 (RSV).

the *Chicago Daily News*. In that sense, not in some merely technological sense, the human medium *is* the message.[24]

Farmer then applies the instance to our preaching. You and I are not the Gospel, God knows. But the Good News cannot be known unless someone like us proclaims it. If Christ is not preached, Christ will be forgotten in his present redemption. We are not the Gospel, but without us, sinful people speaking to sinful people, the Gospel is not known. So we are one with the news. Think of that! If you do, you will be "lost in wonder, love and praise"![25] We asked if the word of Paul about the Gospel ("the dynamite of God for salvation"[26]) is true only of the Gospel or also of our preaching. Necessarily *both*, for news is not news unless proclaimed. You and I are one with the power of the Gospel. We are baptized into Christ's death if we are willing, and girded with the might of his resurrection.

So Christ has assured us, "As the Father has sent me, even so I send you."[27] Mark closely that "even so." It means that Christ sends us with all the joy of the incarnation, all the cleansing of the cross, all the unending

---

24. Buttrick mistakenly attributed to Farmer the specific analogy of the newspaper as the medium of the news, when in actuality it was Buttrick who *on another earlier occasion* (cited below) had crafted the newspaper analogy himself to illustrate in a different way the following words of Farmer: "The content, the preaching and the message, are indissolubly one and cannot be separated from one another. The activity of preaching is to the faith as blossom is to the plant: it is part of it, gathers into itself all its vital forces, all its life history, all that makes it its specific and distinctive self, sums it all up and reveals it in a potent recreativeness. Preaching and message are one organic whole as a man's body and spirit are one organic whole—even though we do find it convenient to think of the one mainly as the instrument and vehicle of the other." See Herbert H. Farmer, *The Servant of the Word* in The Preacher's Paperback Library, ed. Edmund A. Steimle (Philadelphia: Fortress Press, 1964 [New York: Charles Scribner's Sons, 1942]), 5. In 1943, Buttrick had employed the newspaper analogy as his own illustration of Farmer's claim that "the Gospel is an Event, *the* Event" requiring proclamation that is "one with the Event" of "The Good News," to which Buttrick added, "But any news, and perhaps especially The Good News, by its very nature as news, needs telling; and the telling is plainly 'part and parcel' with the news. That is why a newspaper is sometimes called *The Evening News*. The bearer of glad tidings becomes himself in some sense the tidings, for the tidings is [sic] now on his lips and in his heart. So the preacher, becoming one with the Gospel, *becomes one with its power*." See George A. Buttrick, "Power—and the Man," *Review and Expositor* 15, no. 3 (July 1943): 287, from the E. Y. Mullins Lectures on Preaching given by Buttrick at Southern Baptist Theological Seminary in Louisville, March 15–19, 1943.

25. From the last stanza of the hymn "Love Divine, All Loves Excelling" by Charles Wesley.

26. Rom 1:16, "The power [Gk. *dynamis*] for salvation."

27. John 20:21 (RSV).

daybreak of Easter: "even so." Listen again: "All authority in heaven and earth has been given to me. Go therefore and make disciples of all nations."[28] Mark closely that "therefore": the present Christ is the preacher's "authority." Listen again: "It shall be given you in that very hour what you shall say."[29] That is no cheap assurance of cheap success. The context tells of heralds of the kingdom being brought before the thrones and powers of the world.[30] Yes, "in that very hour," but only at the point of risk gladly taken and suffering gladly borne, not least in the pain of sermon preparation.

Perhaps we should here say plainly that the power of the Holy Spirit is no pledge of a cheap or easy "success." Kipling has rightly told us that "success" and "failure" as we understand them are both impostors. The words are safe only in God's keeping. Any preacher can fill a church: all she need do is to advertise that she will hang from the main chandelier by her left leg, and so preach, and the church will be crowded to hear her. If she has a group of millionaires putting her picture in every newspaper and on every screen, and if she then persuades the president to deliver a political speech, this plus massed choirs and mass psychology, she can fill even a stadium. Christ drove away his congregation: they all forsook him and fled. Was he success or failure?

The main question is this: Is our preacher open to the Spirit? Is the preacher intent to know "the mind of the Spirit"? Oh, the preacher's pride—I being a preacher! A carnal imagination is *gross* pride. Laziness is *indolent* pride. Ecclesiastical ambition is *worldly* pride. Conservatism is *fear-stricken* pride. Modernism is *rebellious* pride. The penalty? "Pride hath no other glass to show itself but pride."[31] *The Divine Comedy* shows an angel striking Dante's forehead to erase the pride mark, so that every other sin in him grew pale.[32] But we can be used of the Holy Spirit despite the

---

28. Matt 28:18-19 (RSV).
29. Matt 10:19 (GAB, in the Greek word order).
30. Matt 10:17-18.
31. Shakespeare, *Troilus and Cressida*, ac. 3, sc. 3, li. 47–48.
32. *The Divine Comedy of Dante Alighieri, Purgatory,* Canto XII, 97–99 (New York: P. F. Collier & Son Co. 1909), 195.

pride mark: the apostle Paul had blood on his hands and conscience; and through our prayers we become better servants of the grace of our Lord.

VI

Therefore, glad prayer morning and night. Yes, and as the sermon is begun and continued and ended. Yes, and before it is preached—and after. Yes, and in the home, lest the preacher keep an open face to her flock and sour face before her own family. The seductions of our time are so alluring, its distractions so distracting, its skepticisms so rife, its materialisms so second nature that only God's power through the Holy Spirit can fortify the preacher and save the church.

> Come, Holy Ghost, our hearts inspire,
> And lighten with celestial fire.[33]

Maybe that hymn is sequel to a legend that tells how the crusaders, becalmed at Marseilles, prayed thus for a favoring wind; and that the wind came even while they sang.[34] The object of preaching is to herald the kingdom, the instrument is our seemingly feeble word, the herald herself is such a fool as any preacher, the power is God's through Christ and the Holy Spirit, and the agelong cry of the church is "Maranatha: even so, Lord Jesus, come."[35]

---

33. Latin hymn attr. to Rhabanus Maurus, eighth to ninth cent., trans. by John Cosin, 1627. See n34.

34. Possibly a story associated with the tragic Children's Crusade of AD 1212. If so, then the foregoing Latin hymn "Come Holy Ghost, Our Hearts Inspire," containing the phrase "Keep far our foes, give peace at home," would have preceded that crusade by some three to four hundred years.

35. Rev 22:20 (GAB).

CHAPTER FOUR

The New Preaching

One early morning a young couple were married at the fountain in Seneca Park, the place where he had proposed to her. She wore no coat, though the weather was chill; she wished to show her pretty wedding dress. The guests wore overcoats. During the service a garbage truck rumbled past, and that was only one of the hazards; nature has terrors and malignities as well as meadows and sunshine. The preacher admitted to a reporter that he thought weddings should be in church but that the bride had said, "Church services are so formal." Thus the current revolt. She might have added, "and sermons are so dull." Changing times call for the new preaching.

I

Sermons are briefer now. On the ledge of the pulpit in the First Reformed Church in Albany, New York, there is an hourglass, memento of a time when the preacher preached it empty, turned it over and preached it empty again. But that age was leisurely; and the church was concert hall, community center, and "homecoming week," as well as church in a pioneer world. Besides, people knew the Bible then, whereas now it is kept unopened—as a sacred horseshoe. They rejoiced in the Book, and never wearied of the good news. Now the world is filled with flashing lights, catcalls, and the yap-yap of radio and television, not to mention "future

Chapter Four

shock"[1] already present. Was it ever so hard to concentrate? How few people contemplate anything? As for worshipping God, the very name is an oblong blur.

So sermons should be brief. Not too brief. A love letter is longer than a telegram. But twenty minutes now is a wiser span than forty-five. There are exceptions. I blundered lately in a black church by preaching only twenty minutes. They therefore assumed that I assumed that they were unequal to a longer sermon. But black people are not as distracted or artificial as whites; they know their Bible and rejoice in the proclamation of the word. Yet they are the exception. I now write six and a half pages in a sermon manuscript instead of the ten pages of my first pastorate. So, the new preaching is in briefer compass, though, let us add, the clock is no more than a casual norm.

II

More importantly, the new sermon is not rigorously structured. Why? Because structure is static, and a sermon should move. It should move in itself so as to move both preacher and congregation. It should flow, march, climb—in Christ, through Christ, and unto Christ. We shall discuss soon the main traits of a sermon "triptik" (that's the word, not plan or outline), and shall then stress more emphatically this essential momentum. In past days a sermon could perhaps have a ground plan almost like the blueprint of a house. I've preached some after that fashion. But in our swiftly changing world such preaching is "out," if indeed it was ever "in." A sermon now "opens" like the acts of a play. It leads the congregation on a pilgrimage.

We take contrasting instances. A "how-not-to-do-it" instance might be a preachment on Galatians 5:22-23 (RSV): "The fruit of the Spirit is love, joy, peace, patience, kindness, goodness, faithfulness, gentleness, self-control." The typical "outline" sermon would have a hook-up here, holding a horizontal bar, from which there would be nine pendants in a row. In short, a static sermon, a deadly summary. Of course, if the preacher remembered that the Stoics loved lists of this kind, and that Paul was thus

---

1. A reference to Alvin and Heidi Toffler's *Future Shock* (New York: Random House, 1970).

appealing directly to the interest of his hearers, and that he was claiming a far better treasury of gifts than they and their former faith could ever claim; and if the preacher then pondered the Spirit, the very presence of Christ, with all his riches to be received and shared; and if the sermon then came on the clinching word, "against such there is no law"[2]; and if then it dared the further word to the effect that "those who belong to Christ Jesus have crucified the flesh,"[3] the sermon with such ingredients might smolder, then flame, then become light and heat and power.

The positive instance might be a sermon on the three appearances of Nicodemus in the fourth Gospel.[4] In the first instance he speaks with Jesus on the housetop at night. The night wind stirs, and also the wind of the Spirit. Nicodemus professes bafflement, but the mists have parted. He is troubled, but is now ill-content with his Sanhedrin life. In the second instance he half defends Jesus at a meeting of the Sanhedrin. He knows more clearly now that the council is trapped in its own pride, and that Jesus has words of eternal life. But how hard for such a man to cross a river and then burn the bridge! In the third instance he helps another member of the Sanhedrin to take down from the cross the body of Christ. Why did he bring far more spices for the embalming than were needed? Were both men now defiled, having touched a corpse? Were they both thus barred from the Passover? Why break with a cherished world when it was too late for the new loyalty? What happened when they found it was not too late? Such a sermon would not have a plan; there would be three scenarios in a movie, three episodes in a journey.

III

Again, the new preaching is not by argument: it is proclamation, quiet exclamation, yes, sometimes a shout of need, or joy, as in the "maranatha"[5] of the early church. The wise preacher does not debate, for debate almost

---

2. Gal 5:23 (RSV).
3. Gal 5:24.
4. John 3:1-21; 7:50; 19:39.
5. Aramaic for "Come, O Lord."

always divides people: he speaks in such a way that his hearers find what the Quakers call an "opening." We are not now proposing any dearth of thought. The word *think* is no simple term, a fact to which the IBM slogan is blind.[6] We can think *analytically* after the manner of the scientist who dissects, probes, and even destroys, dealing in postmortems. This is a valid thinking—in the realm of science. We can think *socially* as in economics, having first constructed a necessary but nonexistent model called "economic man." We can think *receptively*, not intent to control but to be controlled by the Stranger (capital *S*) who is no longer Stranger. This is the way of the poet and the prophet. Need it be said that the preacher's thought is more akin to the thought of the poet than to that of the scientist? Now: since "man is that strange creature who can view his own life" (Heidegger's dictum),[7] the preacher *thinks in that self-transcendence*.

So the imagination is focally involved. That word is tragically abused. It does not mean daydreaming, still less wandering of mind. True imagining is the thrust of mind become incandescent. The parable of the two prodigals, the older prodigal being a main reason why the younger prodigal left home, is not bereft of thought: it is instinct with thought. But it is imagination. Therefore, it is not coercive. It nudges us just when we are trying to turn life into abstractions. Most of us could tell a story now and then. That Nicodemus sequence would beckon a story. There are dangers. One preacher has great gifts in this method: he impersonates a Gospel person: "I was walking down the Jericho road." But he is so skilled that at the sermon's end the congregation says, "What a clever story!" instead of "I saw the Lord." But a licensed imagination is nevertheless the stuff of preaching.

---

6. "Think" was IBM's and its predecessors' trademark through most of the twentieth century.

7. While set in quotation marks, this is not a direct quotation but rather Buttrick's paraphrastic summary of Martin Heidegger's premise set forth in his seminal essay "Being and Time," *Existence and Being* (Chicago: Henry Regnery Co., 1949), namely, that human beings ("Dasein") are both subject and object to themselves, able to look upon and transcend themselves while being agents of their own thoughts and actions. See George Buttrick, *Christ and History* (New York: Abingdon Press, 1963): "That is to say, man lives creatively on a vertical line as it cuts the horizontal" (56), which is "implicit in his [Heidegger's] whole discussion of 'Dasein'" (162n37).

Thus preaching is not intellectualized, still less logical: it is thoughtful on a deeper level. It is existential in that it prompts the comment, "Yes, life is like that." James Stewart's sermon in *The Gates of New Life* on "Why Be a Christian?" doesn't belong.[8] I speak gratefully; he is a cherished friend. But faith in Christ isn't *reasonable*: it is a "scandal": "Blessed is he who is not scandalized by me."[9] Besides, the Aristotelian approach has scant power to move people. Conduct is governed by the subconscious as well as by the conscious mind. Why do we forget our appointment with the dentist? We do really forget. Because we don't want to go, the subconscious takes over. So alert preaching addresses both levels. It says, "You don't wish to be governed from 'below the threshold.' More deeply you do really wish to go, don't you?"

So preaching in its rightful thrust does not elicit "That sermon was intellectually powerful" but "That sermon found me where I live"; not "He was rationally convincing" (who is?) but "The Lord Christ walked into my life." Students nowadays ask for a "philosophy of life," but that item is not on the New Testament agenda. The preacher says, "There's a shadowy third to every conversation, a stranger listening to every secret pondering. Invite him in, and you will find him friend in whom all friendships live." The "Jesus freaks" say, "Jesus is the answer," and offer no supporting argument: they testify to an encounter. They don't go far enough: into war and racism, for instance. Maybe they should say, "Jesus is the question." But, thank heaven, they do not turn faith in him into a thin rationalism. Preaching is not intellectual cogency: it is proclamation from experience.

IV

Therefore, the language of preaching is of paramount importance. What immediately follows is a series of comments on that momentous theme. The preacher's sentences are *dialogical*. He engages the congregation in a conversation. The person in the pew does not make audible reply (too bad that he doesn't sometimes shout "Hallelujah!"), though the feedback now gives him

---

8. James S. Stewart, *The Gates of New Life* (New York: Charles Scribner's Sons, 1940).

9. Matt 11:6 and Luke 7:23 (GAB).

that chance, but he nods as he listens. The sermon doesn't tell him what to believe but rather shows him what he already believes. The preacher doesn't fulminate from Mount Olympus, despite the sound of some broadcast sermons. He says, "Behold the Man! Now you and I are picked out—and loved." Preaching proclaims; it doesn't declaim. A recent letter tells me that a forthcoming ministers' conference seeks a "famous pulpiteer." Let's hope they don't find him: the old pulpit rhetoric is gone. It has almost destroyed preaching. You and I speak as sinful people to sinful people, testifying to the grace of Christ. All right: the language is *dialogical*: as when Paul preached, saying, "Who shall separate us from the love of Christ?"[10]

The language is *contemporary*. The older versions of the Bible, because of their "thees and thous," their "beholds and untos," are a roadblock, besides being poor translations. I asked a priest about the Vatican and birth control; he said, "Nineteenth century." I went to a church that nostalgically revived the "John Wesley Order of the Sacrament," and a college teacher in the pew said, "Nineteenth century." I heard a sermon that could have been preached in the nineteenth century almost without a change of word. *You* are concerned with a traffic jam in the local supermarket or with the headlines in today's news. Ask yourself as you write, "How would this sound to that person walking down Lexington Avenue?" Theological jargon and a holy tone will not move him except to exasperation. You and I stand on the border between the church and the world. We speak the world's language (not slang, at least not often), never forgetting that the dear canonical language is just behind our back. All right: *contemporary language.*

Instant language springs from primal pondering. A true sermon doesn't borrow words except in a cogent quotation. In a way of speaking there are no new words or new thoughts, but if the preacher "waits" and listens, even a trite phrase is not trite if it has come firsthand. "There is a river whose streams make glad the city of God."[11] The reference is probably to a wellspring across the valley from Jerusalem, the stream being carried into the city by a viaduct, and then channeled into the various streets. Preaching comes from the fountainhead. It is not "flat" water drawn from a thin

---

10. Rom 8:35 (RSV).
11. Ps 46:4 (RSV).

stream down the thoroughfare. To say this doesn't imply that the preacher shouldn't "do his homework." That is the means of his pondering. But he can't piece together a sermon from books, cut-and-paste fashion. The "joins" show, and they are gummy, and they tear. He reads the psalm: "Be still, and know that I am God."[12] Then he isn't such a fool as to preach on the blessings of silence: every crime is planned in silence. Controls are involved. No, he gets the right translation: "Let your hands hang slack," meaning, "Let the weapons fall out of them." Okay: then the pondering. "Chariots" and "spears" have yielded to tanks and planes. But this power is not power. *Our* killings are worse. "Where have all the young men gone? When will we ever learn?"[13] When we know that God is God! Soon comes the instant language: the "deep" in the preacher "calls to deep" in the congregation.[14] *Instant language*!

Again, preaching language is *eventful*. The linguistic analyst tells us that words have shaped culture, not vice versa. Is this true? Who knows? We were not there. It might be truer to say that the speaking person shapes culture, which then shapes the person. But that still points to the tremendous power of speech. Is preaching passé? Jerry Rubin does not think so![15] Words are the most instant means of communication, the most colorful, the most personal. Visual aids are secondary. The Bible from first to last tells us that the ear is more trustworthy than the eye. "*Hear*, O Israel"?[16] "Let anyone with ears to hear listen!"[17] The Hebrew verb *hear* carries in it the further verb to *obey*.[18] Why? Because the speaking person becomes a new event. An event is invasive. It is *ecstatic* in the original meaning of the word, that is, it requires us to stand outside ourselves and ask, "What now shall I

---

12. Ps 46:10 (RSV).

13. From Pete Seeger's 1955, 1962, 1964 political protest song, "Where Have All the Flowers Gone?"

14. Ps 42:7 (RSV). "Deep calls to deep at the thunder of thy cataracts."

15. Jerry Rubin, a 1960s and 1970s social activist and leader of the anti-Vietnam War movement.

16. Deut 6:4 (RSV).

17. Mark 4:9 (NRSV). Buttrick translated as "Whoever has ears to hear let him hear."

18. Heb. *Shama*.

do?" It "takes place": our place! It "comes to pass": our door. In the faithful preacher that word in the Spirit becomes the Word (capital *W*). Now you understand why the new homiletics centers in "the sermon event."

Still discussing sermon language: it is addressed to a person's *total life*. There is no such person as an individual. A hermit is unthinkable: he grows his garden and weaves his clothes by skills bequeathed to him by his community. So the "individual Gospel" is sheer fiction. Ditto the "social Gospel": it also is fiction because every group is composed of persons, each of whom lives in a strange secrecy. Why do we cringe before a paradox, that our life is individual-social? No one splits a paradox. You were not born an infant-hermit: you were welcomed into a home, and soon you went to school. The Tennessee Baptists tried to believe that sin lives only on the private sector. So? Youths in their colleges wanted to dance, and the Convention said no. Next there was a picture of a black youth talking to two white girls, and the Convention (through its officers) again said no. Then came the busing controversy, and the establishment asked local Baptist churches to open their doors (for segregated schools in some instances, not alone for meetings) to antibusing groups; and this time the churches said yes. I have strong convictions on all three issues. But that is not now the nub. Other Baptist conventions challenged the Tennessee actions. The nub is this: a denomination that has tried as persistently as any to be "individualistic" is now torn apart by social concerns. Why? Because it is impossible to live in only one term of a paradox.[19]

> How "total" preaching should be done is hard to answer. The question is on our agenda. There is no rule of thumb, because no two thumbs are alike. People left of center insist on "action" without consulting the compass to find which way is forward, while people right of center try to stay "put" in a moving world. We should say at once that preaching refuses all earthbound party cries. Every human-made scheme is transitory—and streaked with sin. But there is no evidence that "soundly converted" folk will then reshape our world, for they may join the forces of reaction. A revivalism unconcerned about the genocide in Vietnam is a form of self-indulgence.

---

19. Buttrick gave these lectures during the 1970s to students at Southern Baptist Theological Seminary of Louisville, Kentucky, as well as at Louisville Presbyterian Theological Seminary of the same city. The school busing controversy was at its peak, based upon the Supreme Court ruling of April 20, 1971, upholding busing as a means to school desegregation.

To return to our main "drag": sermon words are addressed to life as life is lived. Sin goes far beyond the private sector. How to preach to the total life we shall later discuss, and hope for discrimination to walk a perilous path.[20]

V

You have noted in all this discussion of the "new preaching" that we have been aware of the *Presence*, that is, the guidance and power of the Holy Spirit. "Comparative religion" is a dubious title: we should speak of "comparative and contrastive religion." For instance, Christian mysticism is not one of a kind, standing with other instances on a horizontal line, as Evelyn Underhill seems to propose.[21] Rather it is a devotion to a person, and therefore unique. The Hindu doctrine of reincarnation is a bold attempt, however unsuccessful, to answer the ancient enigma of pain and evil. Buddhism has idol replicas of Buddha, but even these go counter to classic Buddhism, for the Gautama insisted that he knew "nothing about the gods." There is an unavoidable distinctiveness, a singularity and a particularism about faith in Christ that is not answered by our modern so-called tolerance. Tolerance is conceited ("I'm a tolerant person!"), evasive in its attempt to sidestep a clear-cut choice, and contemptuous (am I supposed merely to "tolerate" my neighbor?). Humans are choosing creatures. The new preaching is still focused in Christ. To treat all people of whatever faith in his love, that is, without any tincture of disparagement or proselyting, goes far beyond our wretched "tolerance."

> If we had love,
> We can melt all the guns
> And then give the new world
> To our daughters and sons.[22]

Yet the new preaching asks *new questions about Christ*. When I was in seminary the doctrine of the *virgin birth* was a main issue, but now

---

20. See chapter 12.

21. Evelyn Underhill, *Mysticism: A Study in the Nature and Development of Man's Spiritual Consciousness* (New York: E. P. Dutton & Co, 1961 [1911]).

22. Dionne Warwick, "If We Only Have Love" (1972).

a college student said, "If Christ is a copout, no unreal birth could save him." That student came to tell me that Christ *is* a copout. The answer was not in an *argument*; we have noted why. In my seminary years the *miracles* were in the forefront of people's minds, but now there is a new approach, for another student said, "It was a cinch for him: he could always turn clay pigeons into live pigeons." Again, it would have been no answer to tell him that that story is not canonical, for the turning of water into wine *is* canonical. I'm only suggesting that the new preaching should not spend time answering questions that the coming generation is not asking.

What are they asking? It is New Testament doctrine that the Holy Spirit moves in the hearts of hearers whom we reckon alien, and therefore we may find lodgment where we think there is no soil—and fall on barren ground where we think there *is* soil. Here are some questions: Is the church ready to lose its life for Christ in a hostile world? Does he bring history to focus, since history without a plot is like a game of Scrabble in which no letters make any word, and no words make any sense? Is life lived in a personal loyalty, since even in Russia, which once renounced the "cult of personality" for the sake of economics, the grave of Lenin is a shrine? Has Christ any answer to the culpable fault in human nature, including the downward drag in every corporate structure? Does Christ have a solving word in the dark enigma of pain and death, an answer not in thin logic or metaphysic, but in the piercingness of events? And, since a person "is that strange creature who can view his own life," one leg in time, the other leg in the everlasting, does Christ bridge both dimensions, Son of God and Son of man; God's Son and Human One?

The book *The Future Shape of Preaching*[23] seems to me to lose sight of both preacher and Gospel for the sake of an abstraction labeled "communication." But the book has this virtue: it knows that a new day has come for the pulpit. We do not dodge the issue of communication. But we hew to the one Gospel, and to the gifts and graces of the preacher.

---

23. Thor Hall, *The Future Shape of Preaching* (Minneapolis: Fortress Press, 1971) was listed for reading in Buttrick's courses on "The New Preaching" at Louisville Presbyterian Theological Seminary, Spring 1972, and Southern Baptist Theological Seminary, First Semester, 1972–73 (George Arthur Buttrick Papers, Harvard University Archives, HUG FP 90.15, Box 6, Extra Homiletic Outlines Used in Louisville).

Part Two
PRACTICALITIES

CHAPTER FIVE

Background Preparation

Sermons are not born out of due time: they have pregnancy. They do not come from beyond, as the infant King Arthur is said to have been carried into shore on a "seventh great wave of the sea." Come to think of it, perhaps they do, as gift from the beyond, but only for those who wait and pray on the beach. To change the metaphor, a sermon is a harvest: there is no reaping without prior ploughing and seeding. We are now concerned with that prior labor, since a preacher can't live from hand to mouth. The true preacher is never a preacher in the "preachy" sense but always a preacher in a certain glad urgency. So what of the background labor in which the preacher sets about specific preparation?

I

The first priority is constant study of the Bible. That makes fertile ground, as witness the fact that seminary students find next Sunday's sermon in their biblical courses. A certain notable preacher claims that he now reads "nothing but the Bible." He should add, "so I become more and more ignorant of the book." Besides, he is probably not telling the truth. Presumably he still reads the news or watches the news on a screen. What version does he read when he reads the Bible? Presumably in this case the King James Version. So he comes to the last chapter of the Epistle to the Hebrews, which incidentally was not written to the Hebrews, for

Chapter Five

it is written in almost classical Greek, and finds this: "Remember them which have the rule over you, who have spoken unto you the word of God: whose faith follow, considering the end of their conversation."[1] The Bible does not tell him that the Elizabethan word *conversation* is almost our word "biography." To retranslate: "Remember your leaders pondering how their (martyred) days were ended." Indeed, the great succeeding word eludes the preacher in its subtleties, for it does not say, "Jesus Christ, the same yesterday, today, and forever," but, "Jesus Christ yesterday and today the same, yes, and forever"—meaning, to those ready to die for the faith. The faithful preacher reads both the Bible and about the Bible.

As our preacher thus reads, the question of inspiration blocks her path. She may not say casually, "The Bible tells us," for the Bible tells us many things, as for instance that the sons of heaven came down and saw that the daughters of earth were fair, and therefore usurped the hopes of the eligible men.[2] Literal inspiration is a contradiction in terms. If God uses a person as if the person were a tape recorder speaking out what has been spoken in, then that person is no longer a person (rather a machine), and God is no longer God (rather a machinist or tyrant). Besides, the whole notion is blasphemy against the Holy Spirit, thereby made to languish with the unemployed. In any real doctrine of inspiration the whole Bible is involved: God's way with chosen Israel, for instance, without which the New Testament would be robbed of meaning. The total event of Christ brings that whole history to climax. The inspiration of the scriptures is by God's Spirit; the word itself carries that meaning. The preacher need not now defend some Old Testament brutality but echo the Old Testament word about "all the paths by which the Lord has led us."[3] So the preacher is now made free in Christ, who is Lord of history and Lord of the Book—in present light and power and love.

The question of biblical criticism also is raised. Criticism: what an unhappy word! It does not mean carping. The art critic studies Giotto[4]—gratefully. The Bible critic comes to the scriptures, comes with a gratitude

---

1. Heb 13:7 (KJV).
2. Gen 6:4 (GAB, humorous paraphrase).
3. Deut 8:2 (GAB, paraphrastic appropriation of the text in the third person).
4. Giotto di Bondone (1267–1337), Italian painter and architect.

as deep as heaven and earth. Some radio preachers accuse the scholars of tearing apart the Bible, though without the scholars those same preachers could never have read the Book. As for "higher criticism" (unhappy word), there is guidance in the fact that the manuscript of Daniel is sprinkled with Greek words, a startling evidence of the conquest of Israel by Antiochus; and that the hero Daniel finds no other mention in the roster of Israel's great hearts. As for lower criticism (unhappy word), if the term *church* in Matthew's Gospel, coming from the lips of Christ when manifestly there was no church, is redaction, that is, a throwback from the life of the early Church, that does not falsify the word. At least it does not if we travel by a true doctrine of inspiration: it proves that the incarnate Christ and Christ the Holy Spirit speak one and the same language.

So the preacher keeps reading the Bible and about the Bible. The Book is her home base. She reads not on the hunt for a text for a sermon but that the inspired word may be her food and drink. She studies Francis Beare's introduction and exegesis of the Letter to the church in Ephesus in the *Interpreter's Bible*, yes, and Dr. Wedel's exposition[5]; and Father Raymond E. Brown's monumental and presently definitive study of the Fourth Gospel in the Anchor Bible,[6] or Günther Bornkamm's new story of Paul.[7] The preacher should be more assiduous in these studies than a doctor is in keeping track of new medical knowledge. Meanwhile she should not neglect the half-truth of that preacher who brags about reading nothing but the Bible. The "nothing but" is silly, but the other two words, "the Bible," are a glad imperative. There's a sly story of a recent graduate from seminary whose sermonizing almost required him to read his Bible. He tapped the book, turned to his wife, and said, "This Book throws great light on what I studied in seminary."

---

5. George A. Buttrick, gen. ed., *The Intepreter's Bible*, vol. 10, *Corinthians, Galatians, Ephesians* (New York: Abingdon Press, 1953). To bring the advice more up to date, she should read the masterful commentary by Pheme Perkins on Ephesians in *The New Interpreter's Bible*, edited by Leander Keck (Nashville: Abingdon Press, 2002).

6. Raymond Brown, *The Gospel According to John*, 2 vols., Anchor Bible (Garden City: Doubleday, 1966, 1970).

7. Günther Bornkamm, *Paul* (New York: Harper & Row, 1971).

Chapter Five

II

> ### Further Reading to Guide Your Preaching
>
> Thomas H. Troeger and Leonora Tubbs Tisdale, *A Sermon Workbook*, 2013, 9781426757785
> Thomas H. Troeger, *The End of Preaching*, 2018, 9781501868092
> Paul Scott Wilson, *The Four Pages of the Sermon*, 1999, 2018, 9781501842405
> Frank A. Thomas, *Introduction to the Practice of African American Preaching*, 2016, 9781501818943
> Frank Thomas, *How to Preach a Dangerous Sermon*, 2018, 9781501856839
> Will Willimon, *Preachers Dare: Speaking for God*, 2020, 9781791008055
> Joni S. Sancken, *Words That Heal*, 2019, 9781501849688
> Lisa L. Thompson, *Ingenuity: Preaching as an Outsider*, 2018, 9781501832598
> Lenny Luchetti, *Preaching with Empathy*, 2018, 9781501841729
> Peter Jonker, *Preaching in Pictures*, 2015, 9781426781926
> *The New Interpreter's Handbook of Preaching*, 2008, 9780687055562

Another background area that prompts sermons is the world of books, special and general, beyond the immediate study of the scriptures. By special reading we mean books that inform our vocation. The Gospel is "once for all," but every generation finds new promises. Barth's *Church Dogmatics* gave the theological journey a new turn. As for Marty's *Righteous Empire*, what light it throws on church history in our America! Fletcher's *Situational Ethics*, though rife with fallacies (even in the title) raises the contemporary question. So does Boyd's *The Underground Church*. There are books[8] that will be read beyond our time: Pannenberg's *Jesus—God and Man*, and Küng's *The Church* come to mind. These titles are at random.[9] They are suggested only to show our need to keep abreast in our particular task. We are "called." *Vocation* is the word, not "profession" and not "career" (that latter word comes from the French *carrière*, which means a

---

8. Buttrick gave these lectures to seminary students and clergy conferences in the early 1970s.

9. Karl Barth, *Church Dogmatics*, 4 vols. (Edinburgh: T & T Clark, 1932–1967); Martin Marty, *Righteous Empire* (New York: Doubleday, 1971); Joseph Fletcher and John Warwick Montgomery, *Situational Ethics* (Philadelphia: Westminster Press, 1966); Malcolm Boyd, *The Underground Church* (New York: Sheed & Ward, 1968); Wolfhart Pannenberg, *Jesus—God and Man* (Philadelphia: Westminster Press, 1968); Hans Küng, *The Church* (New York: Sheed & Ward, 1967).

racecourse: the rat race). Therefore, there is obligation under God to do our homework in our own calling.

By general reading we intend books of common interest beyond our vocation, not least the books "everybody is reading." The best way to counter those who scream against communism is to read Karl Marx's *Das Capital*[10] or the essays of Plekhanov,[11] thus to know not only why communism is blind, but that it travels not by its sophomoric theories but by its valid indignations. A debilitated body invites hostile germs! Again, a random sampling: *Portney's Complaint* and *Love Story*[12] have both had wide reading in any parish, so the preacher reads them—with a whole saltshaker in his hand, not merely the proverbial "grain of salt." *Future Shock* is not profound; *The Greening of America* is naive yet interlaced with sharp diagnoses; *The Myth of the Machine*, though word-cluttered, arrests us on our way.[13] Perhaps dramatists and novelists and poets foresee the erosion of our culture more quickly than the eyes of the church. They shouldn't, for we have the instant norm. But perhaps they do. So, Faulkner, Becket, and Ionesco beckon us, always under the touchstone of the New Testament.

You are asking how the preacher can compass the reading task. The excuse "I am too busy" is worse than excuse: it is self-condemnation. "Too busy" because of what? Because we must scurry round an ecclesiastical squirrel cage? In many instances the local church is overbuilt and overorganized. It runs printer's ink instead of red blood. Many a church club (unwittingly, *club* is precisely the right word) lives for its own perpetuation, and can be left by mighty labor to bring forth its mouse without claim on a ministerial midwife. Even creative ventures in the church can be trusted to lay leadership. There are ways and means of warding

---

10. Karl Marx and Friedrich Engels, *Das Kapital: Kritik der politischen Oekonomie*, 3 vols. (Hamburg: Verlag von Otto Meissner, 1867, 1885, 1894). English translations under the title *Capital: A Critique of Political Economy*.

11. Georgii Valentinovich Plekhanov (1856–1918), Russian and Marxist revolutionary.

12. Philip Roth, *Portnoy's Complaint* (New York: Random House, 1969); Erich Segal, *Love Story* (New York: Harper & Row, 1970).

13. Alvin Toffler, *Future Shock* (New York: Random House, 1970); Charles A. Reich, *The Greening of America* (New York: Random House, 1970); Lewis Mumford, *The Myth of the Machine* (New York: Harcourt Brace Jovanovich, vol. 1, 1967; vol. 2, 1970).

off telephone calls. Books nowadays are slim in size because of mounting publication costs. The preacher should certainly read one book a week. Some of the reading should be for entertainment; my wife reads murder mysteries, though it is mystery to me how anyone so gentle can be intrigued by grisly death. "Talk of the Town" in *The New Yorker* is sometimes closer to the New Testament than some denominational journals.

Then how to choose a few books from the inundation? How to salvage furniture from the flood? The average preacher has little cash and shamefully less vacation. But she can read reviews of current books and learn to trust certain reviewers. In seminary and beyond she consults her roster of professors. Some seminaries publish basic lists of books, old and new, by which the preacher can build a worthy library. The local library can be guided to include books in our vocation. A church library is a "must," for how else can members become literate in the faith? There are national lending libraries for our calling. Groups of preachers can buy and share new books. The best strategy is to go to a church bookstore and read a few pages of a new book, for someone has said that if an egg is bad there's no need to eat more than half a spoonful. A major rule is that we read the "big" books that have manifest life, such as Reinhold Niebuhr's *Faith and History* and Barth's commentary on Romans.[14]

III

Of course, life itself is an obvious background for our sermons. Preachers have no union; if they had, there would be some very engaging junctures. Many a congregation, despite its promise, does not set the preacher "free from worldly cares." She has no eight-hour day or five-day week: fourteen hours every day would be a closer estimate. She keeps a smile on her face, and it is not a forced smile. Presently she is cuffed by both rightists and leftists. Far from living in an ivory tower (whence that nonsense?), she "sees everything." All right: it is precisely this involvement that is her armory. It was true of Cleopatra in letters and legend that

---

14. Reinhold Niebuhr, *Faith and History* (New York: Charles Scribner's Sons, 1949); Karl Barth, *The Epistle to the Romans* (London: Oxford University Press, 1933).

Background Preparation

>Age cannot wither her,
>nor custom stale h*er infinite variety.*[15]

It was not true of Cleopatra as a person: she would have withered if the asp had not forestalled that event. But the words are true of life, even though all history is under "the tooth of time."[16] So the preacher should celebrate life, her own life and the manifold life in which her life is held. More especially she should be grateful for those who are not against Christ, whatever their lips may say, and who are therefore bravely for her. The preacher finds sermons on her left hand in the world, and in the Bible in her right hand.[17]

Pastoral fidelity is involved, so momentously that we shall give a whole chapter to "Preaching and Pastoral Care." Here we ask only this: Can any persons preach effectively for very long to people they don't know? The visiting evangelist depends on the pastor even for those claimed as converts of the mission, and when the mission is ended the evangelist must refer the converts to the concern of the local church. The chief reason why "activist" preachers lose their jobs is because of the dubious hostility of rich people who, prating about Bible preaching, are pitiably ignorant of the Bible. But in some instances, the preacher is to blame: forgetting to preach to our appalling loneliness and our worse transgressions, and not personally sharing the joys and sorrows of the flock. A true pastor has a tolerable freedom in the pulpit, more than the local doctor or lawyer can claim. So the immediate area of involvement is the parish.

But the preacher is no recluse: enlisting in the life of the present time, she finds sermons as the Bible comes alive in the world. Bonhoeffer's "worldly Christianity" is not the best caption, for Jesus warned us, "Love not the world," a caveat that lays a shadow on the adjective *worldly*. "Secular holiness" is under the same danger of misunderstanding: its advocates are already driven to distinguish between secularity and secularism. If only we had kept the Bible words: sacred and profane! All things are sacred, for

---

15. Shakespeare, *Anthony and Cleopatra*, act 2, scene 2.

16. An idiom derived from the prominent mountainous rise in the shape of a tooth near Cimarron, New Mexico.

17. A play on Karl Barth's adage that the preacher should read with the Bible in one hand and the newspaper in the other.

God made the world; but all things can be profaned by our transgressions, the word *profane* (*pro fanum*: before the shrine) being still unable to escape God. The preacher, even while the church has lead in its shoes, can make common cause with the poor and with victims of racial contempt. This the preacher should do, not as a lone-wolf adventure, but with groups resolved to cross the barrier from the comfortable to the dispossessed. I know of one preacher who refused a call to an ultrawealthy parish by asking, "But how would I preach the Gospel to the poor?" Blessings on him! Yet he could have found ways and means. To cite another instance: the preacher can no longer preach piously about the prince of peace while blessing each new war—by silence. I believe (it is a faith, not a wretched Jeanne Dixon[18] pretense to read the future) that the church can be reborn to become in larger actuality the body of Christ. Yet I am more and more sure that so-called conversion (from what, to what?) may become a sticky self-indulgence. The creative preacher shares gladly and painfully the life of the world, where sermons are conceived—for pregnancy, at least some of them.

IV

Therefore, the main "background" of sermon preparation is glad and constant prayer. That word has become a refuge. At a church meeting I was challenged for saying that some prayers for bodily healing meet with God's no. The challengers forgot that Christ's prayer—that the "cup" might "pass"—was denied, and that Paul's prayer that his grievous ailment might be cured was denied. They told me in effect that any ailment, for instance, my friend's brain tumor after three operations, will yield to prayer "if a person has faith." That phrase, "if a person has faith," so used, is not faith: it is pious pride and nasty slander. Did Paul lack faith? As for me, I hope the church does not degenerate into a vast Lourdes;[19] and

---

18. Jeanne Dixon was a popular and controversial syndicated twentieth-century astrologer and psychic.

19. A small town in southwest France to which millions of pilgrims come seeking healing at the Sanctuary of Our Lady of Lourdes, the site of an apparition of the Virgin Mary in 1858.

I pray and pray that it does not yield to an Oral Roberts circus.[20] The preacher's prayer can become an escape. So can any endeavor, such as music or psychiatry. But prayer need not be an escape. Rightfully it is both consolation and commission. The preacher's job is now so onerous in its multiplied demands, so caught in the pagan crosscurrents of our time, that she cannot travel in her own strength. She knows even more than others that she, too, is ignorant, transient, and wicked. Emerson's essay on "Self-Reliance"[21] is essentially a farce and a fake: how can mortal dust be self-reliant?

So the preacher prays. She prays with the morning light, for otherwise the day is a brush heap, not a tree. She prays when she reads, "Lord, that I may know that your eyes are on this page!" She prays when she begins her sermon: "Lord, for the light and joy of the Gospel!" She prays for her home lest she offer an open face to the world and a clouded face to her husband and children. She prays for her flock, not least for those caught in the stress of life. She writes prayers for use in the pulpit: she does not necessarily read them, but she prepares them, lest she offer God a jumble and a sloppiness, a mixed grill of pious phrases and out-of-context quotations from the scriptures. She prays at night, offering God her weariness if she has no better prayer. She prays especially at night, for then she can ask pardon for her blunders, God's fulfillment for unfinished tasks, and praise God for the love her ministry has received and the "golden moments" that God has given.

V

So, the preacher lives in joy, above the pinpricks and jabs the task always brings. Because the Gospel is Gospel, Masefield's faith has a deeper meaning:

> Best trust the happy moments. What they gave
> Makes man less fearful of the certain grave,

---

20. The Pentecostal Holiness and Methodist televangelist, Granville Oral Roberts (1918–2009), founder of Oral Roberts University.

21. A famous 1841 essay by the New England transcendentalist Ralph Waldo Emerson.

Chapter Five

And gives his work compassion and new eyes.
The days that make us happy make us wise.[22]

Such words outside the Gospel can become a whistling in the dark. There are other days. Masefield wrote those words for me in a copy of his poems, and the book was stolen from a table in my living room. Even so the words are true: "Who for the joy that was set before him endured the cross, despising the shame."[23] That joy is now confirmed—for the preacher, for the preacher's faith. The background of all such labors is joy in Christ.

---

22. "Biography," a poem by John Masefield (1878–1967), English poet laureate.
23. Heb 12:2 (RSV).

CHAPTER SIX

Foreground Preparation: Text and Context

Nowadays we should know that the announcement of a text means one strike on the preacher before swinging the bat. A text has an old-world sound. Besides, people do not now read the Bible, so the text is in a foreign tongue. Besides, the Bible has been made packhorse for many a narrowness, and people are now on guard:

> What damned error, but some sober brow
> will bless it and approve it with a text.[1]

Witch burning is only one item in the criminal charges. Besides, the original manuscripts have no verses, and the person who mutilated them by slicing them into verses was either an ignoramus or a butcher. Besides, a text belongs in its context, and to isolate it is like separating out the left cheek of Venus de Milo: the picture is lost. Harry Emerson Fosdick[2] kept his text until the last paragraph, for reasons given.

---

1. Shakespeare, *The Merchant of Venice*, act 3, scene 2, lines 78–79. "In religion, What damned error, but some sober brow will bless it and approve it with a text Hiding the grossness with fair ornament?" (lines 77b–80).

2. Harry Emerson Fosdick (1878–1969), a decades-long close friend of George Buttrick, was the most well-known Protestant preacher in the United States during Fosdick's years as senior minister of the Riverside Church in New York City. His sermons were broadcast by radio throughout the nation. Buttrick was considered a possible successor to Fosdick at Riverside, according to the diary entry of Buttrick's secretary, Elizabeth Stouffer (*Elizabeth Stouffer Diaries: 1932–2007, inclusive*, Schlesinger Library, Radcliffe Institute, Harvard University), Thursday, December 20, 1945.

Chapter Six

Yet there are important advantages in the use of a text. It focuses the mind of both preacher and congregation, a "consummation devoutly to be wished" (Hamlet)![3] *Furthermore*, a text is memorable in the sense that it offers the hearer a clue by which to remember the sermon. Henry Sloane Coffin[4] preached on "How to Live with Life's Second-Best" under the text "Shields of Gold, Shields of Brass"[5]; the context was dramatically rehearsed, and the sermon is still memorable through its striking text. *Furthermore*, the text sets the sermon squarely in the inspiration of the Bible; the preacher is not now on his own: he speaks in the power of the word. So a text honestly used within its context, even though the context must be explained (Bible stories and Bible history turn present-day writing into sputtering candles), is still the best starting point. That is to say, expository preaching is still the root of all effective preaching.

For so-called topical preaching has its own hazards. It may succumb to a cult of thrills, and thus become a refuge for mountebanks.[6] W. E. Orchard listened to one such meteor man declaiming to a crowded church, and said sadly to his wife, "I could not fill this church." She answered, "No, but you could empty it." Jesus emptied it: they all forsook him and fled. *There is a further danger*: the preacher may now try to preach "off the top of his head." He may exploit his own intellectual or demagogic interests. Because he sits loose to a lectionary he may pluck and pluck on one string. His head hardly compares with the majesty and mercy of the book, which circles in mystery the throne on which the Lamb is slain "from the foundation of the world." So topical sermons may soon resemble that counter in the department store labeled "notions"! Yet we should realize that the biblical context is itself "topical": it sets forth the human condition more instantly and constantly than any newscast, with agelong and incisive truth under the power of the Presence.

---

3. Shakespeare, *Hamlet*, act 3, scene 1, lines 63–64.

4. Henry Sloane Coffin preceded George Buttrick as senior minister of Madison Avenue Presbyterian Church, New York City.

5. From 2 Chr 9:15-16.

6. Frauds and deceivers.

Foreground Preparation: Text and Context

I

So we shall give our exemplary preacher a text. What text? Preferably one provided by a lectionary. Why? Because *negatively* the preacher is rescued from his own dominant emphases: he is no longer guilty of harping on one string, the repeated demand for civil rights, for example, on the one hand, and on the other the repeated reassurance of the private solace of the faith. There is also *positive* gain in a lectionary: it may persuade the preacher to travel the full orbit of the Gospel. Any sermon, if it keeps unity as it should, is inevitably disproportionate. If it proclaims the tenderness of Jesus, it may do only scant justice to his realisms and his flinty courage. The cure for these overemphases is not within the compass of any single sermon, for that would be impossible (or, if possible, boring), but within a well-rounded ministry. Granted the use of a lectionary, fewer sermons would have the dubious trademark of "This is what I think," and more would have the poignant, piercing word of the Bible under the light and power of the Holy Spirit; and the preacher would not be trapped in "What shall I preach next Sunday?"

But granted the use of a lectionary (which wisely enlists the reading of the church also), *what text to choose?* Here the preacher's own mind, since he like other persons is unique, may properly prevail. If, as the preacher reads in a certain paragraph, one sentence is suddenly illuminated, so that the preacher stands at salute or is awestruck, he is under command to preach on that text. Suppose he is reading the Daniel story of the three youths who refused to worship Nebuchadnezzar. They stood firm before the king: "We have no need to answer you."[7] (In matters of judgment second thoughts may be wise, but in issues of faith and obligation first thoughts should prevail.) "Our God is able to deliver us" (if that is God's will), "but if not"![8] There the preacher is stopped in his tracks; and his world is stopped, and he can't sidestep. Now he confronts the God-is-dead theology,[9] the world's skepticisms, and his own blank misgivings.

---

7. Dan 3:16 (RSV).

8. Dan 3:17-18a (RSV).

9. The death of God theology of the 1950s and 1960s, proponents of which were Thomas J. J. Altizer, William Hamilton, John A. T. Robinson, and Gabriel Vahanian, among others.

Chapter Six

"But if not, we will not serve your gods."[10] When God beyond seems lost, unable to deliver any person, perhaps not caring, perhaps not anything, God within, the same God, "I AM WHO I AM,"[11] takes over and gives peace because God gives no escape. How does this relate to the protests of our time? How to the word and presence of Christ? The preacher has his sermon. He can hardly wait to preach it.

II

But a certain honesty is required. He must be honest with the meaning of the text. If he knows the biblical languages, he consults the early manuscripts. Otherwise he turns to a worthy modern commentary. He is "under orders" and must obey. He has no warrant to twist the text to his own purpose. That dishonesty has brought preaching into disrepute and ridicule. So he may not take at face value "I can do all things in him who strengthens me."[12] Can he pitch a tent on the sun, or grow a new leg on the stub of an amputated leg? The meaning is "I am enabled in all things through Christ," whether it be suffering or summons. In "I know that my redeemer lives,"[13] the word is actually *vindicator*; and in "Though he slay me, yet will I trust in him,"[14] the right translation is "yet will I argue my case against him."[15] In these three instances and many another the New English Bible is plainly superior. Generations of preachers *have imposed their meaning* on the text instead of searching for the *text's own meaning*. Thus the Inquisition, witch burning, and racism! The honest preacher doesn't presume to be lord of scripture. He doesn't twist and traduce the word. Initial honesty will rob him of some sermons, but will give far more than it takes, not least because truthfulness frees the mind.

---

10. Dan 3:18 (RSV).
11. Exod 3:14 (RSV).
12. Phil 4:13 (RSV).
13. Job 19:25 (RSV).
14. Job 13:15 (KJV).
15. Job 13:15b (GAB). The RSV: "I will defend my ways to his face."

Foreground Preparation: Text and Context

Another honesty: the preacher must be true to the context. The Bible consists of paragraphs, not snippets. There are verses that because of their universal appeal may perhaps be treated as units: "The Lord is my shepherd," the Golden Rule, "God so loved the world," "The just shall live by faith" (which could better be translated "Those who are justified by faith shall live") among others, but even these have more incisive power within their respective settings. So any sermon should be a sermon on the whole paragraph, which then may be highlighted by a chosen text. Suppose Jacob's dream is the pericope, a word that means "cut around" and thus defines the unit. The sermon could rightfully stress (a) God's grace in granting a liberating dream to a man who had deceived a blind father and who was a refugee from an angry supplanted older brother; or (b) the ladder that was set up by God, not for our climbing (we would fall from dizziness after the first steps) but for the angels; or (c) Jacob's making a pillar to memorialize a blessing; or (d) his attempt to bargain with divine mercy in how human a pride; and (e) centrally Christ's own use of the account, and his declaration that he is himself the ladder between heaven and earth. Whatever the chosen text, the dynamism of the pericope should be honored. What verve such honoring would give to the sermon!

Another honesty: fidelity to the whole book in which text and context are found. The preacher's day-by-day study of the Bible now brings its blessings. Proverbs is obviously in texts, but it is Wisdom literature. That is to say, its distillate of human experience may all too easily end in self-regarding shrewdness, and so forget the vast panorama of creation, redemption, and the consummation! The book of Esther never mentions God: it stands on the borderline between a worthy patriotism and a dubious nationalism; compare it with the Johannine Epistles! Or contrast Mark's earlier account of the storm scene, "Master, we are sinking. Don't you care?,"[16] with Matthew's later, "Save us, Lord; we are sinking."[17] How and why the difference? The answer goes back to the two books in toto as to their dates and purpose. Or read First Peter with its heartbreaking courage of martyrdom for Christ with the much less convincing Second Peter:

---

16. Mark 4:38 (GAB, colloquial "don't").
17. Matt 8:25 (NEB).

honest sermonizing reflects that difference. To add one other instance: the form critics' proposal that the "form" of the miracle accounts—especially in Mark, namely, (a) trouble: "We are sinking. Don't you care?"; (b) the sovereign word: "Hush" (waves), "be still"; and (c) awestruck worship: "Who can this be?"—is almost a command to preach, for that form is a paradigm of our life. So once more a gentle but emphatic protest against the pulpit cliché, "The Bible says." It says much on many levels in many centuries. It is not a handy book of home medicine. It is not a level tableland. It is ruled by Christ and understood only under the light of his Spirit.

The other honesty? Fidelity to the mood of the text. The forsaken cry of dereliction, "My God, my God, why hast thou forsaken me?,"[18] peers over a dread abyss and rends our hearts. Even rats desert a derelict ship. A preacher may not use that text to survey the various doctrines of the atonement, so as to indicate the preacher's own preference. That would be like kneeling at the sacrament to examine the silver. The sermon should reflect the mood. The story of the Emmaus Road, which prompted the hymn "Abide with Me," is in another climate; it dwells in the light of all golden sunsets. The sensitive preacher, true to text and context, "feels" the mood. "Come to me all whose work is hard, whose load is heavy"[19] is all compassion. So is "Who set me over you to judge or arbitrate?,"[20] but the compassion now is peremptory. When the Bible is honestly studied it meets *our* varied moods. So, the preacher as he sermonizes must be more than perceptive: he must "see" with the eyes of the heart. Suppose he reads "a sea of glass mingled with fire."[21] He knows already the marks of apocalyptic writing. He does not use the book of Revelation as a fortune-teller in present politics. He knows also that the "fire" is no naturalistic crimson sunset but the red of the blood of the cross freely shed, cancelling the impotent blood of Pharaoh's slaughtered forces. Across the new Red Sea, the people are led to the promised land.

---

18. Matt 27:46b (KJV).
19. Matt 11:28 (NEB).
20. Luke 12:14 (NEB).
21. Rev 15:2 (KJV and RSV).

III

Preachers should choose the great themes. It is better to wave at a mountain than excavate a molehill. Tricky sermons on such a word as *until* or thin psychological advice are under the ban. The preacher travels the boardwalk. His congregation is on one side: the auctions, stores, factories, "white" homes and (pushed back inland) "black" homes. On the other side is the ocean, fit symbol of the majesty and cleansing mercy of the Gospel. The devoted preacher finds his themes on the ocean side, not among the sideshows, which could not live without the sea.

So the questions Jesus asked beckon the preacher. "What are you looking for?"[22] (how little we know, and what swift refusal of the world's prizes if we did know!); or, "Will ye also go away?"[23] (we turn the issue of courage into an alleged bafflement of mind!); or, "Whom say the people that I am?"[24] (they examine you, Lord, as if you were a bug on a page, and so they sidestep the challenge!). The questions asked of Jesus are as surefire as they are poignant: "Rabbi, where do you live?"[25] (not at the end of our itchy roads, or maybe he does!). Or "Are you the one who is to come, or are we to expect some other?"[26] (what other could so meet our need and joy?); or, "Who is my neighbor?"[27] (everybody, but we wish Christ to bless our wretched fences). These themes are pointed and perennial because they are the dialogue between heaven and earth. God speaks, every person hears the voice and answers, and Christ is himself the answer, quietly demanding a lived-out response.

The words of King Lear describe the true preacher, though such an application might have shocked even that homeless monarch. Driven from

---

22. John 1:38 (NEB).

23. John 6:67 (KJV).

24. Luke 9:18 (KJV).

25. John 1:38 (GAB, following the Greek sentence order); Good News for Modern Man: Today's English Version (TEV) reads, "Where do you live, Rabbi?"

26. Luke 7:19 (NEB).

27. Luke 10:29 (NEB).

his palace by his ungrateful daughters, Lear found solace in a shanty with a hobo, and was strangely content:

> So we'll live,
> And pray, and sing, and tell old tales, and laugh
> At gilded butterflies, and hear poor rogues
> Talk of court news; and we'll talk with them too,
> Who loses and who wins; who's in, who's out;
> And take upon 's the mystery of things,
> As if we were God's spies: and we'll wear out,
> In a wall'd prison, packs and sects of great ones,
> That ebb and flow by the moon.[28]

The preacher is God's spy. He tells God in prayer what he finds in the world, and then discovers that God already knows. Then he carries into the world "this mystery, which is Christ in you, the hope of glory."[29]

How does the preacher avoid sameness in his themes, since that dull fate may fall despite the lectionary? How does he escape the violent oscillation of mood, now *adagio*, now *impassionato*, now tooting on the Matterhorn—which the small boy defined as "a large horn to be blown when something is the matter"—now reassuring folk that "all is well"; now declaring that the truth is "not hidden," and now that "we see through a clouded mirror dimly"?[30] The answer may be in an occasional series of sermons even though that may mean a temporary break with the lectionary. A series should not be a life sentence but consist of six or seven topics, such as those found in the Lord's Prayer, the Apostles' Creed, the marks of the true church in Ephesians, the pre-Gospel in the book of Jonah (four topics paralleling the four chapters), and for titles, "Adventures in the Book of Psalms," or for Lent "The Figures of Redemption" such as ransom, sacrifice, atonement, justification. The preacher drinks from an ever-flowing spring. Granted his faithfulness, he need not fear: the word is given to him day by day, through the Word made flesh.

---

28. Shakespeare, *King Lear*, act 5, sc. 3, lines 11–19.
29. Col 1:27 (RSV).
30. 1 Cor 13:12 (GAB).

CHAPTER SEVEN

Foreground Preparation: Gathering Material

Our exemplary preacher is in her study, so located that she is fairly free from interruption. She has said her brief prayer of preparation. The time is Tuesday morning, for Monday is her day off. She is ready to be honest with the Bible. That is why she is exemplary, a member of a rare breed. She has chosen a text, with its context, and topic. The text and topic spring from the fact that the Bible situation finds its echo in our modern life, that is to say, in every person's biography. What shall our preacher now do?

I

Step one: verify the meaning of the text, within the message and color and mood of the context, within the drive of the particular book, within the beckoning of the Gospel. That is, expository preaching and so-called life-situation preaching are not two kinds: they are one blend. Expository preaching unrelated to contemporary experience is not preaching; it is a Bible class study of dubious worth; and life-situation preaching divorced from the scriptures is—divorced: the house is lonely. Suppose the text is from the story of Jacob: "There wrestled a man with him."[1] Our exemplary preacher does not proceed to talk about Christ wrestling with us, at least

---
1. Gen 32:24 (KJV).

not at once. Jacob's crossing the brook Jabbok was disputed by the river god, for the story is old, as far back as animism. The god tried to hide its name, for it was then believed that to know a god's name was to seize its secret power: "Tell me, I pray, your name."[2] A god feared the dawn: "Let me go, for the day is breaking."[3] This made plain, the preacher may then use the story of our midnight wrestling with Christ. Not till then! All right; our preacher clarifies the whole realm of meaning. A deliberately dishonest preacher can't preach.

II

Step two: our preacher next jots down her own thoughts about her text, before consulting any commentaries. She asks why this text has come alive for her: all preaching is in that sense autobiographical, though the personal "I" is usually excised. She asks how the text invades the current scene, for all preaching is "now": the hearer should not be given chance to dismiss the text as being "back there in the Bible." If the preacher begins (after the clarification) with her own thoughts, the sermon will be at firsthand. She will not be dummy for some expositor's ventriloquism. The preacher is always tempted to cull here and cull there, and then glue together the borrowings, but the "joins" always "show," and the sermon is a cut-and-paste affair. It should be true of every sermon that only *that* preacher could have preached that sermon.

Let's take an instance of step two. The text is Pilate's "Behold the Man!,"[4] or, "Here is the man!"—*Ecce homo*! What thoughts occur? They throng. This: the words were almost certainly a slur ("Look at the pitiable wretch!"); then why and how have they become a tribute? Why does the whole world now keep vigil? Death by execution was common enough, and Jesus long ago and faraway should have been forgotten. Who's behind this business? Then this: Isn't there a famous Munkácsy painting of this

---

2. Gen 32:29 (RSV).
3. Gen 32:26 (RSV).
4. John 19:5 (NEB).

very scene?[5] The library has it; I must see it. Maybe there's a story back of it. Then this: Do we behold him? There's a picture of him down the street, with a notice: "Wherever you stand, the eyes follow you." People try it and nod their heads. Then this: of course, Jesus was judging Pilate. Then this: When we do look at him, what happens? It's dangerous to go to church. What wonderful things we see, wonderfully disturbing, wonderfully redeeming! These seminal thoughts have "come" in their own order or by random, but they are enough to make the sermon an original, not a copy; a voice, not an echo, still less a dubbed-in voice.

III

Step three: our preacher can then turn to commentaries and other allies. Many public-domain commentaries are out of date because they rest on faulty translations, but even they yield some treasure, for they may tell how a writer back there in the Victorian era was found by Christ. But by and large there isn't much percentage in consulting, say, Clark's commentary.[6] Our exemplary preacher turns to other books as they come to mind: J. M. Barrie on "Courage"[7] or Josiah Royce on "Loyalty."[8] She asks if there is any account of the origins of that Munkácsy picture or how much the history books or legendry tell us about Pilate. Our preacher flees from sermon outlines published in periodicals, for these at best are pedestrian and at worst unwitting comedy. Besides, they sidetrack the preacher from her own word. There are no prefabricated sermon houses, if because a sermon outline is no longer like a house. It is more like a series of sunbursts on an April day. It can be one sunburst as in a Frederick Buechner sermon.[9]

---

5. Mihály Munkácsy (1844–1900), Hungarian painter known for biblical scenes and those of peasantry and the poor.

6. Adam Clark (ca. 1760–1832), British Methodist (Wesleyan-Arminian) biblical commentator.

7. The rectorial address delivered by J. M. Barrie at St. Andrew's University, May 3, 1922.

8. Josiah Royce, *The Philosophy of Loyalty* (New York: Macmillan, 1908).

9. Frederick Buechner, Presbyterian minister, writer, and novelist, attributed his conversion to the Christian faith to George Buttrick who introduced Buechner to Union Theological Seminary in New York, championing him as a preacher of paramount importance. Buechner spoke at Buttrick's memorial service held at New York City's Madison Avenue Presbyterian Church.

Chapter Seven

Still concerning step three: here are the questions. Does this item really belong in this sermon, or would it be a digression or even a distraction? Is it dull or shining? Is it trite or penetrating? (It had better not be dull in a psychedelic world!) Does it meet the life of my congregation, since, whatever I may believe, I am not preaching to a whole world waiting with bated breath, but to this church at this time? Is this illustration an asset, or does it "thump down" like a block of granite in a meadow? Or is it cheap humor or mere glitter rather an instant interweaving? So our preacher gathers material for maybe two mornings. She doesn't try to force inspiration. She can't; the Holy Spirit is not hers to cudgel, let alone domesticate. Our preacher works along quietly and trustfully, her thought steadily revolving round her theme. Her subconscious mind aids and abets her in sleep. She is surprised to realize how much clearer the sermon becomes "next morning." That cemetery text is a bad translation: not, "He gives his beloved sleep,"[10] but, "He gives to his beloved in their sleep."

IV

> The recommended examples in this section, of course, reflect tools available in the mid-twentieth century. The preacher now has so many thousands of tools available that a bibliographic resource, supplemented by many web bloggers, is necessary for building a personal library. Among the basic options are the following:
>
> *An Essential Bibliography for the Study of Scripture*, Jack Fitzmeyer, 1990
>
> *Multipurpose Tools for Bible Study*, Frederick W. Danker, 1993
>
> *Essential Bible Study Tools for Ministry*, David R. Bauer, 2014

As to reinforcements for step three, our preacher has her tools, as a doctor has medical references or a lawyer law books. They should be within reach of her hand. Some are indispensable: (a) *The King James Version* (KJV) alongside a worthy modern version, such as the *New English*

---

10. Ps 126:2 (RSV).

Bible (NEB).[11] (b) A concordance of large size if you are interested in the derivation or long use of certain words, a short one for most occasions and most budgets. (c) A dictionary large enough for tracing the history of words will give you many an illustration; a short one is quicker to hand and easier on the bank account. (d) A "harmony" of the Gospels such as Throckmorton's *Gospel Parallels* is the best.[12] To compare, for example, the story of the baptism of Jesus in the Synoptic Gospels, is a rewarding venture. (e) A dictionary of the Bible. The *The New Interpreter's Dictionary* and the *Anchor Bible Dictionary* offer fine choices.[13] Others claim consideration, such as Davis's and Westminster.[14] Of course, a preacher who knows the languages will turn gratefully to her Hebrew Old Testament and her Greek New Testament.

We must itemize a second group of tools that claim almost daily use. (a) A book or web site of quotations. Many titles come to mind: Stevenson, Bartlett, Mencken, Bergen Evans.[15] Stevenson has perhaps more

---

11. The New English Bible (NEB, 1961, 1970) was frequently employed by Buttrick in addition to the Revised Standard Version (RSV, 1951), alongside his own translations from the biblical Hebrew and Greek. He quoted from the King James Version (KJV, 1611, 1881, 1901) for its linguistic beauty while now and again pointing to its faulty translations. Since Buttrick's death, of course, the student has many translation choices, such as the Common English Bible, the New Revised Standard Version, and the New International Version.

12. Burton H. Throckmorton, Jr., ed., *Gospel Parallels: A Synopsis of the First Three Gospels* (New York: Thomas Nelson & Sons, 1949, 1957). This English version follows the arrangement of Albert Huck's Greek language *Synopsis of the First Three Gospels*, 9th ed., ed. Hans Lietzmann & F. L. Cross (New York: American Bible Society, 1936). Also available: the *CEB Gospel Parallels* (Nashville: Abingdon Press, 2013).

13. The *Interpreter's Dictionary of the Bible* that Buttrick cited here is no longer in print, though available in some digital collections, so see *The New Interpreter's Dictionary of the Bible* (Nashville: Abingdon Press, 2009). The six-volume *Anchor Bible Dictionary* (1992) did not exist at the time of Buttrick's writing.

14. Writing in the early 1970s, Buttrick recommended: James Hastings, ed., *Hastings' Dictionary of the Bible* (New York: Charles Scribner's Sons, 1909, 1963); George A. Buttrick, gen. ed., *The Interpreter's Dictionary of the Bible* (New York: Abingdon, 1962); John D. Davis, ed., *A Dictionary of the Bible* (Philadelphia: The Westminster Press, 1898; Grand Rapids: Baker Book House, 1972); John D. Davis & Henry Snyder Gehman, eds., *The Westminster Dictionary of the Bible* (Philadelphia: The Westminster Press, 1944).

15. Burton E. Stevenson, ed., *The Home Book of Quotations* (Toronto: Cassell, 1934, 1967). John Bartlett & Emily Morison Beck, eds., *Bartlett's Familiar Quotations* (New York: Little, Brown, and Company, 1855, 1968); H. L. Mencken, ed., *A New Dictionary of Quotations* (New York: Alfred Knopf, 1942); Bergen Evans, ed., *Dictionary of Quotations* (New York: Delacorte Press, 1968). Or see www.quotationspage.com, www.brainyquote.com, www.bartleby.com/quotation.

material, and its dictionary plan brings it into quick avail. Mencken is pungent, and kills many a sacred cow; I use it for its sassy realism. (b) A thesaurus is a "must":[16] it gives synonyms and antonyms, and so rescues the preacher who is preaching on compassion from using that word, even that word, to the pitch of boredom. The new edition of *Roget's* is on the dictionary plan; the old edition, though not as convenient to use, is richer in content.[17] (c) A book of Christian verse is required. Hill's *The World's Great Religious Poetry*[18] and J. D. Morrison's *Masterpieces of Religious Verse*[19] are certainly "indicated," but they are a mixed grill and they include some doggerel; the preacher might be as well off with the *Oxford Book of Christian Verse*.[20] (d) If our preacher can find in a secondhand bookstore *The Reader's Digest of Books*, her drilling has released a gusher.[21] Helen Rex Keller is the compiler. She gives a digest of great novels and poems. For instance, she identifies the Grand Inquisitor in Dostoevsky's *The Brothers Karamazov*. Another secondhand treasure is *The Reader's Handbook*, which traces characters and incidents in literature. The author or compiler is E. C. Brewer.[22] You wonder about Mrs. Poyser, and this handbook identifies her in George Eliot's *Adam Bede*. (e) There's another help: Alan Richardson's *A Theological Wordbook of the Bible*.[23] It is inimitable in its tabloid studies of the great doctrines of our Faith.

---

16. Or see www.thesaurus.com.

17. *Roget's International Thesaurus*, 3rd ed. (New York: Thomas Y. Crowell Company, 1962).

18. Caroline Miles Hill, ed., *The World's Great Religious Poetry* (New York: Macmillan, 1942).

19. James Dalton Morrison, ed., *Masterpieces of Religious Verse* (New York: Harper & Row, 1948).

20. Lord David Cecil, ed., *Oxford Book of Christian Verse* (New York: Oxford University Press, 1940).

21. Used copies can be located on eBay and abebooks.com.

22. E. C. Brewer, ed., *The Reader's Handbook* (London: Chatto and Windus, 1925).

23. Alan Richardson, ed., *A Theological Wordbook of the Bible*, 5th ed. (New York: Macmillan, 1962).

A third group of tools consists of commentaries. Of one-volume commentaries,[24] Dummelow[25] and Gore[26] are simply out of date. Peake (in the recent revision) and Abingdon are probably the best, Peake more scholarly, Abingdon more practical yet well informed.[27]

Of the larger commentaries, *The Pulpit Commentary*[28] and *The Expositor's Bible*[29] are outmoded: we no longer live in their world, though a few volumes cannot be ignored, such as George Adam Smith on Isaiah.[30] Maclaren's *Expositions of Holy Scripture*[31] are to me (because of my stubborn heart) a heap of sawdust, but Parker's *The People's Bible*[32] sets my mind on fire. The chapters are interlaced with his pulpit prayers: they leave any reader "surprised by joy." Sometimes it can be bought (forty volumes or more) for the proverbial song, though my singing would ruin any bargain. Moffatt[33] and the Westminster[34] are perhaps too scant, though generally

24. Since Buttrick's time, many one-volume commentaries have appeared, including the *Interpreter's Bible One-Volume Commentary*, and the *New Interpreter's Bible One-Volume Commentary*.

25. J. R. Dummelow, ed., *A Commentary on the Bible by Various Writers* (New York: Macmillan, 1909).

26. Charles Gore, Henry Leighton Goudge, and Alfred Guillaume, eds., *A New Commentary on Holy Scripture, Including the Apocrypha* (London: Society for Promoting Christian Knowledge, 1928).

27. Matthew Black and H. H. Rowley, eds., *Peake's Commentary on the Bible* (London: Thomas Nelson and Sons Ltd, 1962); Charles M. Laymon, ed., *The Interpreter's One-Volume Commentary on the Bible* (Nashville: Abingdon Press, 1971).

28. H. D. M. Spence-Jones, ed., *The Pulpit Commentary* (New York: Funk & Wagnalls, 1909–1919).

29. W. Robertson Nicoll, ed., *The Expositor's Bible*, 24 vols. (New York: A. C. Armstrong, 1905).

30. Sir George Adam Smith, *The Expositor's Bible: The Book of Isaiah*, 2 vols. (London: Hodder & Stoughton, 1888, 1890).

31. Alexander Maclaren (1826–1910), *Expositions of Holy Scripture*, 33 vols. (London: Hodder & Stoughton, n.d.).

32. Joseph Parker (1830–1902), *The People's Bible*, 25 vols. (New York: Funk & Wagnalls, 1885–1895).

33. James Moffatt, *New Testament Commentaries*, 16 vols. (New York: Harper & Brothers, 1927–1950).

34. Buttrick was likely referring to the limited (thus, "scant") number of commentaries available at the time of the scholarly Old Testament Library series published by Westminster Press, beginning in the 1950s, and to which were added later volumes including a New Testament series after 2000.

trustworthy. *The Anchor Bible* is like the curate's egg:[35] good in parts. Some volumes are too scholarly; the Ugaritic antecedent of Psalm 23 doesn't bring much grist to the mill, but Father Raymond Brown's two-volume study of the Fourth Gospel is already definitive.[36] The best commentary for the average preacher is still *The Interpreter's Bible*.[37] Its expositions provide "openings" for the preacher's own thinking.

A sharp word about two other "helps." One is the twenty-volume *Great Texts of the Bible*.[38] Here we find three or four hundred sermons. Each sermon is pieced together from twenty or thirty sermons printed on that text. The material is gathered into an outline. I use it whenever it bears on my sermonizing, but I try to remember that when I am lazy it is the devil at my elbow. That is to say, it is a fairly good servant if kept in place—and a tyrannous master. It has recently been reprinted, though not revised. Its illustrations are Victorian, and therefore always suspect. The other devil-angel is *The Expositor's Dictionary of Texts*.[39] It has the same plan and method as the *Great Texts*, though the material covers more texts in much smaller compass. Again, the caveat: don't be tyrannized. Besides, these two sets assume a style of preaching that is "gone with the wind."

V

Our exemplary preacher's wider reading is now her friend. She reads the big books. They may not provide instant resource, but they fertilize the mind and come to harvest after many days. If she knows her Shakespeare,

---

35. See the Wikipedia article about the "curate's egg" and its cartoonery, https://en.wikipedia.org/wiki/Curate%27s_egg.

36. Raymond E. Brown, *The Anchor Bible: The Gospel according to John*, 2 vols. (Garden City: Doubleday & Company, 1966, 1970). The first of over eighty volumes of the Anchor Bible series of Old and New Testament translations and commentaries was published in 1964 and continues. The project was conceived under the leadership of the late William Foxwell Albright (1891–1971).

37. George Arthur Buttrick, gen. ed., *The Interpreter's Bible*, 12 vols. (Nashville: Abingdon-Cokesbury Press, 1951–1957).

38. James Hastings, ed., *Great Texts of the Bible*, 20 vols. (New York: Charles Scribner's & Sons, 1910–1915).

39. James Hastings, ed., *The Expositor's Dictionary of Text*, 2 vols. (1910–1911).

and needs an illustration for the failure of all human panaceas to cure our transgressions, she may quote Lady Macbeth's,

> Will all great Neptune's ocean wash this blood
>   clean from my hand?
> No, this my hand will rather
>   the multitudinous seas in incarnadine,
>   making the green one red.[40]

But that would be negative. Our preacher would then remember lines from *Hamlet*:

> What if this cursed hand
>   be thicker than itself with brother's blood,
> Is there not rain enough in the sweet heavens
>   to wash it white as snow?[41]

But there might be handicaps even in that wonderful contrast, for too many congregations Shakespeare would seem literary: they would be turned off. The preacher might be better fortified by Ionesco or Becket. To cite another instance: if the text is "Depend on the LORD, and he will grant you your heart's desire,"[42] the wise preacher will turn to Tennessee Williams's *A Streetcar Named Desire*. If our preacher couldn't find a sermon there, she is dead in mind. We're anticipating what should be said about illustrations, but that won't hurt; we may be more on the alert.

In two mornings our preacher has gathered twenty or thirty items of varying importance. Each as it is gathered should be written on a worksheet in the preacher's own words, except for coveted quotations, which should be accurately copied—and acknowledged. So, in both instances plagiarism is avoided. Plagiarism is a besetting sin the preacher must rigorously refuse. Whenever our exemplary preacher is in doubt as to whether or not she should acknowledge her sources, the answer is "Yes, she should acknowledge." (A famous book of sermons consists almost entirely of stolen

---

40. *Macbeth*, act 2, scene 2.
41. *Hamlet*, act 3, scene 3.
42. Ps 37:4 (NEB).

Chapter Seven

material. Many a paragraph has been "lifted" with hardly the change of a word.[43]) If this gathering includes illustrations, and if any such can pass the proper tests, they can be starred; they are worth a king's ransom.[44] But they must give the countersign before being allowed to enter camp; and they are for a later chapter.

After two days labor and two nights for the gifts of the subconscious mind, our preacher is ready for the next step.

---

43. Plagiarism was a subject Buttrick addressed with the editor in his 1974 interview. Since Buttrick was often plagiarized, during his lifetime he restricted recordings of his sermons and lectures to library holdings that could be listened to but not borrowed on loan. Plagiarism was an issue he invariably addressed with his students. One, by the name of Lawrence Black, who in the early 1950s studied homiletics with Buttrick at Union Theological Seminary, New York, recalled the day that Buttrick came into class fuming and saying, "I've just discovered that most of the sermons [in a book of sermons recently published by a well-known preacher] were plagiarized from my sermons." Buttrick then added, "I want to tell you something. If you steal your thoughts from somebody else, at least have the courtesy to tell your wife you've done that, so that she won't publish them after you die" (editor's interview with Lawrence Black, October 10, 2016). During his tenure as senior minister of Madison Avenue Presbyterian Church, Buttrick published one sermon a month in that congregation's *Church News*. In 1968, when corresponding with the Rev. Wayne Blankenship of Plainville, Texas, he wrote the following: "Since we had four hundred ministers on the mailing list and since I was fairly certain, on clear evidence, that many of them were guilty of plagiarism, I rarely published any sermon which included materials that I might later wish to use in published form" (Letter to the Rev. Wayne Blankenship, December 17, 1968, HUG FP 90.9/1, Box 1).

44. In his sermon outlines Buttrick "starred" with an asterisk particular items that, metaphorically, were worth "a king's ransom" as illustrations.

CHAPTER EIGHT

Foreground Preparation: The Sermon Outline

Lord Bryce, who, though a Britisher, wrote wisely and well about our American history, once said that the mark of an intelligent person is the ability to prepare an outline.[1] The preacher, with text and context chosen, can't "just begin to write." In rare instances a wonderful road may open to that gambit (or lack of gambit), but the odds are that such a person may resemble the famous general who leapt on his horse and rode off rapidly in all directions. The preacher should have a "triptik."[2] That is a better metaphor than blueprint. A house doesn't move, whereas a sermon should "open" like a drama. So, a sermon-journey inevitably has a beginning, a main stretch, and a conclusion. To change the metaphor, the preacher dives into the pool, swims the pool's length, and (hopefully) emerges. Too bad that so many preachers drown.

1. Lord James Bryce, "Address by the Right Hon. James Bryce on the Teaching of History in Schools: Delivered at the First Annual Meeting of the Association, Jan 1, 1907," Leaflet No. 5 (London: University College), 7. "Although the study of special subjects is extremely valuable, and indeed necessary, still the one essential thing is to know the subject in broad outline; for the teacher to help the pupil, so to speak, to look back through a long vista, to see clearly the trees nearer, and to see the trees receding at the end of the vista until one gets only an outline and cannot see the small boughs—that is a very difficult art, because it is a thing the imagination of the child does not easily take in." (It is not known whether these words or other words of Lord Bryce were the source of Buttrick's paraphrase.)

2. Triptik: a travel planner.

Chapter Eight

I

So what of the introduction? It should be brief. The preacher should clear decks, cast anchor, and go. He should not spend five minutes announcing his departure. Sometimes he can say as the ropes are loosed, "We're bound for the compassions of Christ." More often he will keep the occasions of surprise. If the final manuscript has seven pages (that's probably too many), the introduction should not claim more than half a page. Suppose the sermon concerns the soldiers gambling at the cross for the garments of Christ, the introduction could begin, "The drugstore clerk asked, 'Mister, who won the third race?' I guessed that he meant a horse race, not the human race, but there my knowledge and interest ended. But the issue for him was a fever. Not new: soldiers gambled for the garments of Christ—while he watched from the cross. What were the garments?" That sermon would be launched—in fifty-five words. So: brevity.

The introduction should be worthy. A smart-aleck opening has no passport. Incidents reported in *The Reader's Digest* are usually far below the level of the Gospel. So is *The Reader's Digest*. Its articles on the National Council of the Churches of Christ were slander and a pack of lies.[3] Humor in an introduction is okay provided that it is the kind that is cousin to tears. The little black girl was asked cruelly, "Do you prefer to be called 'Black' or 'Negro'?" She said, "I'd rather be called Carrie." That might be a worthy kickoff for a sermon on the biblical doctrine of names. So, humor, yes, sometimes. Our faith is too serious to be solemn. But triviality and cheapness are not servants of the Presence.

---

3. Buttrick was referring to Clarence W. Hall, "Must Our Churches Finance Revolution?" *Reader's Digest*, October, 1971, 95ff; and "Which Way the World Council of Churches?" *Reader's Digest*, November 1971, 177ff. In his December 7, 1972, letter to De Witt Wallace of *Reader's Digest*, Buttrick said, "My substituting 'National Council' for 'World Council' was a slip-of-the-tongue" ("Reader's Digest," HUG FP 90.9, Box 13).

Foreground Preparation: The Sermon Outline

The introduction should be fitting: it should fit the theme. It should directly pertain to the text and context. You read a striking story; what a temptation to use it even though it doesn't "belong"! A stranger sought shelter on Saturday night in a Scots croft. After the evening meal the father examined his family in the Shorter Catechism. The stranger was drawn into the exam. His question was, "How many commandments are there?" He answered, "Eleven," while the children tittered. "No," said the father: "Ten." "Eleven," the stranger insisted: "This is my commandment that you love one another: as I have loved you, that you love one another." The stranger added: "The eleventh has swallowed the other ten." That story (the stranger proved to be a famous bishop incognito) would be okay if you were preaching on "the Eleventh Commandment," but where else would it fit? So: the introduction should be apt and deft (not daft).

The introduction should be interesting, or attention may be lost almost before the sermon begins. Yet the opening words should not be a bombshell, or the sermon proper may be anticlimax. Harry Fosdick used to advise students, "Tell all you know in the first sentence." Good counsel for a Fosdick: genius goes beyond convention. But if I tried it, the sermon after the explosion would be a shower of ashes falling in darkness. Yet the first moments of a sermon are crucial. This the preacher should know. Yet one should not begin therefore in a compulsive urgency. It might be wiser to appear casual. But one should be at pains to enlist at once the interest of the hearers. I've tried already to offer instances.

The introduction should be timely. It is almost an inviolable rule that every sermon introduction should have some sentence that says in effect, "This is your concern here and now." The introduction should not be allowed to be "only back there in the Bible." Suppose our preacher is preaching on the valedictory of Jesus: "It is for your good that I am leaving you."[4] The point of contact is that we don't believe him. So our preacher begins, "Do you believe that? Wouldn't it be wonderful if Jesus lived down your street, and you could ring his doorbell and ask, 'Master, what would you do in my case?'" That sermon would have an instant thrust into our daily life.

II

The main body of the sermon (perhaps we shouldn't say *body*, much less corpse; *impulse* or *journey* might be a better word) has certain marks. One is singleness. A sermon has one theme faithful to one context. Some preachers boldly announce the theme or indicate it in the bulletin. My predecessor in New York City used to write over his sermon manuscript, "My intention in this sermon is...," but he wouldn't print it. If asked to print it, he would answer, "Oh, no: let me surprise them with it!" But he knew the theme, and kept to the highroad, as witness his sermons in such

---

4. John 16:7 (NEB).

a book as *God's Turn*.[5] But many a preacher does not so govern his work. He tries to sit on two chairs that are three feet apart, or even on three chairs spread around the room. Singleness should be as rigorously observed as in the unity of a Greek drama with its oneness of time, place, and plot. Admittedly singleness leads to disproportion. If we preach on the courage of Christ, we can't in that same sermon centralize the other traits. A fine student in seminary preaching would be impelled by honesty to stop and say, "In a certain sense the very opposite of this is true." Thus, the sermon collapsed with a broken spine. Disproportion can't be corrected within the limits of a sermon, but it can in a year's ministry, especially if the preacher cleaves to a lectionary. The sermon in any instance comes to focus in a single theme.

Unity should be heeded even in the choice of illustrations. If the text is, "No one who sets his hand to the plough and then keeps looking back is fit for the kingdom of God,"[6] the pictures should all be drawn from the world of plowman and field. An illustration about the rigging of a ship or about a lamp on a dark street would obviously be out of place. There are plenty of "openings" if our preacher ponders the plowing of a field. For instance, a plowman keeps his eye on the plowshare lest he drive it into a boulder, yet he keeps lifting his eye to the distant mark. Isn't that the way to live? As another instance, there is a great passage in Masefield's "The Everlasting Mercy," a poem that is an outright study of conversion:

> O Christ, who holds the open gate,
> O Christ who drives the furrow straight,
> O Christ, the plough, O Christ, the laughter
> of holy white birds flying after.[7]

That passage climbs and climbs. You can see how the unity of the sermon would be tightened if the very illustrations serve the singleness of

---

5. Henry Sloane Coffin, *God's Turn* (New York: Harper & Brothers, 1934).

6. Luke 9:62 (NEB).

7. John Masefield (1878–1967), "The Everlasting Mercy," in *The Oxford Book of English Mystical Verse*, ed. D. H. S. Nicholson and A. H. E. Lee (Oxford: The Clarendon Press, 1917). Masefield was poet laureate of the United Kingdom, 1930–1967.

Chapter Eight

the theme. One theme at a time is the rule. A preacher should not curse his sermon by a divided mind.

The sermon outline should be simple. Complexity is barred. If the major turns are clearly marked, that is no demerit provided the sermon does not bring the journey to a halt but invites the hearer to look eagerly around the corner. Yet how many preachers say foolishly, "There are three main considerations" (a dull phrase in itself), and then add regarding the first consideration: "We are here confronted by two truths," though it is not the preacher's job to peddle "truths." A recent preacher said, believe it or not, "We must now dwell on ten points." "Dwell"! By that time, he had so many headings and subheadings that we were lost in a maze. That preacher some years ago was in my homiletics class. After church my wife asked impishly, "Wasn't he one of your students?" Please don't let me down! The outline shouldn't be like the government department of Health, Education and Welfare, with bureaus within bureaus.

Obviously, singleness and simplicity are mutual. The singleness requires simplicity, and the simplicity reinforces the singleness. The preacher says, "We are traveling on Route 69." At the proper time he says, "We are turning onto Route 83." Soon he says, "This is the clear Route 74," and never hints that it is the homestretch. There's a classic outline credited to a Scots Highlands pastor. It concerns the younger prodigal, as follows: (a) Sick of home; (b) Homesick; (c) Home. That sermon if wisely implemented would be memorable, that is, easily remembered—for years to come.

Simplicity as one trait of a sermon outline brings us directly to another: imagination. The difference between effective and ineffective preaching lives beyond our human ken; the wind of the Spirit blows where it wills. But humanly speaking the difference lives in the realm of the imagination. The word *truth*, especially in the Fourth Gospel, means nothing abstract or intellectualized but "the unveiling." Penetrating writers regarding creativity, such as Berdyaev[8] or Koestler,[9] agree that all discovery, whether literary or scientific, comes when the mind is off guard. Yes, there is prior

---

8. Nikolai Alexandrovich Berdyaev (1874–1948), Russian philosopher and Christian existentialist, wrote *The Meaning of the Creative Act*, trans. Donald A. Lowrie (New York: Collier, 1926 [1910]).

9. Arthur Koestler (1905–1983), *The Act of Creation* (New York: Macmillan, 1964).

discipline, without which no "unveiling" comes. But the sudden insight *comes*; it is not manufactured. So a sermon outline is not like a syllogism: it is like a Kipling Ballad with two or three verses and a repeated refrain.[10] The preacher thus waits. Then he will not be trapped in such an outline as, (a) international, (b) national, (c) individual. That order is right, but, oh, the dull abstract words and the cheap newspaper titles!

How is imagination born and encouraged? It is given and then cultivated. How? By lively reading in fiction, drama, and poetry, more especially by brooding over text and context. Under that brooding the context offers its own "natural" outline, unlike any other. An Easter carol, with its refrain about the two disciples on the Emmaus Road, gave this outline: (a) Two men walking down the road, broken in mind and heart by Calvary, (b) Three men walking down the road, and what a difference!, (c) One man walking down the road: "he vanished from their sight," and the only way to keep him was to go with him. Requests then came: Would I please preach that sermon? So I hid it for fear I would soon be saying it instead of praying it. Do you see how that outline prints *pictures* on the mind? Preaching is not a list of reasons for believing; it is more like the acts and scenes of a drama. No preacher can flaunt this fact, and still preach. The word *preach* means to herald. Can't you hear the trumpets?

The momentous trait? That adjective is the clue: momentum. The outline travels and climbs. It is like the Tchaikovsky "Fourth." There may rightfully be an intermediate *adagio* movement, but the third movement does not merely echo earlier themes; it gathers them into a climax. The words of Christ precisely describe a sermon outline: "first the blade, then the ear, then the full grain in the ear." Thus, such a text as "I am the way, the truth, and the life" presents hard problems, for we are tempted to regard it as a horizontal bar with three pendants. But no sermon should be horizontal. The preacher could preach a "moving sermon" (note *that* adjective!) were he to say, "he is truth, unveiling"; then, "not in heaven but dwelling in our tent of flesh"; then, "That would not help us, but he walks the way with us." You and I are asked to preach "moving" sermons.

---

10. Rudyard Kipling (1865–1936), British Indian poet and novelist.

Almost we can resort to diagrams. The *pudding-bowl sermon* begins and ends well, but sags in the middle. The *igloo sermon* begins and ends badly, but climbs in the middle. The *begin-with-an-explosion sermon* is like fireworks: a brilliant flash soon lost in darkness. The *airfield-runway sermon* is a stay-there level flatness: the plane takes off, but the runway never. *A true sermon climbs the mountain*, pausing here and there to admire the view, and the mountain is crowned by an empty cross. Or it starts at the mountain like a skier, climbs this hill from sheer gift of speed, quickens wonderfully down this slope, and ends in the village where we all live, the mountain air and the mountain vision now redeeming our common life. The Gospels are rich with "moving" stories, as for instance, that about Zacchaeus.[11] Why was he the most hated man in the town? Why should he crave the sight of Jesus? Why would Jesus ever want to stay in that man's house, and what would the neighbors think? Why and how did Jesus knight the little rascal, giving him the title every Jew coveted? What was the issue? Most sermons hardly "move" us. Why? Part of the reason is that the sermon doesn't "move."

III

The conclusion is as crucial as the introduction or more crucial. If only it could be written first when the mind is fresh! But it can't, for a sermon sometimes insists on going its own way, a better way than the preacher planned. So the conclusion must sometimes wait until the sermon journey has been traveled. But the conclusion in its preparation should not be hurried. The preacher should not say, "Let's get this finished," for that carelessness may botch the whole endeavor.

What are the marks of an appealing conclusion? Brevity. Heralding is not garrulous. A conclusion is like the final chord of some great music. It honors the humanity of the person in the pew. So it never exploits the emotions either by fake tears or by organ music with the tremolo stop pulled "way out." If the preacher believes, as should be the case, that every person is host to the mystery and candidate for the grace of Christ, the

---

11. Luke 19:1-10.

sermon conclusion should so treat the ones listening. It should fulfill the message of the sermon, yes, and the sermon's mood. If the sermon warns, the conclusion should warn: warn, not threaten; though we must add that only Christ can end a sermon with, "It fell with a great crash."[12] If the sermon is hope and the only hope, the conclusion should be a *sursum corda*: "Lift up your hearts!"

There are other marks. The conclusion should confront people, not with the preacher (heaven forbid!) but with the present Christ: "What think ye of Christ"[13] when all's said and done? There was a moment when Pizarro drew a circle round the feet of each wavering follower, and said, "Now, for me or against me, before you leave that circle."[14] The conclusion is serious, but that means that humor is not ruled out, though it should be of the kind that beckons glad tears.

Can we suggest how conclusions are determined? Not easily or confidently, for each sermon "leads into" its own conclusion. But a main guidance might be this: the preacher asks under the eyes of the Presence, "What purpose do I covet for this sermon?" Again and again we have heard as conclusion a summary of the sermon, and nothing is much more dull or unappealing than a summary. Again and again we have challenged a student: "What would you like to happen because you have preached that sermon?" and he has said eagerly, "Oh, I want them to go home with their chins up and their eyes shining!" Then we have said, "Splendid! Tell them so! Say: 'Now you can go out into the world glad!'"[15] Then a lame conclusion begins to sing and dance.

Some instances? You would have to hear the sermon to understand. But it might be this: "One man walking down the road. When you go to bed tonight and draw the window shade you can see him going down your street. If you invite him in, he will come, and his breaking of bread will once more be a sacrament. But he will not stay. There are other broken

---

12. Matt 7:27 (NEB).

13. Matt 22:42 (KJV).

14. Francisco Pizarro (1476–1541), Spanish conquistador in South America, reputedly said, "Choose. You may return to the poverty of Panama or cross this line and come with me through infinite dangers but eventual wealth."

15. Mark 16:15 (GAB paraphrase).

Chapter Eight

folk. The only way to keep him is to go with him—to the other side of the tracks, the other side of the world." Is the sermon on the soldiers gambling at the foot of the cross for his garments? They gambled. Pilate and Caiaphas gambled, and thought they had a sure thing. Christ gambled: "Father, into Your hands," though he couldn't see any hands reaching down from the sky. We must gamble—and we have the same options. Such might be the outline of the sermon. Then the conclusion, and it might be in one line if you were preaching in a college church: "Jesus is here. Do you hear what he is saying? 'I'll throw you for it!' Do you hear him?"

No person can tell another person how to preach, for each is his own person under God. All this one teacher can do is to say, "I've tried, and fallen into these snares; maybe I can save you from them." Preaching is never learned. That is why it is so joyous a craft. Every preacher is a novice to the end of his days. But why not? What apprentice ever had such a Master? By the way, that's a conclusion.

CHAPTER NINE

Sermon Illustrations

We use the word *like* as both verb and adverb: "I like lobster," and, "That cloud is like a ship." We like what is like. Deep issues are here involved. Does thought travel by analogy? Its vehicle is certainly not logic or proposition; or, if so, the vehicle doesn't provide its own power. Is analogy the filling station? Science is not profound in its basic assumptions, but even science can't escape analogy or metaphor, for it speaks about the *field* of force (strange field) and the *wave* of light. Are figures of speech the lifeblood of speech? We begin to understand that simile, story, and symbol are far more effective carriers of truth than any syllogism. So we turn from the Cartesian fallacy; it has led us into a desert.[1] Thought becomes incandescent through imagination, and imagination lives in metaphor. The Gospel comes through the power of parables.

---

1. The Cartesian fallacy consisted of using circular reasoning to validate dependent conclusions derived from equally dependent premises in logical discourse. Yet Buttrick makes the larger point that human reason (rationality) is neither the sole nor the supreme conveyor of truth. As to René Descartes (1596–1650) and his famous dictum, "I think, therefore I am," Buttrick wrote that "the nonsense in the Cartesian catastrophe is multiplied, as follows: first, the 'I' is 'snuck in' at the beginning of the sentence, and inevitably comes out at the other end, turning the whole sentence into assumption pretending to be argument. Second, we cannot just think; we have to think about something or someone. Therefore, he should have said, 'I think about my world: I am and my world is: we and the world share is-ness. Third, thinking philosophically implies the use of only one dimension in our many-dimensioned mind: e.g., we are aware of ourselves thinking: we live in self-transcendent mind which is the real land of mind. Fourth, the whole sentence puts the cart before the horse, for he should have said 'I am, therefore I think.'" See George A. Buttrick, *God, Pain, and Evil* (Nashville: Abingdon Press, 1966), 111.

Chapter Nine

I

All this does not remove the threat of illustrations. Illustrations may eclipse the sermon. Wise homiletics now questions the value of any *stated* illustration. It is too chunky: it is like a boulder fired into a meadow. A certain capable preacher was asked how soon a sermon could be repeated in a given church. He rightly answered that it shouldn't be repeated: the first "try" should reveal weaknesses, which should be healed before the next occasion. Then he added, "If you change the illustrations you can probably repeat that sermon in the same church on the same day." There's the ominous threat. How do we remember a sermon? This way: "Didn't the preacher tell a story about...?"! Even the story is not confidently remembered, and the sermon is forgotten.

Charles Dickens wrote, "Preaching is not worth a farthing without innumerable illustrations."[2] But "innumerable illustrations" would sink any sermon ship. Yet a sermon should be picture(sque), not Aristotelian.

Despite every hazard, preaching should appeal to the senses—eyes, ears, smell, taste, touch. This is "mod" doctrine. We shouldn't try to refute it. For decades our thinking has been *first* Cartesian (you know: "I think, therefore I am"), dealing in dreary concepts; and then scientific, proceeding by neutral analysis (as if the mind could ever be neutral), shrouding the exciting instance in so-called "universal law" until life became a flat insensitivity. Language must recover color and music, and the pulpit can lead the way. The words of Jesus are pictures ("a city set on a hill"; can't you see the white houses by day, and the tiny flickering lights by night?), and his Gospel came from his lips by stories, each story with a central flame. So the preacher should master the art of illustration, with eyes alert for the pitfalls. Here are some guidances.

II

Illustrations should always be brief. That warning should be repeated and repeated. The preacher says, "This picture comes to mind" but does

---

2. Explicit source unknown. Charles Franklin Thwing, *A History of Education in the United States since the Civil War* (Boston: Houghton Mifflin Co., 1910), wrote, "Dickens somewhere says that criticism is not worth a farthing unless it be accompanied with innumerable examples" (108).

not dwell on it. A sermon told of a man resolved to be happy, who was therefore "put down" wherever he went. One neighbor cited human greed, another reminded him of nuclear threat, a third spoke of a neighbor's death, a fourth asked if he had ever heard of Vietnam. Served him right! Realism is seeing life steadily and seeing it whole. He was going through life looking "for the silver lining," and so was in danger of being soaked by rain or blown off the map by a hurricane. The story went on and on—for six or seven minutes. Incidentally, it came from *The Reader's Digest* and should have been left undisturbed in that dubious home. The text, believe it or not, was the word of Christ: "that my joy may be in you, and that your joy may be full."[3] The joy of Jesus is not in the same world as a superficial happiness. That preacher had done no homework. Tell me: What have I remembered of that sermon? Prose quotations should not be more than fifty or sixty words, simply because prose is prosy, and because a preacher should not let another voice steal the instancy of her own voice. Poetry illustrations can be longer, for they have rhyme and rhythm, but not too long. Chunky illustrations are "out": they are bomb craters in a harvest field. So, brevity, lest the illustration should steal the show.

Illustrations should be few in any sermon. Dickens was wrong: not "innumerable illustrations." Yet how many preachers peddle stories instead of preaching. One well-known preacher spoke to a men's meeting in a certain church and sold us sixty-eight illustrations. I know: I counted them. To collect catchy stories and sell them is about as worthwhile as collecting and selling brightly colored marbles. Marbles can never pass as breakfast food. No, retract that; say that they are about as nutritious as the average breakfast food. One of our forebears, himself a preacher, used to laugh at what he called "anecdotage," and dismissed it as a form of "dotage."[4] Illustrations should be woven into the toil of mind and heart. They should be infrequent lest they become a cheap substitute for toil. Maybe our illustrations should closely resemble metaphor.

---

3. John 15:11 (RSV).

4. See H. T. Henry, "Sermon Anecdotage," *The Ecclesiastical Review* (Philadelphia: The American Ecclesiastical Review: The Dolphin Press, 1922), 374–85, with reference to J. P. Mahaffy, *The Decay of Modern Preaching: An Essay* (New York: Macmillan and Co., 1882), 125.

An illustration should be on target. It should illuminate *that* verity in *that* sermon. Always a preacher is tempted to use a striking story even though it doesn't "fit." But a piece of mosaic, though it is solid gold, if it is out of pattern, simply makes confusion. By the way, that's an illustration, and it is brief. An old book of illustrations (you should flee such a book as from a pursuing plague) under the caption "Courtesy" tells of two Civil War generals of equal rank, so that neither would defer to the other. One remembered his Christian faith, and so bowed to the other. A cannonball at that very moment passed over his bowed back and neatly decapitated his rival. That story was not on target, whatever may be said for the cannonball. The incident raises far more questions than it settles, not least about a doctrine of providence. Why didn't that sermon tell of Robert Louis Stevenson sending a check to an impecunious hack writer with a message, "Please be kind, as from one man of letters to another"?[5] If the illustration is not on target, it centers an overlapping circle, and so introduces a new theme. Some metaphors are out nowadays. "Like a mighty army moves the Church of God"[6]: like a bombing squadron? Let's hope not! The illustration should be fitting and cogent.

An illustration should be interesting, but not too interesting. If it is not interesting, it doesn't illustrate; if it is too interesting, it distracts. The sermon itself should be interesting, and the illustration should be woven into the fabric as the weaving proceeds. Paul Tillich's story of the Jewess running away from the Gestapo, and giving birth to her first child in a newly dug grave, and of the gravedigger finding her there, and exclaiming, "The Messiah! Only the Messiah could be born in a grave!" is almost like a lightning flash. And Tillich's sermon carried it because it was the only illustration in a sermon that was sheer thought. Tillich himself was unsure of it. I know because he told me. But he was so excited about it that he could not resist it. But I've heard him preach again and again with

---

5. Source unknown.

6. From the second verse of Sabine Baring-Gould's 1864 hymn, "Onward, Christian Soldiers."

virtually no illustrations—with Harvard students hanging on every word.[7] So: few illustrations, and those congruent in interest with the preacher's own message. Don't you see that preaching is a fine art?

An illustration should be worthy in itself. This demand doesn't rule out humor (of course), but it does rule out cheap humor. One seminary student's sermon informed us that the Holy Spirit is "like Wrigley's spearmint gum: the flavor lasts." My shoe itched to make contact with the inviting part of his carcass. Illustrations should befit the preciousness and depth of the Gospel. Would you say when preaching that one person who is committed can put to flight a hundred? You could illustrate by saying that if one note on the keyboard is dead the music is ruined. But that picture is negative and would more readily fit a sermon that says, "If your voice is missing...." Here is the positive illustration: Channing Pollock, the dramatist, was lunching with a friend when they heard a woman at the next table say, "In this kind of a world, what can one person do?" Pollock said, "Shall we go over there and tell them that every fine endeavor in history began with one person?"[8] Would you say that all our gadgets, including 747s,[9] are worth nothing compared with one child? Okay: the teacher hipped on gadgets and talking about them interminably, asked his class of small boys, "What's in our world now that was not here even ten years ago?" Jimmy raised his hand, and answered, "Me." That child should be sent to Washington, which rarely hears such wisdom. That illustration is not "flip." If it were, it should be shown the door. Illustrations must be worthy.

They should be new and contemporary, not old, not hackneyed, not heard again and again. Not the small boy with his hand in the dyke. I've always believed that story to be highly apocryphal; if the boy had tried it, he would have been washed five miles inland. Biblical illustrations are

---

7. Buttrick and Tillich were colleagues and friends during the years they taught at New York's Union Theological Seminary and subsequently the Harvard Divinity School. They and their wives lunched together every Thursday during their Harvard years. (From 1974 editor's interview with George Buttrick.)

8. Channing Pollock (1926–2006), world-famous magician and actor. The source of the quotation is unknown.

9. Boeing 747 aircraft.

always new if properly used, but people nowadays don't read the Bible, and so biblical illustrations have to be explained, and such an illustration therefore doesn't illustrate. Yet if a preacher uses a lectionary she finds again and again that her whole context is illustration, and that she can gratefully live there. Books of illustrations are of little worth if only that they belong to the past. Novels, films, and dramas now commanding attention are a better source. Daily life is a treasure house, that is, provided our preacher yearns and gladdens in the Gospel. The pictures should be contemporary because we live in the contemporary world. Compare the worldview of three astronauts. One said, "I am an eagle," a voracious bird. Another, "I didn't find God anywhere," the word of a fool so blind that he thought God is a flying saucer.[10] Another said that the planet Earth is so small and beautiful from "out there" that he wondered why we can't live in peace. Tell me if that illustration "bites." So much for the characteristics of illustrations.

III

Is there guidance about the use of them? Not much. There are no blanket rules because a sermon is not a blanket, and because every sermon is its own instance. But there are some rules of the road. This is one of them: illustrations should not be bunched. If they are bunched they cut into each other, so that each is robbed of power, and the hearer is distracted. So: one picture centered on a wall gains attention. A dozen

---

10. It was eventually discovered that the Russian astronaut, Yuri Gagarin, never said "I went up to space, but I didn't encounter God." Those words apparently were falsely attributed to him (placed in his mouth) by Nikita Khrushchev as Russian propaganda. Gargarin was a devout Russian Orthodox Christian who actually said, according to a friend, "An astronaut cannot be suspended in space and not have God in his mind and his heart." See https://www.beliefnet.com/columnists/on_the_front_lines_of_the_culture_wars/2011/04/yuri-gagarin-first-human-in-space-was-a-devout-christian-says-his-close-friend.html. Also http://www.pravmir.com/did-yuri-gagarin-say-he-didnt-see-god-in-space/. As a critic of communism, Buttrick wrote, "Sin is the egocentric pride of the creature which often flaunts property, but which has many another form, such as administrative control, public adulation, even vodka and caviar, and above all political power. Meanwhile every time Khrushchev accuses his enemies of bad faith he introduces norms far deeper than the play of economic force." See George Arthur Buttrick, *Christ and History* (New York: Abingdon Press, 1963), 73.

pictures of different kinds cause confusion. There's an illustration for *that* rule: a small boy at a seven-ring circus in Madison Square Garden began crying as he complained, "There's so much to see that I can't see anything." This counsel joins hands with the suggestion that illustrations in the new preaching are few in number. Metaphors can perhaps be bunched, but even in that area the method is of doubtful worth. Christopher Fry's *The Lady's Not for Burning*[11] would be even more appealing if its metaphors were not multiplied.

Another guidance might be this: an illustration is not more effective at the beginning of a sermon's stretch of the road, even though a main thought is clinched. But there is no fixed rule. An illustration can sometimes introduce a sermon, even in such a way that the whole sermon is pendant.[12] Or the right illustration can thus introduce a main plea. Even the conclusion can carry an illustration if it is brief and "central." A sermon on "perfect love" (only God's love is perfect) "casts out fear," could end, or, rather, almost end, with the motto over the fireplace in an English inn: "Fear knocked at the door. Faith got up and answered. There was nobody there." But that should not be the final word: a preacher should not yield the final word to even the noblest surrogate. So a poem (it is usually doggerel) should never end a sermon, for that introduces an alien voice at the final, crucial moment. By and large an illustration may or may not sometimes come as a clincher.

Another counsel: the few illustrations should be drawn from varying fields. Rural illustrations are right for rural folk, city illustrations for city folk. Human illustrations—that of Dennis the Menace bringing home a black boy and saying to his mother, "He's different from me: he's left-handed"—are for all folk. Scientific illustrations are called for in a scientific time; an ocean vessel takes its bearings not from flickering shore lights or from passing vessels but from the stars. Carry that picture further: the vessel must always turn to help a ship flashing the SOS! If all the illustrations are literary, the preacher may appear remote and "bookish." If

---

11. A play first produced in 1948 and published in 1949 by Oxford University Press.

12. The entire sermon rests upon the illustration like a jewel (pendant) hung upon a necklace.

Chapter Nine

they all come from *The New Yorker*, the preacher may be called dilettante. There were over a hundred medical doctors in my New York parish, so I rarely traveled a month with a medical illustration, but that I would check it with one of the doctors so carefully that the others would sometimes accuse me of having taken some medical training. The best illustrations are obviously those that "find" everybody, that is to say, those drawn from our shared experience under God.

IV

Where are illustrations found? They are not found. If we search for them, and find them, and drag them into a sermon, each will appear like an effigy at a wedding. (By the way, that's a metaphor, and better than a "stated" illustration). Illustrations "come" of themselves; otherwise they are ill-at-ease at the banquet. Books of illustrations in most instances are a chamber of horrors, and even the horrors are out of date.

Whence are we "found" by illustrations? *By and from the Bible*, because the Bible under the Holy Spirit makes contemporary the sovereign Lord. If our preacher uses a lectionary, as indeed she should, both text and context, brought from one human situation to our situation, come alive. The instances are almost legion: "Jacob's ladder" was never Jacob's despite a favorite spiritual. The word in the Hebrew is "staircase." Presumably it had no handrail, for it was for the use of angels "ascending and descending." *We* can't climb it; we would fall from dizziness after a few steps. Now the sermon looks to its true home; we can't climb to heaven, but there's no need for us to try: "For us and for our salvation he came down from heaven, was incarnate and became truly human."[13] There's a living staircase: "the angels of God ascending and descending upon the Son of Man."[14] Church people by and large are ignorant of the book. But they

---

13. From the modern version of the Nicene Creed in the Presbyterian Church (USA) *The Book of Confessions* (1999). Buttrick quoted the traditional version, "who for us men and our salvation came down and was made man."

14. John 1:51 ("man" RSV, "Man" NRSV, "Human One" CEB).

can be told—by sermons, which are their own illustration from what is rightfully called "the living word." That is our source beyond compare.

A second field for illustrations is the preacher's reading in history and letters, in science and biography, yes, in the daily press. If the preacher is absorbed in her job ("Woe is me if I preach not"[15]), pictures beset her. Loneliness? That photograph in our newspaper of a solitary man standing beneath a huge embankment gazing down an empty river. Racial concord? That other photo of a legislator in close conversation with an eight-year old black page-boy. The subtlety of omnipresent evil? Ionesco's play *The Killer* shows a reformer proposing first social reform, then economic re-patterning, then revivalism. Each proposal, including that third, is greeted by mocking laughter offstage. Then the reformer finds the killer's calling card in his own briefcase and has no idea how it got there! If the preacher reads faithfully, refusing to be caught in church machinery, she finds that for illustrations she lives among "acres of diamonds."[16] After a time, her problem is how to drive off illustrations or how to choose among them.

Of course, her main source is the teeming life around her. If she is "busy with many things like Martha," she will lose imagination. If she "muses," the "fire" will burn, not in anger as in the original context of that quotation but in the kindled mind.[17] While she broods, illustrations will knock at her door; while she walks, they will tug at her sleeve. Once I was challenged to find illustrations at noontime between lectures in a drab city. I went walking. Soon iron gates and pillars invited me. Inside violets bloomed in the grass—amid factories! Soon a tiny church with a hand pointing upward, a hand instead of a steeple: the function of the church! A man came from that little building pushing a wheelbarrow filled with garden tools, so I said, "I thought it was a church," and he said, "It used to be, but we turned it into a tool shed"! On the way back to the lecture hall there was a sign in a jewelry store window: "Crosses for sale: Cheap"! The preacher shouldn't look for illustrations. If she does, she'll come up

---

15. 1 Cor 9:16 (GAB).

16. A play upon the title of Russell H. Conwell's famous essay, *Acres of Diamonds* (Philadelphia: John Y. Huber Co., 1890), given as a speech worldwide more than six thousand times. The thesis is that "diamonds" are to be found in one's own backyard.

17. The original context is the Mary-Martha pericope of Luke 10:24-42.

with artificial flowers. Illustrations come of themselves if she's not scared of solitude.

V

What of sermons that are all story? There's a place for them, especially if they are children's sermons, and if the preacher has the gift. Jesus spoke from a text in the Nazareth synagogue, yet the scant record seems to show that more often he told parables. But we are not Jesus, so we may more wisely interpret his stories than venture on our own. If we can dramatize our faith there is always danger that someone in the pew may say, "Wasn't that novel and interesting?"—and so forget Christ. But sometimes a story begs entry and should not be refused. Simon of Cyrene traveling to Jerusalem for the great festival, lodging in a village, coming through the little booths of reeds and rushes, guided by the gold roof of the temple, on the *qui vive*[18] to hear the summoning trumpets. You finish it. The title is "The Strangest Thing Happened to Me on the Way to the Temple." But our best queue is a lectionary—and a licensed and dedicated imagination. The Book has no rival.

The effective preacher therefore preaches an accustomed sermon in an unaccustomed way. She cleaves to a vision in the marvelous circle of grace. In a time of national crisis, the preacher can forsake the lectionary. When President Kennedy is assassinated, our preacher chooses Isaiah 6 as the text: "In the year that King Uzziah died I saw the Lord sitting on upon a throne, high and lifted up; and his train filled the temple."[19] But the lectionary is her traveling map. Expository preaching, granted that it is not a silly whittling away at a text (that is whittling, not preaching), is still the most effective plea. Where else is there comparable light? The Bible has its own doctrine of God, its own doctrine of humanity (which makes our humanisms sound like kindergarten chatter), its own doctrine of history, its own doctrine of life and death—and of life beyond death. The other books sail up and down Long Island Sound. Only this Book

---

18. On the alert, as in asking, "who goes there?"
19. Isa 6:1 (RSV).

does "business on the great waters."[20] So our preacher broods and broods on the Book.

What about autobiographical illustrations? Never if they involve pastoral confidence. Rarely at any other time. Occasionally if they come urgently, humbly, gratefully, as when a person says, "I know: God stood by me in sorrow!" Always that capital "I" should be challenged. Often it should be shot at sight. The remarks of the preacher's children are not as smart as the preacher reckons them: they are usually "out." The church that sends its preacher to the holy land asks for trouble: they'll hear about it for the next five years. "I" can all too easily get in the way of Christ—and often does. Take this instance—about me. *Life Magazine* asked me to write a life of Jesus in one thousand words.[21] What an exercise in what to include and what to exclude! So which words, which actions? What happened to him? What has now happened to us? That next Sunday, I didn't say "I," or tell them about *Life Magazine*, though the editor was in the congregation.[22] Instead I began, "Once upon a time. Soon some hearers smiled. Some began to weep." The editors struck out only one sentence in the published manuscript. Why? "That's preaching!" They meant, "That sounds preachy." Of the rest even they were moved. In the middle of the reading one said to the other: "It's damned good!" I've said "I" to you, and for you. But not in that sermon, which (come to think of it) I could revive.

VI

So here's an illustration—one more among many just offered you free, gratis, for nothing. An artist in a mountain village led his new friends round the curve of the hill each evening so that they might see the sunset.

---

20. Ps 107:23 (RSV).

21. George Arthur Buttrick, "The Life of Jesus Christ," *Life Magazine*, Dec. 28, 1936, 44ff.

22. The editor was Henry Luce, a member of Madison Avenue Presbyterian Church and a close friend of Buttrick's, despite their many differences. (From 1974 editor's interview with George Buttrick, and 2014 and 2016 interviews with David Buttrick).

Chapter Nine

A man from the valley, hearing of that habit, asked with a trace of disdain, "Haven't you seen the sunset before?" The villagers answered, "Yes, but we never really saw it till he came." Our world hears the rumor of Christ. It is beset by many a false picture. But because he is present, we all know when a picture distorts him. He hardly belongs in that monstrous trench in My Lai—except to die there.[23] Perhaps after next Sunday's sermon someone will say, "I never really saw Christ until that preacher spoke." The true preacher is the world's benefactor because she is Christ's apostle.

---

23. Editor's note: On March 16, 1968, in the village of My Lai, South Vietnam, US soldiers from Company C, 1st Battalion, 20th Infantry Regiment, 11th Brigade, 23rd Infantry Division, murdered more than five hundred unarmed Vietnamese men, women, children, and infants, some of the women and girls having first been raped and mutilated, in what thereafter became known as the "My Lai Massacre." Buttrick, a lifelong pacifist, was saying that only a false picture of Christ would depict him in that "monstrous trench" as a soldier or seek to justify war in Christ's name. Rather, the only legitimate picture of Christ to be found in any such place is that of the "Crucified One" choosing to die as one of the massacred.

CHAPTER TEN

The Delivery of the Sermon

The sermon should be written, but the manuscript should not become a bondage. Only by disciplined work can the right word be found; only so can the sentences find persuasive rhythm. Advertising has stolen all the adjectives. The preacher must now reclaim for the kingdom of God words that Madison Avenue has perverted to soapsuds. Here is guidance: fine diction consists not in the use of unusual words (he should let Spiro Agnew have them[1]), but in the unusual linking of usual words as in the Shakespeare comment: "Parting is such sweet sorrow."[2] Words are not peanut shells: they are jewels, and they have claim to their favorable setting. In T. S. Eliot's *The Cocktail Party*, Celia's death is reported—at the very party she foreswore to serve as a nurse in an African village. Someone asks casually how she died. "She was crucified very near an anthill."[3] Why does that sentence boggle the mind? Why? The sermon should be written, even though it is then consigned to the round file. Otherwise the mass of drab words that compose (or don't compose) the average sermon!

---

1. Spiro Agnew, vice president of the United States, spoke of the media as "nattering nabobs of negativism," a phrase coined by his speechwriter, William Safire.

2. Shakespeare, *Romeo and Juliet*, act 2, sc. 2, line 185.

3. T. S. Eliot, *The Cocktail Party: A Comedy* (New York: Harcourt, Brace & Co., 1950), "It would seem that she must have been crucified very near an ant-hill" (175).

Chapter Ten

I

The writing helps the preacher observe limits of time. He can more easily comb out the verbiage. Jesus had something to say about the "idle word,"[4] that is, words that do not work.[5] We live in a neon-flashing world. Sermons should be far briefer than our parents knew. Television assigns its speakers so many minutes. The preacher should set his own wise limits and keep them. The preacher in a university church, knowing that the nearby clock would boom out twelve noon in booms heard miles away, should not be such a fool as to offer his sermon's conclusion to that loud death. Oriental hearers have remarkable powers of concentration whatever the surrounding clangor, whereas our congregation is waylaid by the buzzing of a fly. So our preacher writes every word, and keeps faith with the clock.

He keeps faith also with the proportions of the sermon. We have cited a Scot's outline regarding the younger prodigal: (a) Sick of Home; (b) Homesick; (c) Home.[6] But those three moves can't claim "equal time." The Gospel is first hinted, then brought into view, then proclaimed in joy. So, the page assignments might be respectively one page, one-and-a-half pages, and three pages. A wise preacher notes this assignment in the margin of the sermon outline, and then rigorously obeys his own instructions.[7] As he writes, the inevitable word may come to mind. A recent sermon spoke of the memory of forgiven sin as "a precious discipline," and the congregation was blessed. The "right" word has power. It comes—by long pondering. Then he can say, "Of course that is what the book means

---

4. Matt 12:36 (KJV).

5. See George A. Buttrick, *Jesus Came Preaching: Christian Preaching in the New Age* (New York: Charles Scribner's Sons, 1931), "How many idle words there are in the average sermon—words that do no work, that are not felt, that are merely sound! Let the sermon be written, and when it is written, let the redundancies be pruned away with an unsparing hand. Let the commonplace phrases be given short shrift. Let them yield place to phrases that glow, that move in the imagination like a drama. Let the cumbersome words of Latin origin be pushed aside: they make any style lumber along like a procession of elephants" (159).

6. See chapter 8.

7. Buttrick did so with his own sermon outlines.

when it says…" Thus, the powerful word is gathered into the power of scripture inspired by the Presence.

II

There are further guidances. This: the preacher writes with his congregation looking at him over his desk. He writes to be heard, not to be read. There's a difference. It tells us why printed sermons are flat. Maybe sermons shouldn't be printed; maybe they should be a flame on an altar, and so disappear as a glad offering. Their value is for those who have heard them, that is, in kindled memory. When we read a book and a sentence confuses us ("How's that again?"), we can go back to check and reread. But if we are confused by a sermon sentence, we can't go back, for our preacher "has gone on!" So, sermon words should be instantly simple and clear. You and I are not tripped by such words as *transcendence* or *existential*, but the average congregation is not only tripped, but lost in fog. Clichés are "out." You know: "all those with whom we come in contact." Such phrases run off the mind like water from a roof: they do not sink into the ground like fertilizing rain. Scripture quotations out of context, as if they were magic incantations, are also taboo. So is any ponderous diction. There's a wicked story of a preacher who wished to say, "He went home and read the newspaper," but who actually said, "He proceeded to his domiciliary residence and perused the chronicle of contemporary transactions."

In any clear sentence the driving force is the verb. "The farmer *went* to town": the verb gives movement. An adverb trims the verb: "The farmer slowly went to town." No great hurt done, for we ask, "Why slowly?" An adjective trims the noun: "The sad farmer went slowly to the deserted town." Again, no harm done, for we wonder why the farmer was sad and the town deserted. But if adverbs and adjectives are multiplied, if there is too much trimming, then the force of the sentence is lost, as a tree may be killed by a creeper. So beware the trimming. There is beauty in a bare tree—and in a bare sentence. Polysyllables, such as the word *polysyllables*, should be denied entry. Words of Latin and Greek origin should be suspect. Anglo-Saxon words such as *bread* or *break* gleam and beckon. Use them. You will not find them, or they will not find you, unless the sermon is written. The simplicity and arresting clarity of the speech of Jesus shines even through the opaqueness of the translation. "I tell you" he said, "that people will have to answer on Judgment Day for every useless word they speak. By your words you will be either judged innocent or condemned as guilty."[8] There is no exemption, least of all for preachers.

III

As for the use of the manuscript, there are three extremes. One is to read the manuscript. This is not totally *verboten*, for fine preachers have used this method. The famous Thomas Chalmers[9] in the nineteenth century, and Henry Sloane Coffin[10] in the twentieth century are instances. It should be noted that Coffin read as Jehu drove:[11] no one quit listening. But not every preacher knows how to read, and few congregations accept a sermon that is read. They feel that the preacher is more concerned about what he has written than about them. A second dubious way is to memorize the manuscript. Again, this is not necessarily taboo. Harry Emerson Fosdick and E. Stanley Jones came close to employing it.[12] Their effectiveness was not impaired. But most congregations are turned off by sermons learned by rote. They sense half-consciously that the preacher has focused on a photostat copy of a manuscript rather than on them and the Gospel. A third questionable method is to half-memorize the manuscript, and then to preach without any prepared page. The preacher may still travel by

---

8. Matt 12:36 CEB; Buttrick had quoted the RSV: "men will render account for every careless word they utter."

9. Thomas Chalmers (1780–1847), minister of the Free Church of Scotland.

10. Henry Sloan Coffin (1877–1954), Buttrick's predecessor at New York's Madison Avenue Presbyterian Church (1910–1926) and subsequently president of New York's Union Theological Seminary (1926–1945).

11. Jehu, king of Israel (842–825 BCE), drove his chariot "furiously" (2 Kgs 9:20, RSV), "like a maniac" (NRSV).

12. Harry Emerson Fosdick (1878–1969), Baptist minister of New York City's Riverside Church, professor at Union Theological Seminary, national radio preacher, and author; E. Stanley Jones (1884–1973), Methodist missionary evangelist to India, friend of Gandhi, and author of *The Christ of the Indian Road* (New York: Abingdon Press, 1925).

The Delivery of the Sermon

rote, or memory may suddenly fail him, or he may ad lib until the sermon becomes sloppy, or he forgets the location of the terminal bus station.

So there are three methods that are better for most of us. One is to carry into the pulpit a brief synopsis of the manuscript. This method gives the preacher a large liberty, but does not avoid the same dangers of preaching without any prop: memory may fail and the sermon may wander. The second method is to use fuller notes. The preacher is thus close to what he has written, but is not unduly dependent. It is probably true that most preachers choose this road. A third method with many advantages is to carry into the pulpit the full manuscript, without reading it or memorizing. Thus it becomes a guide map. Roman numerals show the main "turns." The underlining of the first sentence of each paragraph reminds the preacher of "what comes next." Thus, he stays on the track, and keeps faith with both effective diction and the limits of time, yet has a certain freedom. If key sentences "come back" as written, his liberty is not impaired. There is no right or wrong about these alternatives. Each preacher chooses the method that best matches his own gifts. Maybe he should try several methods from time to time to find which is best for his mind and the needs of his congregation.

IV

As for the delivery of the sermon, clear articulation and interesting modulation of the voice are so important that if they are neglected a sermon filled with promise in the manuscript may be a dud when it is preached. A preacher with speech defects should consult a speech counselor. To listen to a recording of one's own sermon has no sure value: the preacher may repeat the tragedy of the centipede that resolved to understand how its legs moved, and fell on its back and died because it couldn't get right side up. But if the preacher has a voice habit such as dropping the tone every five words, and doesn't know it (most such drones don't know it), a voice recorder, if he is willing to listen, may save him. But to write about the delivery of the sermon is like teaching swimming by means of a diagram. Yet some "don'ts" are focal. They are not censorious or merely "negative." They recall a teacher's failures, and are offered to save others from the same pitfalls.

Don't mark off the passage of time. Such phrases as, "as I have already pointed out," or, "as I shall soon show," or, "as you have noted," are a blunder. They invite the congregation to watch the clock. The dreary sequence of "firstly, secondly, thirdly" is worse: it almost obliges the congregation to wonder how many *-lys* are in prospect or threat. Some preachers can so enumerate, as witness James Stewart,[13] but they succeed in spite of the method, not because of it. A certain professor of homiletics would challenge his students with this: "Don't count one, two, three, four. Just sit in silence, and raise your hand when you think one minute has passed." If you try it with any group, almost all hands will be raised before forty-five seconds elapse. "A watched pot never boils." Any marking off of time shackles the sermon.

Don't be pretentious or ponderous in tone, as if proclaiming supernal edicts. You are not Jove on Mount Olympus. You need not be like Daniel Webster on his deathbed, saying with solemn priggishness, "Friends, physician, wife, children, have I on this occasion said anything unworthy of Daniel Webster?"[14] Such unction would turn any sermon into a deathbed. The preacher should remind himself frequently, "I'm another person traveling between the twin mysteries of life and death." He should so speak. If he rejoices in his faith he can say with Paul in self-forgetfulness, "For to me to live is Christ, and to die is gain" (of Christ).[15] Such a credo carries its own tone and accent.

Don't use a martyred voice, as if you were a new Elijah in distress: "I, even I only, am left; and they seek my life, to take it away."[16] You will probably survive until the next Sunday, whatever may be the fate of the

---

13. James S. Stewart (1896–1990), minister of the Church of Scotland, pastor, professor of New Testament at the University of Edinburgh, author, one of the most influential preachers of the twentieth century, and friend of George Buttrick.

14. Buttrick often paraphrased from memory. Danial Webster was remembered as having said, with witnesses surrounding him: "Have I—wife, son, doctor, friends, are you all here?—have I, on this occasion, said any thing unworthy of Daniel Webster?" See "The Death-Bed of Daniel Webster," *Appleton's Journal: A Magazine of General Literature*, March 5, 1870, 274.

15. Phil 1:21 (RSV).

16. 1 Kgs 19:10 (RSV).

congregation. There is no need for a voice with a sob in it. The church is now polarized. The main guilt rests on comfortable people who listen for any word that is left of center, or not squarely right of center. Others listen for the preacher's "cowardly silence." But there are always some who hunger for the word of Christ. In any event the Gospel is just that: good news. The preacher's voice and bearing should proclaim the great gladness. He should not succumb to any paranoia as if he were standing blindfold with his back to the fatal wall. Needless to add, a smart-aleck, jaunty, hands-in-pocket voice is an even worse offense. Always a preacher brings glad tidings of great joy. Surely that fact should govern his glad voice.

Don't, oh, don't use a pulpit voice. A Broadway play portrayed a preacher murdering a text torn from its context, drawing little moralisms that were absurd in their unrelatedness. But worse than the sermon was the mimicked voice, solemn, officious, pompous. The audience rolled in the aisles. This was caricature, but it was instantly recognized—from multiplied instances.

Don't use a "holy tone," a pious twang, a sainted voice as if you were looking for a vacancy in a stained-glass window. Perhaps nothing has contributed more to the ridicule of the pulpit. The danger is not as easy to avoid as laypeople guess, for the preacher has to speak in larger volume of sound and with emphasized clarity. Thus, his speech is measured, his manner formal. Congregations can be too large. Smaller churches would give the preacher a better chance to gather his folk in dialogue. But there are ways and means, by manner and substance, to flee the holy tone. A preacher can follow the naturalness of Christ as he pointed across the valley and said, "Look, there's a sower going out to sow." A preacher can use the voice God has given him.

V

Our revolutionary time demands realism. The pious ranting of revivalists, not least those who preempt the radio or screen, may be sincere; we should not judge lest we be judged. But surely sincerity will issue in intensity rather than in bluster, in steadiness of tone rather than in a throbbing tremolo. The rebellious young believe rightly or wrongly that the typical sermon is "full of sound and fury, signifying nothing."[17] They forget that they themselves are sometimes guilty of the same nonsense in their crowd harangues. But two instances of nonsense do not make sense. The preacher should not pretend to a deeper knowledge of God than others can claim. He should be more aware of our mortal ignorance. He should be quick to cry,

> Hide me, O God, between the gates
> of saving flesh and bone,
> lest I should know what dream awaits
> the soul escaped alone.
> A veil twixt Thee and me, dear Lord,
> a veil twixt Thee and me,
> lest I should hear too clear, too clear,
> and unto madness see![18]

A certain seminarian fractured all the homiletic rules so that his teacher almost despaired—until he noted that that student always won a hearing, by sheer openness and honesty. Sincerity overleaps all the rules on its way to the city of God. Once I heard a gifted preacher speak with such quiet yet passionate integrity on the text "Love your enemies," that when he ended with an "Amen," the congregation, not predisposed to accept that message, instinctively replied, "Amen."

So now, in a continued concern for the delivery of the sermon, we write about the preacher's own life. Every sermon commends or betrays the preacher, under an unerring Light. Phillips Brooks wrote, "There must

---

17. Shakespeare, Macbeth, act 5, sc. 5, line 7

18. Rudyard Kipling, "The Prayer of Miriam Cohen," *Songs from Books* (Garden City, NY: Doubleday, Page, & Co., 1912), 154–55. Throughout these third and fifth stanzas of Kipling's poem, Buttrick changed the subjective voice from first person plural ("us") to first person singular ("I") in order to personify the verse as the "cry" of the singular preacher. For the same reason he made the following substitutions: (1) "Hide me, O God, between the gates" for Kipling's "Hold us secure behind the gates." (2) "Lest I should know what dreams awaits" for Kipling's "Lest we should dream what Dream awaits." (3) "A veil twixt Thee and me, dear Lord, a veil twixt Thee and me," for Kipling's "A veil twixt us and Thee, Good Lord, A veil twixt us and Thee." These alterations would have been footnoted, had Agnes Buttrick had the opportunity to prepare the citations for publication as was her custom.

be a man behind every sermon."[19] "If you could make all men think alike, it would be very much as if no man thought at all, as when the whole earth moves together with all that is upon it, all things seem still."[20] Sincerity is each preacher's being himself—in the healing, fortifying presence; not just "by himself," for no person is equal to the preacher's task, but under God, where one's very weakness becomes strength. Brooks himself, a shy man in conversation, almost silent before the interviewer, poured out his heart anonymously before his congregation. His sermons prevailed, not because they were sound argument (they were conventional in his conventional world), but because they had the sure "sound" of a sincere man.

The preacher, writing or speaking, is therefore never a copy. Some of us can remember a time that bred a host of little Fosdicks. Little indeed! The sentence, "The spirit of the Lord came upon Gideon,"[21] could be translated from the Hebrew, "The spirit of the Lord clothed himself with Gideon." We are led to believe that the Holy Spirit searches our world for the right person with the right voice. "Whom shall I send?," God asks, looking first on those near the throne. Then a sinner, his lips just cleansed, steps out from the crowd, crying, "Here am I! send me."[22] Then God commissions the sinner! Mark you, that person is not robbed of his distinctiveness, for his uniqueness is promptly heightened. He has lost only his pride. Compare preachers: John and Paul, Augustine and Francis, Edwards and Bushnell, Tillich and Scherer.[23] Each is his own person—under God. Why are we dear to each other? Not because we are copies, not because of traits shared, but precisely because of individualisms, even of idiosyncrasies. Surely, we are dear to God for the same cause. In the mystery of our mortal life God's creativity knows no photocopy machine.

---

19. Phillips Brooks, *Lectures on Preaching: Delivered before the Divinity School of Yale College, January and February, 1877* (New York: E. P. Dutton & Co, 1891), 150.

20. Brooks, *Lectures on Preaching*, 23.

21. Judg 6:34 (KJV).

22. Isa 6:8 (RSV).

23. St. John and St. Paul, St. Augustine and St. Francis of Assisi, Jonathan Edwards and Horace Bushnell, Paul Tillich and Paul Scherer.

Chapter Ten

Every sermon in both preparation and delivery should be a new creation because every preacher is a new creation. Originality is not the fiat creation of the hitherto unknown, for none could comprehend that invasion; it is the re-creation of the ever-old under new forms for a new time. When Luke said, "It seemed good to me also,"[24] he confessed (enviously?) that he had not seen Christ as had those who were "eyewitnesses and ministers of the word," but claimed that he had carefully traced the sources, and had tried to bring them into "an orderly account"; and that he was compelled by love to tell what he knew of the Presence. It was not a secondhand testimony, whatever his fears. What tragic loss had he been silent! Each preacher must say, with whatever misgivings, "It seemed good to me also." Thus, people who know little about the third Gospel may yet be redeemed by the "Gospel according to you." The sermon is spoken in that faith.

Paul spoke often of *the* Gospel. Of course. It is the Event in history, once for all, sovereign over history. Yet it is always coming to new birth. So Paul spoke also of "*our* Gospel,"[25] for the real joy of the kingdom "none but his loved ones know,"[26] and they will not know for long unless they share their joy. But Paul speaks also of "*my* Gospel,"[27] for Paul was a new creation, an apostle "born out of due time"[28] on the Damascus Road. The preacher, lonely in an unregenerate yet shaken time, can use all three adjectives,[29] and should. He need not shrink from the "my," for he is his own person under Christ. If by the Holy Spirit the sermon finds its mark, God in God's kindness may even let the preacher take the credit, yet only for the preacher's worthy hope.

---

24. Luke 1:3 (RSV).

25. 2 Cor 4:3; 1 Thess 1:5 (RSV).

26. From the fourth verse of the hymn "Jesus, the Very Thought of Thee," attributed to Bernard of Clairvaux, trans. Edward Caswall, 1849.

27. Rom 2:16; 2 Tim 2:8 (RSV).

28. 1 Cor 15:8 (KJV).

29. "All three adjectives": "*the* Gospel," "*our* Gospel," and "*my* Gospel."

Part Three
PREACHING IN THIS TIME

CHAPTER ELEVEN

Preaching and Pastoral Care

Pastoral care is in decline.[1] Many a modern preacher shirks the shepherding task. The reasons are many, and they interfuse. *There is this reason*: the preacher feels inadequate and insecure; what to say to a family whose son has been killed in Vietnam? *And this reason*: the image of the present church, and the image of the preacher going pietistically from door to door, are hard to accept. *And this reason*: the conventional prayers of the house-calling pastor seem so out of place in the typical home as to be almost comic. *And this reason*: people are now on the move, so that ringing doorbells is a waste of time. *And this reason*: an activist role shows more promise and far more chance to make an effective witness in our needy world. *And this reason*: as soon as parishioners see the preacher approaching, they adopt a pious pose, and promptly begin to talk as they think the preacher wants them to talk, namely, like trained fish. That's a formidable list of reasons. We asked a group of pastors how many calls they made in a typical week. The average was eight. I made thirty a week for twenty-eight years in a church in mid-Manhattan.

I

Yet from New Testament times pastoral care has been the nature of the church—because it is the nature of Christ. Did he not leave the sheepfold

---

1. It peaked when the troubled veterans came home from World War II.

to find one lost sheep? Has he not charged us, "Feed my sheep"? This concern was in the grain of the early church, as witness the work of deacons. It was in the heart of Paul, as witness the list of names in his Epistles. The name for the church, *the koinonia*, implies both mutual love within the body of Christ and concern in love for the joys and sorrows of the world. So, the preacher, if she is faithful, that is, full of the faith, can't escape the pastoral task. She shouldn't try, whatever the roadblocks. Preacher and pastor are one person. Each without the other lives an amputated life.

II

This course does not focus on the pastoral function. We are studying preaching, not pastoral theology. *But realistic preaching itself invites pastoral care.* The congregation knows from the very tone of the sermon if the preacher has them on her heart. If the sermon breaks here and there in prophetic indignation, they know when judgment springs from love—as Lincoln's anger sprang from his compassion for the slaves. So when the sermon deals with human fear, when the text is, "Perfect love casts out fear"[2] (perfect love being God's love toward us in Christ), some hearer says to herself, "That woman understands my case." On the next day or two she may knock at the preacher's door, saying, "May I talk to you?" Since we have come on that text, it should be said again that though preaching has a place for prophetic indignation, since that flame broke again and again in the words of Christ, there is no place for moralism, still less for censoriousness. "For God sent the Son into the world, not to condemn the world, but that the world might be saved through him."[3] If the preacher preaches the whole Gospel, she will not lack for counselees who overtly may raise side issues (Harvard students would often begin a conversation with the problem of vocation), but soon ask for the meaning of their life. So one person in Harvard, when I took him at his ostensible purpose and began to discuss vocation, interrupted with, "But, gee, Doc,

---

2. 1 John 4:18 (RSV).
3. John 3:17 (RSV).

I don't know who I am." When the sermon thus invites counselees, the preacher may not shirk the pastoral task. She's picked out.

Even when a parishioner comes in angry protest, the pastoral door opens. Suppose the preacher has said in a flashing aside, "the Pentagon, big, brassy and blind," and suppose a member of the John Birch Society (and of the church) arrives at the parsonage to say he "can't stand this treacherous attack on our country," a conversation can ensue that is the very stuff of *mutual* pastoral concern. The critic may insist that the preacher "keep the peace of the church," whereupon the preacher can say with kindness, "If only my job and yours were that easy: we are both asked to keep faith with the Lord of the church." There is common ground to say, "Jesus loved his land, and wept over Jerusalem; you and I," the pastor says, "are both grateful for America." Agreement between pastor and critic would not come easily in that instance. The preacher could say honestly, "You have helped me. Come back soon, and tell me about you, for I want to know." The critic may then take his membership to another church or may not. In any event the breach is not final. The wise preacher goes straight to the critic, not waiting for the critic to come to her.

So there is no "futility in ringing doorbells." Some preachers know that the phrase originated with Harry Fosdick. What they don't know is that after a year or two Fosdick himself had renounced it, and then resumed pastoral calling.[4] Suppose the parishioner is not at home: there is still no "futility." If the preacher leaves a calling card on which she has written a nonstuffy "hello," that household knows that they are not on file in the missing persons bureau. I myself went three times to a home where I was bluntly rebuffed, being told, "Mrs. So-and-so is not receiving today." Then the morning paper told me that the oldest son in that home had committed suicide. I was there at breakfast time on that same morning, and the door opened—because there is no "futility in ringing doorbells." Incidentally that family began to attend church. A church doesn't live by preaching, however eloquent; it grows by pastoral faithfulness, and is kept growing by faithful preaching.

---

4. Parenthetically, see "Dr. Fosdick Writes a Pastoral Letter: He Asks Park Av. Congregation Not to Expect Regular Calls When New Church Is Built," *New York Times*, August 14, 1927.

III

All right: just as preaching leads on into pastoral concern, there is the reverse movement: pastoral concern reinforces preaching. For instance, the preacher learns in the home the need for clarity in the pulpit. She is amazed to find how incredibly, yet honestly, she has been misconstrued. People listen not with their ears but with their emotions, as you and I listen. They hear more with their subconscious minds than with their conscious minds, as you and I hear. In the tumultuous Franklin Delano Roosevelt years, two men came after the morning worship. One said, "Why do you always blast FDR?" The other said, "Why do you always praise FDR?" Actually FDR had not been at all in my thoughts! Each man had come to church predisposed by his not-too-profound political loyalties. The next Sunday I went almost out of my way to say, "Don't accuse me of entering the political cockpit. King Lear had something to say about 'great ones who ebb and flow with the moon.'" There's no sure defense against misunderstanding. But the preacher can resolve on clarity. J. H. Jowett used to warn young preachers, "Say everything three times, though in different words."[5] That counsel is not infallible. Jowett's sermons "read" that way, and so lack content. But his word is worth heeding.

The pastor learns realism in preaching. Ernest Freemont Tittle[6] avowed that he got most of his sermon topics from questions asked by his parishioners. That source is not celestial, but it is useful. For the preacher thus confronts actual issues: "Why has this misfortune happened to *me*?" Or, "How can I ever forgive myself?" Or, "Why does God allow such things?" Thus, the preacher knows that generalizations, however poetic, about goodness, beauty, and truth, don't dig many potatoes. On the National Preaching Mission,[7] I proposed that a modern mission should

---

[5]. John Henry Jowett (1864–1923), English Congregational minister who served as pastor of Carr's Lane Congregational Church, Birmingham, England, then toward the end of his life, Fifth Avenue Presbyterian Church in New York City and Westminster Chapel in London.

[6]. Ernest Freemont Tittle (1885–1949), minister of First Methodist Church, Evanston, Illinois, 1918–1949, author, ecumenist, pacifist, socialist, affiliated with the ACLU and NAACP.

[7]. Buttrick participated in the nationwide National Preaching Mission in the fall of 1936. Leading Protestant preachers itinerated throughout twenty-eight major urban areas for four

invite questions. The team agreed, and one man said, "But let's write the answers." I asked how that could be done until we knew the questions. So for my temerity, I was given the assignment. Here are the first three questions: "Why is my faithful and skillful husband out of work?" "Can Christianity tell me if my love affair is real?" "Communism gives people a chance to die for a cause; why doesn't my church give the same chance?" How many groups of preachers would have "thunk up" these questions? These questions were not final by a long distance, but they were pertinent. Contact with parishioners helps in the choice of sermon topics. A lectionary should still chart our preaching journey. The Bible is always pertinent, and sermons that travel by the lectionary path are already fortified. But topics must still be phrased and pondered so that they live where people live. Many a sermon offers a neat answer, though there are no neat answers, to questions that nobody is asking.

Pastoral concern aids and abets the "liberty of prophesying." If a preacher does not stand with her flock, if she fails from either lack of interest or self-distrust, she has little claim to freedom in the pulpit. "They know not the voice of strangers"![8] Presently people are tense in a tense world. So it is open season on any preacher who tries to declare the mind of Christ. There is no worthy immunity. But a pastor is more likely to be heard in a Gospel that sometimes condemns the church than is a preacher who has not proved to be a friend. Here's an instance: a rigidly "backlash" layman, more notable for hoarded cash than for an open mind, suffered a sudden sorrow—his wife died. His pastor went to that man at once in the middle of the night. The man was angry against God. Such angers flame when a man is his own god. He would not speak to anybody. His pastor waited. When the man walked toward the lake intending to drown himself, the pastor gently turned him back home. There the pastor wisely said, "Catherine was a wonderful person." The tears began to flow. The crisis passed. Yet, an uptight mind in another church (of the kind he favored)

---

days in each place, while churches across the country conducted similar preaching missions locally. See the *New York Times*, August 29, 1936, p. 12, and December 11, 1936, p. 29. Buttrick preached in Albany, Syracuse, Buffalo, Pittsburg, Kansas City, Detroit, Birmingham, Louisville, St. Louis, Cleveland, and Minneapolis–St. Paul.

8. John 10:5 (KJV).

asked the man, "You don't agree with your pastor's communism, do you?" "No," the man replied. Then he told the story of his sorrow, and ended with a thoroughly pardonable phrase: "My preacher can say any damn thing he wants to say to me." But in any event, why should any preacher expect or claim liberty in the pulpit unless that preacher is shepherd of the sheep?

IV

What of the mutuality of preaching and counseling? The preacher is not a psychiatrist, and should not try to usurp that role. Attempting to help a psychotic or even a neurotic is likely to hurt rather than help. Chances are it will aggravate the sickness. The counselee will make the preacher a mother figure, a father figure, or a leaning post, or (worse) demand "spiritual comfort" in lieu of facing reality. The value of psychiatry for a preacher is to show the preacher what not to try to do. Trouble is that most small towns have no psychiatrist. Worse trouble is that if a psychiatrist were available the average person can't afford the treatment, though more and more of such a resource is being brought within reach of the poor. The cost of depth analysis is sky high. What is the preacher to do? A little knowledge in this field is not a dangerous thing if it enables her to "spot" a psychosis, for she can then offer, not a specialized skill that she cannot claim, but quiet friendship within realism; there is no other friendship. We now know that such friendship itself has healing power. At this point a clear warning should be given: no worthy preacher should ever use a counselee as a sermon illustration. Pastoral confidence is a more stringent requirement than even medical confidence. If a counselee were to recognize herself as the preacher says, "A woman came to my office this week," she would be wise to walk out of church and wipe that preacher's name from the slate.

But what of the mutuality of counseling and preaching? Surely it should make the preacher slow to judge. Many an action that seems straightforward is not simple or single: it has twisted roots. The wise counselor does not begin with "What have you done?" but with "Have you asked why you have done it?" A person's slovenliness may be a kickback on parents who in her childhood told her *ad infinitum* to "keep your room tidy." A girl who suddenly goes off the deep end sexually may be acting in subconscious rebellion against a prim, coercive father and the warnings of a fear-stricken mother. When the preacher cannot trace her own motives, she should be slow to preach as a censor. Would you covet a clear instance? The revivalist's first sermon was as usual on "The Sins of Smallville." He seized on an item in that morning's newspaper: a man had been found guilty of exposure. The revivalist cried aloud against this "blatant immorality." But we now know that exposure may be a symptom of acute anxiety, and that in some instances it is so compulsive that the victim has little choice and even little knowledge of what he has done. Any action is both better and worse than it appears. The "heart is deceitful above all things."[9] Each of us is tempted of the devil; each of us is tempted to be a saint. Let the preacher take note.

This mutuality leads the preacher out of an impossible "individualism." Psychiatry itself must make that venture, in a new awareness that the whole culture is involved. Karen Horney's *The Neurotic Personality of Our Time*,[10] and Harry Stack Sullivan's *The Interpersonal Theory of Psychiatry*[11] are harbinger books. The home is a factor. A cash culture brands every poor person a failure. A white man's world turns the black man into a rebel. The cry of "law and order" in a society where law is delayed and unequally administered, and an order that for millions is a dingy disorder, will soon beckon a ghetto filled with flames and staccato with gunfire. So once more: honest preaching is to individual ears in a massed society, to a church too long insulated from a needy world. Should we add that psychiatric metaphor can be an asset? Yes, provided *that* reference is not overdone. Tillich is fond of such a context, as when he says that every person's decision is whether to accept God's acceptance. Part of a preacher's burden is to find metaphors of atonement, for instance, that speak to our

---

9. Jer 17:9 (RSV).

10. Karen Horney, *The Psychotic Personality of Our Time* (New York: W. W. Norton & Co., 1937).

11. Harry Stack Sullivan, *The Interpersonal Theory of Psychiatry* (New York: W. W. Norton & Co., 1953).

time. "Ransom" hardly fits the modern scene. Blood transfusion would make a more instant appeal. But a preacher should be slow to use psychiatric analogies unless informed, and should remember that every human endeavor, science or art or what have you, can become reductionist, that is, forget that its models should not leave home, much less try to rule our whole life on earth.

V

With respect to the issue of preaching and pastoral care, worship is involved. Is real preaching possible except in a context of prayer and worship? Even street evangelism (the Salvation Army provides a courageous instance) begins with praise and prayer, the sermon then being an outright personal witness and confession. Pulpit prayers and the sermon are cut from one cloth. There the two disciplines, homiletics and pastoral theology, walk hand in hand. Maybe we can trace that journey, if not in lectures, then in the give and take of our discussions. A poor order of worship is a handicap for the preacher. So is the absurdity of the "long prayer," which goes counter not only to elementary facts in psychology but also to the clear command of Christ.

The whole congregation is, or should be, enlisted in this dual concern. The congregation largely "makes" the sermon, and every member should be a pastor. Indeed, preaching belongs in the beloved community of faith. The doctrine of the priesthood of believers does not mean that every individual is his or her own priest, but that everyone is one's neighbor's priest. Thus, there is mutuality of love in the church. The root of the word *koinonia* is our word for home. The home spirit spreads until communities, stores, and factories become homelike. We are not here focally concerned with church programs, but it should be said that preaching is crippled in a church that is simply spinning many wheels—out of gear, or intent only on the comfort and continuance of its own life. There are clear signals that the local church must become a task force in the midst of the world's need.

Charles Williams[12] has alleged that if our love were prospered by the Spirit of Christ, we could say of a neighbor's sorrow what we now say about his suitcase: "Let me carry that for a while."[13] How preaching would kindle in that kind of church!

It remains to say that the main gift of pastoral concern for preaching is that it enables the preacher to preach as a whole person. "Whoever loses his life," in the ways of love in Christ, "will find it."[14] The pastor returns home from a round of calls. In each home she has tried to think herself imaginatively into each home's joys and sorrows, not as one merely sharing them but as one lifting the banner of the faith above them. In that venture she is set free. "In God's army only the wounded can serve." Matthew Arnold makes report from East London, which is dingier by far than West Louisville:

> I met a preacher there I knew, and said:
> "Ill and o'er-work'd, how fare you in this scene?"
> "Bravely!" said he; "for I of late have been
>   much cheer'd with thoughts of Christ,
>   the living Bread!"

Arnold, for whom any joyous faith came hard, makes his comment:

---

12. Charles Williams (1886–1945), British poet, novelist, playwright, theologian, critic, and member of Oxford University's "Inklings" along with C. S. Lewis, J. R. R. Tolkien, and others meeting at the Eagle and Child.

13. Charles Williams, *Descent into Hell* (Grand Rapids: William B. Eerdmans, 1990 reprint [1937]). The Williams novel persists throughout with the christological and Pauline theme of carrying the burdens, fears, and agonies of others. "And what can be easier for me to carry a little while a burden that isn't mine? If you give a weight to me, you can't be carrying it yourself; all I'm asking you to do is to notice that blazing truth," p. 98. Since Buttrick often quoted or paraphrased from memory, his sentence, "Let me carry that for a while," is a summary paraphrase. In his own book *God, Pain, and Evil* (Nashville: Abingdon Press, 1966), 177, Buttrick employed the same words when explaining Williams's idea of the "co-inherence" of one person's reality with that of another, thus "if one member [of the body of Christ] suffers, all suffer." Charles Williams examines the meaning of "co-inherence" (Christ in us, and we in Christ) in his book *Descent of the Dove: A Short History of the Holy Spirit in the Church* (Grand Rapids: Wm. B. Eerdmans & Co., 1972 [New York: Oxford University Press, 1939]).

14. Matt 16:25 (RSV).

Chapter Eleven

> O human soul! as long as thou canst so
> set up a mark of everlasting light,
> above the howling senses' ebb and flow
> to cheer thee and to right thee if thou roam—
> not with lost toil thou laborest in the night!
> Thou mak'st the heaven thou hop'st indeed thy home.[15]

Of course, Arnold was wrong in this: the preacher doesn't set up "the mark." Christ is the mark.

The lazy or unconcerned preacher has an arid mind when Sunday comes, for lovelessness has only hollow words. But the preacher-pastor proves faith by faith and love by love. She preaches with a cleansed conscience and an eager heart. The "futility of ringing doorbells" gives wings to her words—because they live within the "Word made flesh."

---

15. Matthew Arnold (1822–1888), "East London" (Public Domain).

CHAPTER TWELVE

Preaching the Whole Gospel (Or the Nonsense Gap)

The nonsense gap is the nonexistent space between the so-called individual Gospel and the so-called social Gospel. There's no gap. There's not even a pencil line. The two words, *individual* and *social*, are conjoined twins. Separated they die. Nobody can split individual life from social life. Yet we try to divide preachers (some are all too willing to accept the division) into those "who stick to the Bible" (they don't), and those who "meddle in politics." Thus, there's a chasm down the life of the whole church.

I

It should help us to remember that this attempt to find a gap is not new. It reappears in every era. There are two New Testament words for time. One is *chronos,* which means the succession of hours, days, and years: thus our word *chronometer.* The other is *kairos,* which means a crux, a juncture that gives a new turn in the road, a new direction. Does anyone here doubt that our generation lives at a crux in history? Our world shakes in revolution and disruption. Preaching is not immune. It must now try a new and hazardous road. The ordered pieties of the old-time sermon are gone.

Chapter Twelve

Such crises are not unknown in the history of the church. The New Testament folk had to choose between being a small troublesome satellite of the synagogue, where it would have the protection of the Pax Romana, and on the other hand becoming a new adventure in the new Gentile world, and so inviting persecution by both the synagogue and the empire. They chose that second path. So despite its wish and fear, they became "involved in politics." That is, they ran afoul of the empire. They did "stick to the Bible." They did not play it safe! They risked turbulence, and were hauled before rulers. Their Lord was himself killed by an empire. Should he have peddled pious platitudes, and died safely in his bed?

What of the Reformation church? It rebelled against the then-existent church. To use blunt terms, the Reformers split the church. Inevitably the Protestants were lined up pro or con with rulers according as the rulers were lined up pro or con with the pope. Incidentally, Protestant mobs destroyed priceless sculpture and paintings, and nuns and priests rushed into marriage with unseemly haste. Then what of those who now propose that the first task of the church is to keep its internal peace? On whose terms?

Now for a modern instance. Those who would have the American church "stay out of politics" are quickest to deplore the fact that the church in Russia did not oppose the Lenin revolution, and that the church in Germany did not oppose Hitler. Both churches were more concerned about ritual and theology than about the sorrows of the poor. Then what about the failure of the American church to speak with clear voice about war, racism, and poverty? Actually, the conservatives are quite ready to hear *their* politics and *their* economics from the preacher's lips. They hurry to provide cash to print the sermon. So the millionaire backers of Billy Graham raised no serious objection when the evangelist invited President Nixon to make a political speech in a Knoxville revival meeting.

We here pause to confess that to preach to a person's whole life, to shed the pretense that sin lives only on the private sector, is an agonizingly difficult task. We are neither begging the question nor evading it. Indeed, we here and now confess that revolutions are usually well-named: they only revolve. Bottom dog becomes top dog, and then is trapped in the same pride. What about the revolution in Russia and Germany? The history of insurgencies, such as the Anabaptists in Europe or the Levelers in England, offers no cause for optimism. So the conflict in the present church is not solved by snap judgments, but only by long pondering in the Spirit of Christ. What we have so far said is this: the church in history has never been able to live on the private sector. There is no private sector.

II

Let's underscore that fact: human nature is both individual and social. How can the proclamation of the Gospel be anything else? Every child born is *individual*, yes, in fingerprint, not to mention deeps of personhood. He is unique, lonely, a prisoner in a hermitage of flesh. He is sentenced to solitary life and a still more solitary death. Always there will be the so-called individual Gospel: our solitude cries for it. Yet every child from the moment of birth is social. He is welcomed into a home, which is interlocked with other homes; and by need for food and clothing and shelter with farms, factories, schools, and governments. Says one psychologist, "The 'I' is nourished by the 'We.'"[1] Sometimes cursed rather than nourished! That fact again raises our question—further back than Amos. So a sermon addressed only to the individual is a fiction; so is a sermon addressed only to "social man." Again, we make admission: *how* to bridge the gap is *the* question; we shall not run for cover.

Notice another paradox of human nature: each of us as body-soul. So what becomes of preaching that seeks to "save the soul"? The very word *soul* is a dubious translation. It savors of Greek gnosticism more than of New Testament faith: its manuscript word is by very sound our word "psyche." "Self" or "personhood" would be a better translation than "soul." "What shall a man give in exchange for—himself?"[2] The New Testament follows the Old in the belief that a person is not an enfleshed soul (the soul

---

1. Source unknown.

2. Mark 8:37 (GAB). Buttrick paraphrased the KJV, "What shall a man give in exchange for his soul?" The Common English Bible translation in 2011 avoided the word *soul* when translating the Hebrew (*nephesh*) or Greek (*psyche*). For example: "What will people give in exchange for their lives?" (Mark 8:37, CEB).

going to heaven by American Express while the unfortunate body festers in the grave), but a body breathed into of the Spirit. "Don't you know that your body is a temple of the Holy Spirit?"[3] So we preach to a person's body in gladness, not in moralistic gloom. If we are on the way to church to cultivate our soul, and we see on the other side of the road a person mugged and bleeding in body, we must not leave them (there's no guarantee of a nearby Samaritan); no, we tend their body and temporarily forget our own soul. The diversion may save both the wounded one's soul—and ours. Each person has a larger body: a house and neighborhood; and bodies on bodies: the whole sheathing of the whole material world. We preach to that fact. Both the ghetto and the suburb now confront us. This total preaching grows harder and harder. As to how, we shall not sidestep.

Still regarding the stuff of human nature: our age is ruled by corporate structures. That fact makes a person more lonely, so that "preaching to the individual" is more and more required of us; yet that loneliness can be ameliorated only as structures are changed, asking for sermons in a wider context than the supposedly isolated "soul." Even in a former pioneer age the sermon could not address only a lonely life, though farms were then almost hermetically sealed: almost, but there was trade, and the question of Native Americans. That latter affair in retrospect is not a shining page.[4] Can we any longer accept the popular assumption that if we save enough "souls," they will then change the world? It hasn't happened. "Saved" from what? "Saved" to what? The very word *soul*, so used, spells public incapacity. "Soul savers" nearly always strengthen the ranks of reactionary minds. We end this discussion of human nature with this truth: "the individual Gospel" is blind in one eye; the "social Gospel" is blind in the other.

---

3. 1 Cor 6:19 (GAB).

4. At this point in the paragraph Buttrick included the sentence, "Cotton Mather was not a false prophet." Since Buttrick did not explain how he meant this statement relative to the context, we simply note it without editorial interpretation. It should be said, however, that Buttrick by no means would have countenanced Mather's degradation of Native Americans, or Mather's morally self-justifying accounts of the Puritan Hannah Duston's killing and scalping of ten "Indians," or Mather's influential role in the Salem witch trials of 1692. Nor would Buttrick have concurred with Mather's substantiating his apocalyptic views of current events with passages from the book of Revelation.

Preaching the Whole Gospel (Or the Nonsense Gap)

III

We now turn to the scriptures, which under the Lordship of Christ are the "only unfailing guide of faith and practice."[5] They confirm and illuminate our study of human nature. Conservative minds in the church plead for "Bible preaching." They wouldn't if they knew the book! Liberal minds sit loose to the Bible. They keep it, but at the edge, not at the center. So they miss the path. The Bible under the light from Christ *underlines the truth that every person is individual-social.*[6] The Old Testament is concerned centrally with the covenant *community*: the individual stands on the vague periphery. Some later psalms and some passages in Jeremiah may or may not strike the individual note. But not until the late-date book of Daniel is the person a prime concern. There we find the promise that the human one of God shall stand in his "allotted place at the end of the days."[7] We must travel into the New Testament to hear in glowing love about "one lost sheep" and "one of these little ones." But we find there also news of a church that is the "beloved community," not a conglomerate of digits.

So we ask about the word and deed of Christ. There's a group in the church (it is not insignificant that they are all wealthy men) who through one of their spokesmen tell us that "Jesus taught spiritual truths to individuals." Few sentences have compassed such total fallacy—to the point of blasphemy. Jesus was not primarily a teacher or pedagogue; he was and is our Savior. He did not deal in "truths" or any other kind of abstraction; he proclaimed a new kingdom. He never severed the word *spiritual* from

---

5. Buttrick employed alternate wording to that of the 1946 Presbyterian Church USA Book of Common Worship's traditional ordination vow citing scripture as "the only infallible rule of faith and practice." The phrase "only unfailing guide of faith and practice" was used by English Wesleyan Methodists and others. During the fundamentalist-modernist controversies of the early twentieth century, as the senior minister of Old First Presbyterian Church of Buffalo, NY, Buttrick stood with those who rejected biblical inerrancy and infallibility. He was one of the original five New York Presbyterians to organize the drafting of the Auburn Affirmation of 1924, signed by 1,274 Presbyterian ministers as the primary vehicle that thwarted reactionary elements within the denomination in their attempt to impose the "Five Fundamentals" as doctrinal standards. See Charles E. Quirk, "Origins of the Auburn Affirmation," *Journal of Presbyterian History* 53, no. 2 (Summer 1975): 120–42.

6. Buttrick's emphasis.

7. Dan 12:13 (RSV).

the body; he talked about houses, lands, horses, seed, and again and again about cash. He spoke to individuals, yes, but also to groups—to his nation, to the Pharisees, to the poor, to rich men often, and in a word from which we shrink (and that we try to cut down to size: our size), about our enemies. He spoke so sharply to his own people as to tell them that other lands would fare better at the judgment. Jesus was not a little holy man peddling platitudes to a group of hermits. The preacher may not preach differently from his Lord, except as a sinner lost without his Lord's grace.

As for the other paradox, body-psyche, that also is under the biblical seal. The Old Testament is an earthy faith: it distrusts rationalisms and even art. As for the New Testament, the word *soul* as now used is an echo of Greek thought (*soma* is *sema*: "flesh is prison") rather than Hebraic-Christian faith. All through the New Testament there is the rumble of a warfare: "Your sons, O Zion, over your sons, O Greece." Our faith never downgraded the flesh: "Honor God in your body."[8] But of course there is no encouragement to fleshliness. Human nature purged by grace is home to the indwelling Christ. There is no dualism. Preaching that severs body and soul, as if "salvation" could ever be torn away from slum housing, or as if a person's public witness could ever be separated from one's secret sins, addresses two halves of a corpse.

IV

So we come to the thorny question of how to preach the whole Gospel. There is no rule of thumb for the sufficient reason that no two thumbs whether in pulpit or pew are alike. But there are guidelines. The preacher is not prophet only, but the shepherd of a flock. His congregation may be sleepy-eyed from an exhausting Saturday night, and may be on edge with many a prejudice and fear. The shepherd begins where the people are and then leads them out to better pastures. He can say in a university church[9] what would raise hackles in a typical suburban congregation. Jesus made his concessions as the Good Shepherd: "There is still much that I could say

---

8. 1 Cor 6:20 (NEB).
9. Buttrick wrote "Harvard" in the margin.

to you, but the burden would be too great for you now."[10] But his word always bridged a paradox and—he was crucified. He would be today. So an honest preacher can't preach nothing but "safe" doctrine in a conservative church, and nothing but leftwing doctrine in a way-out church. His job is not to please the congregation, but to be true to his Lord. His concern is not to "keep the peace of the church" (which has never been at peace, and never will until the eschaton), but to invite the peace of God through the atoning cross. The preacher can't measure so many grams of realism and so many grams of pastoral concern, for he lacks any such pharmaceutical skill. He brings every sermon to the eyes of the Spirit, and then obeys orders.

Thus the overall mandate is that the preacher preach the whole Gospel as Gospel. The approach is after this manner: "I'm not saying this because it pleases my conservative mind or yours, for there's no cheap grace, but because this seems to be the clear word of Christ." At another point he will follow the same path: "I'm not saying this because it pleases my unconservative mind or yours. Christ's first hearers complained of his 'hard sayings.' You and I complain. But isn't this what he said, and what he asks of us?" After a while the congregation knows that the preacher is not judgmental, and not expressing his own convictions except as they are quickened by the Holy Spirit. Yes, Bible class discussions are here "indicated," and discussion groups, and "feedbacks," and the preacher's pastoral fidelity. But the "unconditional demand" is that the preacher be a person in Christ, saying, "Imagine the eyes of Jesus on today's newspaper: what would he say about our priorities?" If a preacher bridles at that approach, he has left the faith, and the church might be fortunate if he left the church. I know of a sermon recently preached on the text "Love your enemies." It traveled by a series of ascending questions: "Is this roseate idealism? Is it merely a far-off goal? Is it only an individualistic ethic?" That sermon was

---

10. John 16:12 (NEB). Buttrick wrote the name Calvin in the margin next to these words of Christ. Absent Buttrick's specific reference to John Calvin, we know that Calvin commented on this Gospel text (16:12) several times in his *Institutes of the Christian Religion*, once quoting from Augustine's *Tractate on the Gospel of John* (53:7): "We must walk, we must advance, we must grow, that our hearts may be capable of those things which we cannot yet grasp. But if the Last Day finds us advancing, there we shall learn what we could not learn here."

so rigorously faithful to Christ that the congregation at the end breathed an audible "Amen."

It follows that the preacher should be slow to endorse any economic or political party or leader. As to the latter, "Let no one boast about human leaders."[11] As to the former, I went once to a Quaker meeting and was not blessed, for person after person rose to make a feeble comment on the last week's headlines. Rich people who condemn "politics in the pulpit" may be running scared; they rejoice when they hear *their* politics. But they have a point, for the preacher is not merely a critic of the news. Here is the dual caveat regarding "politics in the pulpit": every party is doomed by time, and every corporate structure is vitiated by pride. Every movement of any era is doomed by time; communism and capitalism are both changing and passing before our eyes: "Our little systems have their day and cease to be."[12] Meanwhile all human works are infected by pride and the lust for power: labor unions and manufacturers' associations, schools and medical societies—and the church. The difference is that the church daily makes confession of sin, and lives near a "fountain filled with blood."[13] The pulpit should never sponsor what is doomed by transience and corrupted by selfishness. But sermons should still cover both terms of the paradox. The story of Lazarus the poor man and Dives the rich man is not now without pertinence. Yes, sermons are now addressed more than ever to the lonely soul, but therefore also to the world that makes for loneliness. The preacher should still be intent on "individual conversion," but that means conversion from racial prejudice to the "beloved community" of our faith. So no partisanship. Parties are earthbound and pockmarked. Meanwhile we should remember that the early followers of Christ were lit like torches in Nero's garden.

Therefore, the preacher preaches with patience, and must not casually and wantonly rend the church, the body of Christ. But his focal loyalty is not to the church, either local or universal, but to the Lord of the church:

---

11. 1 Cor 3:21 (NRSV). Buttrick quoted the KJV: "Let no man glory in men."

12. Alfred Lord Tennyson, "In Memoriam A. H. H.," *The Poems and Plays of Alfred Lord Tennyson* (New York: The Modern Library, Random House, 1938), 294, st. 5.

13. From the poet William Cowper's 1772 hymn, "There Is a Fountain Filled with Blood."

Preaching the Whole Gospel (Or the Nonsense Gap)

to God "be glory in the church and in Christ Jesus from generation to generation evermore!"[14] There should be chance for the congregation to discuss the sermon. Not to debate it, for debate solves nothing and may divide everything. This discussion should follow a silence, with guidance given, namely, "Do you believe that what has been said is true to the mind of Christ?" There is a migration of seminary students to the inner city. That choice is gain rather than loss. But they will not thus escape hardhat entrenchment. Meanwhile the people whose hands are on the levers of power attend the suburban church, which may therefore offer the harder task. So patience after the manner of Christ, but not surrender. When did he surrender? If there are those in the church who genuinely pray for a new Pentecost, the preacher's patient word will not lack its rightful harvest.

But the preacher should not be too patient. His persistence should catch fire in adventure. His sermons should not ignore the collective term. It is amazing to me how rich persons can prate about "individual freedom" when their very machines and factories require and impose massisms. Sermons that try to live in one half of a paradox lead directly to the verdict, "as dull as a sermon." "Individualism" leads to a dreary pietism; social tracts lead to a shallow transience. Preaching the whole Gospel to the whole person may provoke antagonism, but it will not be dull. No faithful preacher lacks critics who may leave the church, taking with them their dubious cash. To be forewarned is to be forearmed. "The servant is not above his Lord."[15]

So further guidance: real preaching does not camp in one term of the paradox one Sunday, and in the other term the next Sunday. The preacher does not say, "Today I shall preach about unemployment, and the next Sunday about private prayer," for the two are obviously linked in a hundred ways. Private prayer must follow the order of the Lord's Prayer. That is, its first entreaty should be for God's coming kingdom. That means that no one should be deprived of the chance to work, not alone because a joyful life on earth requires joyful labor, but because if one does not work one

---

14. Eph 3:21 (NEB).
15. Matt 10:24 (GAB).

is cheated of the urgency of God's judgment and the heaven of God's favor. So, prayer is never merely private, and unemployment is never merely a public issue: it is as poignant as the poverty-stricken home next door. So true preaching (this is a momentous item) flashes sentence by sentence like electricity between two poles. Here's an instance: the preacher says, "Our politicians promise prosperity—which has always been a curse to any nation." Then the preacher adds, "Do *you* want it, or *you*, or *you*? What has Jesus to say about the 'abundance of things'?[16] I'm sure that in your deep desire you'd rather have his favor." In other words, the sermon comes on "touchy" truths *obliquely* and in flashing asides. Frontal attack with massed batteries is as futile as—well—our bombing of North Vietnam. That's an oblique comment!

V

So every sermon should be Gospel. The wise preacher makes this requirement constantly clear. Thus he says of some word of needed comfort, "I say this not that you may have peace of mind, for I hope you don't ever find that, but that you may know the peace of God, even his conquest over sin and death; and that you may share this peace on Monday through Saturday lest you find it gone." Thus, he says of some comment that treads on political toes, "I'm not talking politics: 'raving politics, never at rest'[17]; I'm talking Christ, and would beg you to confirm me by the study of the New Testament." Thus, the congregation may come to know that the Gospel is no middle-of-the-road affair, but what the New Testament calls "a shout from on high" (the incarnate Word) who puts to shame our earthbound loyalties, without whom our polluted and warring planet cannot live.

Of course, preaching, especially in these particulars, can't be insulated from other labors. Preaching is capsuled unless the preacher is also pastor. Preaching is set in the context of worship. It is child (or victim) of the life of the church. It is robbed of substance without a grateful yet toughminded theology. Take Christian education for instance. (A digression

---

16. Luke 12:15.
17. From Alfred Lord Tennyson's "Vastness," *Poems and Plays of Alfred Lord Tennyson*, 851.

here: when Christ becomes an adjective as in "Christian education," we are on the way to losing him.) So, let us speak about education in Christ. Today's preacher is almost handcuffed because his congregation is illiterate in the faith. As for worship, admittedly it has become formal and dull. Thus the underground church has merit—as a protest. Let us hope that it knows and applies tests in Christ. Otherwise it will barter eternal verities for a dubious novelty. Preaching belongs in a total context.

When all is said, the preacher should not and cannot blink the fact that individual-social is not two facts, but one and indivisible. Preaching without that total view is not only vacuous, but distortion. We preach to *each person* in the *whole world*. "God so loved *the world* that *whosoever* trusts him"—there are the two terms: "world" and "whosoever"! So the Gospel is for every person and for all people on this wayward and shrinking planet, in the mystery made known in Christ, "before whose face the generations rise and pass away."[18]

---

18. A familiar clause in various denominational service books for addressing God during a funeral service. See "Commendation of the Departed," *A Book of Services: The United Reformed Church in England and Wales* (Edinburgh: The Saint Andrew Press, 1980), 94.

CHAPTER THIRTEEN

Preaching to a Skeptical Time

The basic guidelines regarding preaching have been thrown off base by the revolution and disruption of our time. So we now confront explicitly the preacher's contemporary problem, that of *communication*. "No one steps into the same river twice."[1] True. But if the stream is history, the person changes in certain eras as swiftly as the stream. How different today's congregation! Yesterday church members knew the Bible; now the Book goes unread even in the pew. Yesterday there were ethical landmarks; today all the roads seem under flood. Yesterday theology was understood; today "who shall show us any truth?" So we are now concerned with communication. This guidance deals with the prevalent skepticism.

The Gospel is "once-for-all," but that is the very "reason" why it confronts each new age with new demands and new assurances. So preaching changes. The very language of "the old-time religion" has a horse-and-buggy cast. We cherish it, but it clutters the roads in our fast-car, jet-plane time. Any person, preacher, mechanic, or lawyer who defies change becomes a roadside wreck. We can see both the abidingness and the innovation of preaching even in the timespan of the Four Gospels. Mark speaks to a persecuted church, Matthew to the long hope of the Messiah and its strange fulfillment, Luke to the Greek world of the then Middle

---

1. Heraclitus, fifth-century BCE pre-Socratic philosopher from Ephesus.

East, and John to the deeper longing in a gnostic time for the Word made flesh. Each Gospelist wrote in a new disclosure of the Spirit to his own circumstance. Preaching will bring amusement and not grace if it comes in a Prince Albert suit. How to preach to a skeptical time?

I

There is no need to marshal evidence of current doubt, but there is need to understand its origins, for only so can the preacher speak the solving word. That word is not a berating of "the sins of unbelief." There has always been doubt. Perhaps in Christ's day the "lesser breeds without the law" outnumbered the faithful worshippers in the synagogue. Perhaps in the Middle Ages, when the church loomed mightier than the empire, there was a shadowed margin of unbelief where most people lived. The folk of Christ have always been a minority cause. But in our time skepticism is rife not only in the street but in the pew. In the pew it is covert. It would be healthier for the church if it were openly declared. Today's congregation is illiterate in the mighty persuasions of the faith, and still more unaware that these flatly contradict our *prevailing* culture. So some groups in the church gather to hear "an interesting speaker" speak about anything except the Gospel. Even where faith is avowed it has lost its glow, and peddles censoriousness instead of shedding light and joy.

The history of this skepticism can be fairly easily traced, at least in broad outline. It is no modern affair. It began centuries ago. We are its victims, not its authors. It began in the Renaissance, which in some of its fruits was well named: God *did* give new light both on nature and human nature. But there was a dark spot, namely the proposal that "man is the measure of things."[2] How can humans stumbling in unwisdom and doomed to die be the measure of anything ultimate? So the Renaissance dwindled to "the Age of Enlightenment." That was a dubious title; in part it was an age of dreary questioning. In its turn it dwindled into our "Age of Anxiety." W. H. Auden has portrayed it: four people in a tavern getting

---

2. The concept of subjective relativism characterizing and predating the Renaissance and Enlightenment was summed up by Protagoras, fifth-century BCE Sophist: "Man is the measure of all things, of things that are that they are and of things that are not that they are not."

drunk, each talking about himself interminably, tubercular folk seeking cure by breathing into one another's faces.[3]

Skepticism in any time comes not from brainy bafflement but from a life-situation. Our political culture has broken into war after war since the early twentieth century; its toll has been well over one hundred million lives. Our social culture is a glaring contrast between wealth and poverty and between race and race. Our industrial culture is an open lesion between labor and capital. Our marriage is shallow selfishness: "I like you, and you like me, so let's enjoy each other." Our education is self-worship, for it enthrones "learning," an abstract verb with neither subject nor object. Our churches have succumbed to the culture so that there is no "balm in Gilead." Every person is to blame, adding a smoky torch to the prevailing fog. In another sense every person is a victim of the times. Why should anyone expect our culture to issue in a mighty glowing faith? It darkens faith and invites skepticism.

Some observers believe we are entering an "age of longing," and that this will lead on to a new age of faith. Arthur Koestler so believes.[4] Frank Baumer agrees, and even proposes (unconvincingly) the new form of the new faith.[5] We hope and pray, but cannot see the daybreak light. Maybe the ebb tide of doubt has slowed to the tremulous turn; maybe the tide of faith will soon flow. But to our eyes there is yet no sure turn. How can there be when we have made a hell on earth, and still brag about our civilization? Modern humanity speaks in casual assurance about "ethical lag," as if we could at any moment leave our polluted and mechanized world, not to mention our racisms and our indifference to the poor, and quickly catch up in our dealings with God! Have we not so committed ourselves to mortal pride as to be incapable in our own power to fashion any worthy "new order"? There are deeper questions: Can our finite existence, coming from mystery and moving inexorably toward death, ever escape doubt except in a constant surrender to God's grace? The preacher is not free from doubt. Sentenced to

---

3. W. H. Auden, "For the Time Being: A Christmas Oratorio, II, Advent, 6–7," *W. H. Auden: Collected Poems*, ed. Edward Mendelson (New York: The Modern Library, 2007 [1944]).

4. Arthur Koestler, *The Age of Longing* (New York: Macmillan, 1951). Koestler and his wife jointly committed suicide in 1983.

5. Franklin L. Baumer, *Religion and the Rise of Skepticism* (New York: Harcourt, Brace and Company, 1960), in which he addressed Koestler's *The Age of Longing*.

strange freedom in a broken earth, she also feels forlorn. She knows of love "up there" through Christ who "came down," and trusts that the little loop of our history shall one day be gathered back into heaven. Her own misgivings should teach her in measure how to preach to a skeptical time.

II

So we stand in the outer court.[6] From that vantage point we see that doubt, however much our fatal pride is involved, comes always from a life situation. So the preacher should be slow to condemn even unworthy doubt. Shabby skepticism takes many forms. It taxes the patience of the believer. Sometimes it parades an intellectual conceit that despises "gullible faith." But we now know that conceit is the reverse side of an insecurity. So, though vanity may sometimes be rebuked, sermons reach home more quickly by the road of understanding. The world sometimes tries to justify perverse or wanton sexuality by a list of the famous who have chosen that unruliness, and the preacher may sometimes ask, Were they famous "because of" or "in spite of"? But even in that issue the preacher should be slow to judge. The affair is psychologically complex. Home and culture are both implicated. Yes, mortal pride is ever present, but no preacher is qualified for the role of angelic censor.

That comment leads, or should lead, to acknowledgement of the church's guilt. We have surrendered to the world's "success," bragging of buildings, bricks, and budgets. The visiting preacher is shown the loveliest suburbs, not the slums. The word *God* is sometimes pious trimming on sermons, not alone on political speeches. The church has condoned or ignored massive wrongs. What of the slaughter of the natives, which some churches blatantly justified as the right of the new chosen people? What of the silence or worse regarding slave ships? As for the appalling genocide of our wars, the church has impeached war in general in the pious name of the Prince of Peace, and then either canonized each successive war or pleaded "national security." All this should now be said from the pulpit, the preacher confessing her own share in the church's failure. Then she will

---

6. A metaphorical reference to the outer court of the Gentiles within the first-century CE Jerusalem temple.

have some warrant to tell of the wonder of the church that lives on while empires rise and fall—by grace of the indwelling Christ whose word the church has again and again refused.

As for honest doubt, by what right do preachers condemn? Yet the unbeliever has often fallen under Jesuitical persecution.[7] Happily that day has passed: the skeptics outnumber the faithful; there is doubt in the pew. Pulpit arguments, even unaccompanied by the lash, are a blunder, not only because true preaching is rarely argument, not only because argument itself is likely to antagonize but because doubt does not rise primarily in the mind's bafflement. It betokens a life situation. Take a circumscribed instance. Imagine a dominant mother and an aloof father, both officers in the local church. The child's rebellion begins at the age of two, becomes overt in puberty, and gathers supporting arguments in high school and college. How can that kind of doubt be overcome by pulpit argument? The preacher and the church must offer a life climate of acceptance over and against the alien climate of the home. Albert Camus is an instance in a wider context. He hated God rather than denying God; how can God be good in a world of wars and contempts, plague and final death? This question is not wicked. It is answered only in the Gospel. That is why Camus himself pleaded with Christians to be Christian. Sermons that try to show the reasonableness of the faith have gone. All that is left of them is a thin time-bound logic. The faith in any event is not "reasonable." Christ called it a "scandal"—of God sharing life and love with people on earth.

III

We now look at doubt from the inner court.[8] There we note the broad streak of skepticism in the Bible. The Psalms take issue with God: "How long, O Lord?"[9] They accuse God of disappearing when humans most

---

7. *Jesuitism* was a pejorative term coined by the French Catholic and Jansenist theologian Blaise Pascal (1623–1662). In his *Provincial Letters* he attacked the Jesuits (the Society of Jesus) for casuistic reasoning that employed equivocation, prevarication, and placation for the sake of justifying particular ends by unsavory means. "Jesuitism" characterized Catholic persecution of Protestants with widespread Jesuit involvement.

8. As if we were standing within the inner court of the Jerusalem temple.

9. Ps 13:1; 35:17 (RSV).

need divine help: "Why stand so far off, Lord, hiding thyself in time of need?"[10] Job is tempted to say that God is dead. Then he realizes that his indignation against a cruel providence could hardly be aroused by nothing, so he accuses God of being a tyrant: a "vindicator" will justify Job. Camus's hatred and Kafka's bafflement are both in the Bible itself. The New Testament also traces humanity's frustrated yet ever returning hope. The apostles ask Christ, "Lord, is this the time when you are to establish once again the sovereignty of Israel?"[11] Theirs is the short-circuited nationalistic hope, and the enigmatic answer is, "It is not for you to know about dates and times."[12] Instances multiply: the story of the father of the epileptic boy speaks poignantly to our time.[13] The world is not divided into doubters and believers. Every person is both. Thus the father's prayer for his son's healing: "I have faith; help me where faith falls short."[14] The last word of the New Testament is faith, but faith wondering why Jesus doesn't return, and why the church is martyred: "Come, Lord Jesus!"[15]

IV

The preacher can next claim that Jesus chose a doubter to be an apostle. His name was Thomas. Jesus chose him not in spite of his doubt, or in respite of his doubt, but because of it, and because the doubt itself bred a certain courage and love. This latter portent need not surprise us if we remember that doubt springs not from some feeble intellectualizing but from the dynamics of the subconscious. The doubter, alienated in childhood, espouses the cause of the oppressed. So Thomas, though sure that Christ would be killed should he venture by foolhardiness into Herod's land, leads the other apostles in brave discipleship: "Let us also go, that we

---

10. Ps 10:1 (NEB).
11. Acts 1:6 (NEB).
12. Acts 1:7 (NEB).
13. Matt 7:14-18; Mark 9:14-27; Luke 9:37-43.
14. Mark 9:24 (NEB).
15. Rev 22:20 (RSV, NEB).

may die with him."[16] Many a skeptic in our time leads the crusade against racism while church members play it safe. Thomas was a doubter almost to the end. He denied the resurrection of his Lord, and obdurately set his own terms for faith: "Unless I see the marks of the nails in the hands I will not believe."[17] No spook or apparition could ever be his Lord! The answering beatitude may be a dividing line in the history of the Gospel: the age of the flesh has now given way to the age of the Spirit: "Happy are they who have never seen me, and yet have found faith!"[18] By whatever worthy exegesis, the whole story is a blessing for our faith and doubt.

The preacher can therefore say that doubt is always the shadowed side of faith. The doubter cannot doubt nothing. Nothing is nothing. Augustine implied wisely: I doubt, therefore God is.[19] That child who was dominated or neglected in his early years reacted not against Christian faith but against his parents' failure to practice it. Camus's hatred of God failed to account for his own sense of righteousness and impulse of love. He debited God with all the cruelty, and credited himself with all the compassion, as if life were born in sudden portent in him. That father was right: he believed as every person deeply believes, and prayed that he might be saved from the unfaith which always besets our mortal life.

So the preacher stands with the doubter. She says in effect, "You doubt? So do I. But we cleave to faith in the onset of doubt." She knows that doubt builds no Rheims Cathedral and prompts no crusade of mercy. She says again, "Tell me what kind of God you don't believe in? Maybe I

---

16. John 11:16 (NEB).

17. John 20:25 (GAB).

18. John 20:29 (GAB).

19. See George Buttrick, "Faith and Doubt," *Sermons Preached in a University Church* (New York: Abingdon Press, 1959), 23–29. Buttrick concluded the sermon by saying, "Augustine spoke a final word: A man doubts, therefore God is," to which he added a printed footnote: "I have not rediscovered this as a quotation, but it fully accords with Augustine's argument in *De Trinitate*, Bk X, sec. 14" (ibid., 212n12). Likewise, the statement, "I doubt, therefore God is," captures the implication of Augustine's reasoning, namely, that doubt is predicated upon the very thing that is doubted. In the sermon "Faith and Doubt," Buttrick asserted, "Genuine doubt is the reverse side of genuine faith. Even atheism must define itself by theism: it is a-theism, that is to say, not theism. Is doubt not always the doubt of our faith?" (24). Just so, "doubt is always the shadowed side of faith" for "the doubter cannot doubt Nothing."

too don't believe in him. Now tell me what kind of God you could believe in. Then let's see—Christ!" The writer of this book had a group of "atheists" hanging round his house. They would ask in surprise, "Why do you like this roustabout crowd?" He would answer, "Because you are such religious people." They would retort, "Stop kidding us." He would answer in his turn, "I'm not kidding you: you couldn't doubt nothing. What do you deeply believe?"[20] The preacher who condemns doubt is usually a pitiable figure. She has not yet learned to be honest with herself. Still less has she seen how the Bible meets the crisscross of our faith and doubt.

V

Now we approach the holy of holies.[21] We dare to stand at the door because Christ has opened for us a "new and living way" into that awesome presence. Christ also is paradox. Our words poorly describe it, "human and divine," for there is a sense in which every person is divine. No, the terms are between our life as "created" and his as "begotten," between mortal humans and the Word made flesh. But that rightful description etches Christ's genuine humanity while never yielding the conviction of his "Godhead bodily." Perhaps all great thinking is rooted in paradox. That word does not mean puzzle or confusion. It acknowledges that life doesn't travel down our paved conventional roads. *Para*: contrary to; *doxa*: our neat accepted tenets. So Christ genuinely shared our life—and God's life. So Christ met blunt refusal: he could do no mighty works in Israel "because of their unbelief."[22] Why any unbelief in God's world? So Christ shrank from the cup of death's stigma and lostness. Why should there, how could there, be any such cup? So Christ marveled at unfaith: "How

---

20. One of Buttrick's divinity students at Harvard confirmed a similar dialogue. Being an agnostic at the time of his first conversation with Buttrick, he began by saying to Buttrick, "I don't believe in God." Buttrick replied, "Tell me the God you don't believe in. Maybe I don't believe in him either" (editor's oral history interview with the Rev. Wallace McPherson Alston, Jr., October 12, 2017).

21. The innermost sanctum of the Jerusalem temple, into which only the high priest entered on the Day of Atonement.

22. Matt 13:58 (RSV).

little faith you have!"[23] Yet he marveled also at faith in a world that seemed flatly to deny faith: "I tell you, nowhere, even in Israel, have I found faith like this."[24] He knew that for a Roman, a person not born under the covenant, it would be hard to accept discipleship. We cannot dot the *i*'s and cross the *t*'s of Christ's incarnation, but theology has always centrally underscored the book of Hebrews declaration: "For ours is not a high priest unable to sympathize with our weakness, but one who, because of his likeness to us, has been tested every way, only without sin."[25] That is, he knew the onset of both doubt and defection, of discomfort and death.

So we come once more to the "cry of dereliction." There are those who contend that Christ on the cross recited the whole of the twenty-second psalm with its assurance of triumph. They hope thus to draw the sting from this confession of forsakenness. To this we can reply that we have no history to tell us that the whole psalm fell from his lips (this is conjecture, not text), and that in any event the "cry" is a sharp punctuation in the psalm. Christ knew his Hebrew Bible, so line 1 of Psalm 22 had its poignant meaning. Besides, what of verses 6 through 21? Forsakenness is not a captious mood, soon overcome by some Pollyanna optimism. No, it is the ultimate void. Christ bore both our doubts and our transgressions. He knew the emptiness of people who talked then, as people talk now, about "religious bunk." He bore the doubt of Thomas, who thought the Gospel was too good to be true. He carried the weight of our meaninglessness. What joy for the preacher to say, "Our doubts are nailed to the cross!" For the cross is made contemporary by the movement of the Holy Spirit.

Thus we see why Jesus himself is not doubted. Some skeptic may say, "Jesus means nothing to me," but what the skeptic means is, "I don't like the pseudo-Christ preached in a pseudo-church." Meanwhile the now-departing God-is-dead theology sets Christ at the center. The followers of Bonhoeffer's *Letters from Prison* exalt Christ as the "Man for Others." They forget that he was first the "Man for God," but their chosen title is tribute to a love that knew no bounds. The "Jesus People" go back to a

---

23. Matt 8:26 (NEB).
24. Luke 7:9 (NEB), spoken to a Roman centurion.
25. Heb 4:15 (NEB).

Chapter Thirteen

long-disproved bibliolatry, but testify in their own way that "no other name has been given among humans through which we must be saved."[26] The modern trust in Jesus follows directly from his bearing our doubts—and bearing them away. The fire of his love kindles in us the fires of a new faith.

VI

The dual role of preacher-pastor is here involved. The covert skeptic may be in the pew. The open skeptic, perhaps as promising a breed, avoids church. But the preacher has chance to meet him, if the preacher knows her way around. In a summer conference ground, the hippies are round the fountain in the conference park or down near the lakeside, while the "good folk" are attending service. If the preacher is not uptight, the hippies will welcome her, not asking her to use their jargon. The preacher prays for them in her room at night, and thanks God that through them may come a counterculture over against our materialistic, dehumanized world. One counterculture group was brought to confrontation by this challenge: "You can pray. Wait in silence for five minutes. It will seem an eternity. God is, or God isn't. Don't beg the question. Just leave the door open."

At any rate, doubt is impossible without faith. Conversely, faith is impossible for mortal people in an ambiguous world without doubt. Can any reader, ministerial or otherwise, honestly claim that she has never doubted? Has she never doubted what God is doing when a tidal wave sweeps the coast of Pakistan or American bombers obliterate a village? The preacher doubts. No, she doesn't peddle her doubts. In New Testament language that would not be "edifying." That is, it would build no home for anyone. She preaches the faith that overcomes the world. But she deeply understands for her guidance Augustine's word: I doubt, therefore God is.[27]

---

26. Acts 4:12 (CEB), translation substituted for GAB's: "no other name granted among men, by which we may receive salvation."

27. The statement, "I doubt, therefore God is," captures the implication of Augustine's reasoning, namely, that doubt is predicated upon the very thing that is doubted. For further explanation see n37.

CHAPTER FOURTEEN

Preaching to a Dehumanized World

The Gospel is once for all, written in Christ's life, scored deep by his death, brought to triumph by his resurrection, and made contemporary by his Holy Spirit. But changes bring a new world, and preaching is an answering newness in the power of the Spirit. *Relevant* is not the word, for it savors of accommodation, but the Gospel is always *pertinent*. Thus, in the first century there was a new-old approach to the faithful in Judea, and a revolutionary turn as the Gospel leapt like a flame from city to city in the Greco-Roman world. How to preach to our strange apocalyptic time? Our immediate concern is with our facelessness, our alienation from God and our neighbor and ourselves, our loss of self-identity.

I

One invasion that has messed up our time is scientism. It treats persons as objects. It has that right of course, for we *are* objects: we live and die like the beasts of the field. But we are not merely objects: we are *subjects* with power to view our swiftly passing days. This higher dimension science ignores by its own self-appointed bounds. *Science* is aware of its chosen limitations, but *scientism* pretends there are no bounds. It proposes that physical measurement is the limit of the world. Thus it hopes to

Chapter Fourteen

conjure up *homunculus*[1] from a test tube, with scientism in godlike control of the sperm bank. *Science* stays in its own backyard: *scientism* tyrannizes as it regards humans as only genes, cells, and carbohydrates. Thus depersonalization. Preaching should puncture the fallacy, in gentle satire rather than in a long dreariness of (negative) condemnation.

Another troubler is mechanization. A person has become a "hand."[2] The machine invited the factory, the factory invited the city, and the city made people anonymous. They are now lost in the "crowd." Modern people are computerized people, numbers in a zip-code society. We share Harvey Cox's gratitude for city amenities, but we are troubled by his blindness to city threats.[3] In New York City about a thousand people are buried annually in pauper's graves because nobody claimed the corpse in the city morgue. We urgently need a book on theology and technology. Mechanized society becomes uniform, and so dies, for each person is unique and can't be uniform and live. Maybe that is one reason why we are so quickly in uniform.[4]

Another agent of chaos is the impact of our wars. In a military world, a person is even less than a "hand" for being a number on a metal disc that lasts longer than her expendable flesh. How could we ever have believed that wholesale human slaughter could bring order and peace? How could the church have been silent in war after war?[5] The attempt to stop war by means of war is like stopping fires by means of incendiarism. The Vietnam War did not scotch communism: it made a desolation, which is always tyranny's seed plot. It did not encourage democracy: it made an ally of the local dictator. It did not bring freedom: it has been freedom's assassin. A boy and a girl in love walked along a Mekong Delta beach hand

---

1. A preformed "little person" inside a cell, who grows to be a mature person.

2. As in handservant.

3. Harvey Cox, *The Secular City* (New York: The MacMillan Company, 1963). Cox later changed his mind about admiration for the secular city, in his book *Fire from Heaven: The Rise of Pentecostal Spirituality and the Reshaping of Religion in the Twenty-First Century* (Boston: Addison Wesley, 1995).

4. "In uniform" entails not only mechanization but also war-making.

5. Buttrick was a lifelong pacifist and conscientious objector, as were his father and his three sons, John, Robert, and David.

in hand. Our landing forces reckoned them an enemy ruse, and mowed them down. That is a parable of what war does to human love. Small wonder that war has brought not mutual regard but a wholesale cynicism. Again, the logic of events gives the preacher his cue.

The failure of the home is a fellow marauder. The pulpit's pietism, "The child is the hope of the race," was never true, for the child has to live with his parents, as they with their parents. Freudian doctrine, convincing in part, unconvincing in part, has demolished the preacher's foolish attempt to make the home a miniature of the kingdom. Have we not read that "the sins of the fathers are visited on the children," yes, "to the third and the fourth generation"?[6] That is why we have Christ's prayer: "Our Father, in the heavens"! The home now finds mother working in a factory, and father perhaps killed in war by our infantile and bankrupt "statesmanship." Students consult the college chaplain about their "career," a word of French root meaning a racecourse, because the word *vocation* is now forgotten. The proposed topic is often only a front: "But, Doc, I don't know who I am." What need for realistic preaching about the home!

Another thug who leaves our world in disarray is the norm of a false success. Who are the successful people in any town? That question lists the rich. But by that test few can succeed: most are relegated to failure. The planet is largely salt ocean, desert, and mountain. There are only a few arable valleys. We live only in a mutual sharing. But the white race hogs the loaf, leaving only the crusts to other races. Even among the white race many are poor. By our wretched money norms they are "the lower classes." Their mind is dulled, their eyes glazed: they are the "faceless generation." Even the church has catered to "our fine contributors," and rich people try to control the preacher's word by their money power. The news outlets meanwhile travel on an ellipse with two foci: conflict and sensation. This, not Agnew's[7] charge, shows the real threat of the public press. Television meanwhile offers trivial pap for trivial minds, though there are

---

6. Cf. Exod 20:5, 34:7.

7. Vice President Theodore Agnew (1918–1996) pled no contest to the charge of federal tax evasion in exchange for dropping charges of political corruption.

saving exceptions. So faces become a mask, with all masks showing the same compulsive grin.

It is not strange that frustration with an "inferiority complex" marks our time. The counterhero in *Death of a Salesman*[8] tries to "get by on a smile and a shoe-string" because "he never knew who he was." So, W. H. Auden has described our loss of personhood under the horrible term, "It."

> Just how, just when It succeeded we shall never know…
> For nothing like It has happened before.…[9]

What a day for the Gospel! What other word can rekindle life in a dehumanized world?

II

Mark more closely the mindset of our time: violence is its signature. "Don't fence me in"[10] means "or I'll break the fences." So the news headlines exhaust sensation. Televised news feature fire, murder, and rape. Movies peddle sex and horror. Subscriptions offer pornography. Repression, in psychiatry or in police action, brings only a temporary respite. The local ministers' group should realize that to try to stop something, prostitution or the local tavern, is a poor substitute for starting something.

There is also a revival of the occult. Our precious dead, their faults fallen away, their loyalty remembered, visit us (we are told) through "mediums" previously unknown to our loved ones gone or to us. The proposal is bizarre and heartless. A further dabbling in the occult is our modern hang-up with astrology. Jeane Dixon[11] is a reactionary mind

---

8. Arthur Miller, *Death of a Salesman* (New York: The Viking Press, 1949).

9. W. H. Auden, "For the Time Being: A Christmas Oratorio, II, Advent, 6–7," *W. H. Auden: Collected Poems*, ed. Edward Mendelson (New York: The Modern Library, 2007 [1944]), 352.

10. "Don't Fence Me In," a popular song by Cole Porter, 1934.

11. Jeane Dixon (1904–1997), born Lydia Emma Pinckert, was a popular syndicated psychic and astrologer.

trading in probabilities with a few guesses about possibilities. Any perceptive person could play the game better than she, but many a newspaper features her guesses as if they were messages from heaven. Mark this: if events are to happen as she predicts, there is nothing we can do. For the nerve of responsibility is cut, and we are condemned to a robot world.

We should note also the new romanticism. "All the world needs now is love, sweet love."[12] Thus we invoke a rainbow world. What kind of "love"? The New Testament does not say that love is God: it says, "God is love,"[13] and finds God revealed not in some saccharine sweetness but in the rigors of the cross, yes, and in the power of the resurrection. "Everything's beautiful in its own way."[14] Is it? Drug peddling outside a high school? "Everyone's beautiful in his own way": is he? A Gestapo officer shoveling an emaciated Jew into the ovens of Dachau? Thus the new romanticism! The kindest comment would doubt its intelligence. Actually, it's a euphoric flight into unreality.

Add the revival of mysticism, not Christian mysticism, but the cult of a thin "meditation," as in our Western variant of Zen Buddhism. We fixedly ponder not Christ in the scriptures but a tree. This is almost animism, or a hope to find God in the deeps of contemplation. We should not condemn out of hand; the sterile worship of the church is partly to blame. But the fact remains that the Gautama professed "no knowledge of the gods," and that to Buddhism history is only a moving screen. Christ's people see history as so real that Godself is revealed within history. Meanwhile the best mysticism is under threat: it may seek "absorption into the infinite" instead of the glad surrender of our free self to God, and it may easily forget both the sorrows of our neighbors and our flagrant public sins.

Add the Jesus cults. They are partly a rebound from science suddenly become a false messiah. Thus they are tempted to a renunciation of the

---

12. "What the World Needs Now Is Love" a popular song by Hal David and Burt Bacharach, 1965.

13. 1 John 4:8 (RSV), Gr. *agapē* (love).

14. "Everything is beautiful in its own way," from the children's song "Everything Is Beautiful" by Ray Stevens, 1970.

intelligence God has given. Some groups have social concern. Most have sold out to an incredible literalism, so that any Bible phrase is taken at face value—with what hazards! One commentator has said, "They may be freaks, but that's better than being on drugs."[15] Some of them are still on drugs: they have a "jag" on Jesus. The Bible is not a list of magic incantations or a book of recipes for instant dinner. It is not enough to say, "I feel Jesus in my heart": feelings are shifting sand. Contrived ecstasy soon evaporates. A few slaves set free for an hour in ancient Corinth and pondering a letter from Paul know more than the Jesus cults about "the power of God and the wisdom of God."[16]

We should not overlook secular piety. I'm thinking of Harvey Cox's jaunty confidence and jauntier exegesis in the book *The Secular City*. I'm remembering also Dietrich Bonhoeffer's (blessings on his brave witness!) *Letters from Prison*,[17] with its proposal of "worldly faith"—supposing it has not been misinterpreted. The "post-Christian era" proves on examination to be a modern version of Kierkegaard's not-unjustified attack on "Christendom," the Church "establishment."[18] This new theology tells us that God has given human "dominion" over the earth, so we must "go it alone," not running home to "Father," but acting as if God were not. Already this school of thought is driven to define its terms. It distinguishes between secularism and secularity: the former is cursed, the latter blest. Actually, God has never washed his hands of our earth. God has made humans *trustees*, not *owners* of the planet. God keeps coming back, as in our time of pollution, to ask an accounting. True life is never from human to human, but always from God to human, and only then from human to human.

---

15. Source unknown.

16. 1 Cor 1:24 (NEB).

17. Dietrich Bonhoeffer, *Letters and Papers from Prison* (New York: The Macmillan Co., 1953).

18. *Kierkegaard's Attack upon Christendom*, trans. and intro. by Walter Lowrie (Princeton, NJ: Princeton University Press, 1946). Søren Kierkegaard (1813–1855), Danish philosopher and theologian, one of the most important thinkers of the nineteenth century.

III

Now we ask what the pulpit should say at such a time. The word should be biblical, for only that book is *pertinent* in our time. The preacher should set his face against our shallow "isms," and more against the dehumanizing empires. Jeremiah scathingly denounced his nation's foreign policy. Jesus took direct issue with the false nationalistic hopes of his people. Sermons that pretend to be "scriptural," but never make application to our own time, betray the Bible. Jesus warned against resort to the sword. He stood on beatitude ground when the Maccabees were hailed as *the* heroes.[19] The Epistles also are startlingly contemporary: they condemn the nostrums of their time. So the preacher today should deal in irony with the bamboo hideouts cherished by modern humanity. Jesus laughed at the kowtowing to the "mighty" of his day. Our "mighty" are of the same breed.

Thus the preacher peddles no social panacea, but stands against the depersonalizing flood, even though he is a "voice crying in the wilderness." He risks unpopularity? Of course. "Alas for you," said Jesus, "when all speak well of you."[20] When the preacher plays it safe he may more quickly raise the church budget, but there are God's secret eyes. To betray them is to lose wholeness of person, and therefore to speak a dismembered word. Then must the preacher's pipings be lost in the world's greedy tumult? No. To borrow a metaphor from de Rougemont, he, the preacher, and others make a group of reeds in the river, and change the river's flow.[21] The word of

---

19. In contrast to the celebrated violence of the Maccabean revolt and military conquests of the second and first centuries BCE, Jesus proclaimed the beatitude, "Blessed are the peacemakers, for they will be called children of God" (Matt 5:9, NRSV).

20. Luke 6:26 (NEB).

21. Denis de Rougemont (1906–1985), *The Devil's Share: An Essay on the Diabolic in Modern Society* (New York: Meridian Books, 1956). In the face of totalitarian powers, such as the Nazis whom he resisted, de Rougemont writes, quoting Joseph de Maistre during the reign of Napoleon, "'God, who owes no one any miracles, and who makes no useless ones, employs two simple means to reestablish the equilibrium: sometime the giant cuts his own throat, sometimes a greater inferior power throws in his path an imperceptible obstacle which, no one knows how, subsequently grows and becomes insurmountable; like a feeble reed, caught in the current of the river, which in the end produces an accumulation of silt which changes its course.' I say that we can participate in this really *total* victory [God's victory] by becoming, each one for himself, that 'imperceptible obstacle' to evil, and that 'feeble reed' which changes the course of the current" (200). So, by analogy, Buttrick is saying that a "feeble reed" (the

God in Christ is not mocked. Our "practical commonsense" is catastrophic nonsense, but the catastrophe is less than a cloud in the oncoming dawn. "This is the victory that overcometh the world, even our faith."[22]

The rush of the social Gospel, so called, with all its headlong dangers, was bound to come, not because some preachers have suddenly gone berserk, or because they wish to pose as politicians or economists, but because they cannot any longer pretend (with Billy Graham) that sin lives only on the private sector. They know now that wickedness marks our corporate structures, not alone our "individual life." Of course, the preacher should take his text not from his own opinions but from the Bible interpreted under the Spirit of Christ. The preacher should lead a Bible class, even though the group of students is a mere handful—like the eleven apostles!—so that they, a golden heart of wheat at the center of the husk, may unmask the money-greedy and power-hungry persons who usurp public leadership. Some of the rich may hive off into nostalgic tabernacles that revert to their boyhood pietisms. Even so, the church will not be poorer for their cowardice. When the books are balanced, Martin Luther King will be remembered when some current healer or revivalist has been relegated to his proper limbo.

Note, therefore, that Jesus resisted the dehumanizing pressures of his time. Yes, he spoke to individuals. How else? There is no planetary ear. That is not the point. The point is that he spoke about *groups* as well as about individuals. One sentence would challenge a man in his secrecies: "You fool, tonight your soul will be asked of you";[23] the next sentence would rebuke the temple or the empire. The parable of the two prodigals is savingly for two men, but it is addressed also to two groups (see its opening words), to the wanton crowd through the younger son, and to the synagogue community through the older son.[24] He knew the bankruptcy of our wars, forever sowing the dragon's teeth of new wars, and therefore

---

preacher) calls other "feeble reeds" (the church) together as God's "greater inferior power" to alter the course of evil.

22. 1 John 5:4 (KJV).

23. Luke 12:20 (GAB), the parable of the rich man who planned to harvest many crops.

24. Luke 15:11-32, the parable; 15:1-2 (NEB), the preamble introducing the "bad characters" and "grumbling" Pharisees and doctors of the law.

commanded that we "love one another."[25] He knew that our widespread worship of cash, which brands every poor person a failure, makes mock of the kingdom, so he said, "Blest are those of a lowly heart."[26] In our time many a humanist has tried to stem the dehumanizing flood, while many a church has kept a safe pietistic silence.

IV

But of course, the preacher should address also our loneliness, the more because the massisms of our time have made the individual all the more lonely. We must quit kidding ourselves that if enough people are "converted" (from what, to what?), they will set redeemed hands on our twisted society and straighten it. It hasn't happened, and won't happen. People who come down the sawdust trail are among the last to make a brave social witness. Yet each of us lives half his life in an incorrigible loneliness. When Linus asks, bragging about his library card, yet confessing that he was afraid to use it (the library was "too high and cold," and the librarian has such "round, silent eyes"), Charlie Brown comforts him, saying that every person has some place where he feels lonely. Linus asks, "What's your place?" Charlie answers, "Earth." Our finite bounds, even if we are not guilty of playing our own lonely god, betray the fact that our mortal days are torn away from perfection. The loneliest place is therefore "Earth." The social activists easily forget the loneliness of the person next door.

Now we ask importantly how a person knows his personhood. *Not by the body*. The body is both ally and foe inasmuch as it makes each of us individual; foe because it links us with the "beasts that die." *Not by the mind*, whatever the university may believe, for mind can flow into mind for curse or blessing, and mind can succumb to rationalizing. Then how? *By the confrontation of the Presence*. Each of us looks into the mirror and hears a voice asking not "Who am I?," but, "Who are you?" By that voice

---

25. John 13:34 (NEB).
26. Matt 5:8 (GAB), "Blessed are the pure in heart" (RSV).

each person knows that he is mortal, sinful, and short in wisdom. How else? By that voice she knows that here she has "no abiding city." Personhood is realized by faith when we stand before Christ. The Gospels are instinct with the wonder. Even the broken worship of a broken church thus grants a certain peace, especially if the preacher has conscientiously prepared both prayers and sermon. Each of us is named and claimed. Each is gathered home despite "the time disconsolate."[27]

Note this emphasis on the word and work of Christ. He was not silent regarding social ills, but always the cry of individual need stopped him in his tracks. Thus, the centurion whose slave was critically sick, the woman with an issue of blood, the blind man shouting above the clamor of the crowd, the paralytic "lying on a bed," and the little child whom he "set in the midst." His social concern led directly into his love for every person. The word *one* was ever on his lips: *one* lost coin, *one* lost sheep, "*one* of these little *ones*." He was "moved with compassion both for the flock and for each sheep." This instant concern for the individual would stagger our imagination if we had not been anesthetized by scientism and mass pressures. He went out of his way for *one* hated tax gatherer, *one* leper, *one* thief on the cross. The Holy Spirit brings to life every such word, so that at last each of us can say, "He loved *me*, and gave himself for *me*." Individual love and social concern go hand in hand. None has yet succeeded in splitting a paradox. True preaching honors both terms. How long before the church learns that truth?

We are not a fiction because the real has confronted us. It is not true that "we have no importance to love," for we are singled out by God in Christ. "*Who* are you?" Each of us is the child of the Most High God, loved into life by God's love. "*Why* are you?" Each of us is born to respond to God's love by the direct line of prayer and worship, and on an indirect line by trying to love all God's other children as all of us and each of us

---

27. From Henry Wadsworth Longfellow's poem, "On Translating the Divina Commedia (Part I)," published in the December 1864 issue of *The Atlantic*. "So, as I enter here from day to day, And leave my burden at this minster-gate, Kneeling in prayer, and not ashamed to pray, The tumult of the time disconsolate To inarticulate murmurs dies away, While the eternal ages watch and wait."

have first been loved in Christ. This is our true vocation. We are identified all the more as persons as we try to fulfill it.

Abraham Lincoln said that God must love the common people because God made so many of them. We are grateful for that word. But there is need for a comment that Lincoln himself would have endorsed: God has made no common people. Everybody has their own fingerprint, their own unique gift, their own special presence. That distinctive grace is now under threat from the massisms and mechanized pressures of our time. The pulpit must defend each person's distinctive birthright. The *incarnation* of Christ is for everyone, for God's self-disclosure is not through a "universal man" (a horrible notion), but through "the person Christ Jesus." *The cross* is for every separate person: "God so loved the world that whosoever..."[28] *Easter* is for each person, even for Peter who betrayed his Lord, for he was arrested and specifically commissioned, "Feed my sheep." *The Holy Spirit* is for each person, for now Christ's challenge and pleading are not by outward voice and flesh but within the personalized secrecies of each lonely life. Yet the paradox of human nature is still honored in both its terms: we are one flock, while each sheep is called by name. Each of us is commissioned (a task that further ratifies our self-identity), but we are bound together in love.

V

This book concerns preaching. It is not primarily concerned with the church. But the church is the home of preaching, and

> Home is the place where, when you have to go there,
> They have to take you in.[29]

Say, rather, "they *want* to take you in"! Is the present church such a home? Is the person there welcomed who has been bruised by our impersonal world, or who has bruised himself? Would the town prostitute be welcomed? Or the black person or the brown person with the white

---

28. John 3:16 (KJV).
29. From "The Death of the Hired Man" by Robert Frost.

person, each being persons? The local church sometimes contradicts the Gospel being preached from its pulpit! There is a place for mass evangelism. Pentecost is an instance: there we see the power of the Spirit to override and overrule our barriers of nation and race. As for revivalism in our time, who knows? It may have to lie fallow just because it is "mass" in a world bedeviled by massisms. Small groups where each person is known and loved may now be an obligated strategy. The "house churches" give each member the chance to say, "I belong."

Likewise, this book is not focally concerned with pastoral fidelity, but with preaching. The preacher is also pastor, and his preaching is crippled unless as Christ's undershepherd he calls (and calls on) the sheep by name. The doctor now eliminates house calls. He chooses to be scientist rather than friend. Should we add that the new method multiplies his income? His is the richest profession. The church through pastors and lay folk cannot eschew house calls. By mood and manner, not by pious speech, each church member says to each church member, "You are singled out by God's love in Christ." The right kind of psychiatry is gain because its whole method is concerned with each of us as individuals, so that each is "accepted." But psychiatry has no word to speak either about unmendable wrongdoing or about final death. We must ask also why Park Avenue in New York, the avenue of the rich, is the mecca of psychiatrists. Only the Gospel asks the ultimate questions: "Who are you? Why are you?" Only the Gospel answers them. "But, Doc, I don't know who I am." Only God knows. God has come in Christ that we may know that he knows—and loves each of us.

CHAPTER FIFTEEN

Preaching to a Revolutionary Age (I): The Background of the Task

In the midst of revolution and disruption, preaching cannot be content to hold the line, still less to become a coward's refuge. When all things change, the pulpit cannot remain unchanged. It cannot peddle any "old time religion" unless it has a new pertinence. Preaching must be the Evangel, but of today and addressed to the contemporary dilemma. It can be a cloud by day and a fire by night for a generation that has already broken camp and is on trek toward it knows not what.

Can anyone doubt that ours is a revolutionary time? The New Testament has two words for time. One is *chronos*: clock time, the passing of the years, the duration of dynasties; the other is *kairos*, the time of crisis, the pivot on which all life turns in a new direction. Surely our time is a *kairos* time. *Science* now confesses the erosion of its "laws." *Philosophy* tries this and that new gambit. *Economics* may or may not like the Russian Revolution, but must travel in the sight of it for years to come. *Law* is deeply troubled; the claims of people now threaten the ancient rule of property. *Technology* is driving us to the use of creative leisure. The absolutes of *ethic* are under attack by the new situational ethic—if it is new. *Education* is conducting an "agonizing reappraisal" of its goals; on this original manuscript I wrote "gaols" by mistake: that may have been a Freudian slip.

Chapter Fifteen

Sociology confronts the problem of urban poverty and the worse problem of wealth. *Politics* must soon disown its tired, cruel slogans—"A strong army is the best defense of peace"—for now a tinpot tyrant may toggle an atomic bomb, and there is no sure defense against rocket missiles, science having washed its hands of the misuse of the new physical forces which science has given to our hands.

How can the church and its preaching remain unchanged in such a time? A cartoon showed certain Victorian gentlemen with their silk hats and frock coats, floating in the sky, using Victorian umbrellas as parachutes. An angel asked, "Why are you here?" They answered, "Somehow the earth just rolled on and left us." There is no such sky for the preacher. We cannot go back home. The preacher is on our rolling planet! She cannot stop the planet and get off. The journey invites the brave, amid the screaming of a baffled rearguard. For the advance guard the view is clouded by our human dust, but we cannot stop: we are on pilgrimage. The church is bedeviled on the right by money-rich reactionaries who withdraw their subscriptions if the preacher does not keep silence about their vested interests; they starve her out, though a worthy person would not starve even a dog. The church is bedeviled on the left by the contempt of social rebels. In the middle it is being torn apart by acute-minded friends. Then what of the person in the pulpit? She cannot offer safe answers to questions nobody is asking, or mouth platitudes that never hurt or helped anybody, or encourage individuals to try to hide in an impossible individualism, or in any other way prove the damning phrase "as dull as a sermon."

I

Then what of the message of the preacher? It is timeless in the sense that God is God, and in the sense that Christ is the eternal Christ. But it is not like a granite block of doctrine on which the weather beats in vain. It is not a gravestone, which morticians and their sculptors assure us is "everlasting." It is timeless in the sense that God in God's mystery and in God's recurrent disclosures is the only life, beckoning and thwarting our timebound life that is separated from and joined with God's life by the strange gift of our freedom. The message of the preacher is *timely* as well as timeless. As the onset of the world changes, preaching speaks the one Gospel with changing accent. In the first century the apostle James could proclaim a Gospel set in Judaism. But what was the apostle Paul to say as the faith leapt like a flame from city to city in the ancient Near East? His preaching could no longer carry a Judaistic accent; the milieu now was Gentile. The change was revolutionary, for it stripped the infant church of its protection under the Pax Romana, and thrust it into danger and persecution. The episode is a paradigm of what must happen to the church in any age. Our faith is not a set of principles, for that could conceivably remain unchanged; nor is it an inviolable code of laws. It is a history, a community, a person, and a presence. The ark of the Presence is sometimes at rest, the mystery dwelling in the midst of the huddled tents of God's chosen yet often faithless people; but sometimes the ark moves into the desert and beyond the desert, keeping its own mysterious distance ahead lest those who follow shall lose all reverence for life. Our age is on the move. Whither bound? Such a time reveals new wonders in the faith, so that we say, "This is for our time! Strange I never saw it before!"

Then the message of the preacher now is—what? The same message since the year when Christ tore the calendar in two—yet spoken in new speech by a new preacher to a new time. Who can tell that "old, old story," which is never old, as it is woven into a history which is always breaking into new colors? The joy of it silences speech, yet a preacher must speak. This is the word: the mystery from whom we come, to whom we go, to whom all our questions and answers must tend, has come to our planet in our flesh! The very God in Christ has exposed himself to the whips and scorns of our strange life. He has tasted death for us (and what a death!), and was raised from the dead. His resurrection has opened a door for us in the blank wall of our death, and his cross has gathered into his mercy all the poisoned arrows of our hates and greeds, and drawn all their sting. Our way of saying it is always an anticlimax: worse than flatfooted. Of course, for how can a person describe supernal glory stooping to our bedraggled need? Browning tried, his mind and poem studded with exclamation points:

Chapter Fifteen

> The very God! Think Abib; dost thou think?
> So, the All-Great, were the All-Loving too—
> So, through the thunder comes a human voice
> Saying, "O heart I made, a heart beats here!
> Face, my hands fashioned, see it in myself!
> Thou hast no power nor mayst conceive of mine,
> But love I have thee, with myself to love,
> And thou must love me who have died for thee!"[1]

The message is the same in that it is rooted in the scriptures. No, not in any fixed literalism. The proposal that Bible writers spoke out exactly what God spoke in, and that therefore we have a Victrola record[2] engraved in print instead of plastic, could not be a guarantee of inspiration; that would be mechanization. A person so used would no longer be a person but a thing; and God so using and degrading such a person would no longer be God. Besides, the whole theory is blasphemy against the Holy Ghost, for it leaves the Spirit with no work to do, and charges the Spirit with being a dead letter. The blasphemy threatens to make the scriptures a dead letter! The matrix of inspiration is a history, a community, and a person, not a theory or a concept. God chose an outcast tribe, not for its privilege or praise, but that it might make known God's mighty acts: emphasis on the word *acts*, on history. That tribe was thus to be the servant of all nations. These acts—such is biblical faith—are the core and interpretation of all history. Are they not "mighty" in the Old Testament through pioneer, lawgiver, and prophet? Do they not find fulfilment in the New Testament, the community now channeled in a person?

So preaching in any age is from the book in which history and gospel are one, and the home of preaching is the church, whose life is the continuance of "sacred history." This claim for scripture is not an "asinine exclusiveness," whatever our pluralistic age may believe, for the present Spirit of Christ plays upon biblical trust so that it springs to life in our time,

---

1. Robert Browning, "An Epistle Containing the Strange Medical Experience of Karshish, the Arab Physician," *The Complete Poetical Works of Browning*, Cambridge edition (Boston: Houghton, Mifflin & Co., 1895), 340–41.

2. A vinyl record played on a brand-label Victrola phonograph (record player) made by the Victor Talking Machine Company of Camden, NJ.

startlingly, as though written for tomorrow. This claim for the church is not a "ridiculous pride," even though the church on the corner may seem a dull joke with no hooks into the realities of our time. For the church is no sinecure; the word of the prophet may once more condemn it: "The day of the Lord shall be darkness and not light";[3] and any church person may forget that the task of the "new Israel" is precisely that of the old Israel, namely, to make known God's purpose as shown in God's mighty acts (acting in the great acts of Christ), so that any church person, far from being the favored child of privilege, may the more quickly be cast into outer darkness. So the answer to the questions about preaching in our time are found in the book, where this story and that verdict spring into fierce fire in our darkness, for its pages are inspired—breathed into of Christ; and the light from the consuming fire will be shed abroad from the church, which is now the body of Christ, yes, still his, despite its saccharine speech and its timid silences, for Christ still stoops to incarnation in our broken flesh. Yes, there are books God uses beyond the book, especially when God's own people are blind to *the* book; and there are prophets of God beyond the church, especially when the church has lost both courage and understanding. Yet even failure points back to the book as the wellspring, and to the church as God's commissioned people.

It should be said that reading the Bible in church is no trip through a flower garden to a gourmet's restaurant. The book is "star fire and immortal tears."[4] It is judgment and mercy. We listen—in church, the pilgrimage of sacred history, and if we listen well the word we hear is inspired: breathed into of Christ. Such listening is the crux of any time. For we ask, "What does this mean?" and are thus drawn into Bible study. Then we ask, "What does this mean to me?" and are thus brought to confrontation. Then we ask, "What does this mean amid the events and decisions of our culture?" and we are thus saved from easy pietisms. Then we ask, worshipping in the home of faith, "What now must I *do* tomorrow?"

---

3. Amos 5:20 (GAB).

4. Thomas Carlyle, *The Life of John Sterling* (London: Chapman and Hall, 1851), 334. Carlyle recalled his years-long close friend, Sterling, from whom he had received a final poem: "And four days before his death, there are some stanzas of verse for me, written as if in starfire and immortal tears; which are among my sacred possessions, to be kept for myself alone."

Chapter Fifteen

Then the prayers, coming from the tension induced by such questions, will be real, a confession both of helplessness and resolve. Thousands of people come to church determined to keep their prejudice. If the preacher cuts across it, the local banker fears that the preacher is "not safe." But when was the banker's world synonymous with the kingdom? Yet even the dullest of us, even the most stubborn, entrenched in our unexamined selfishness, are not totally closed to the book, for the book is inspired; our little iron curtains cannot stop its secret invasions. Thus the scriptures may "get through," whatever the preacher may say or fail to say. Preaching in any age is from the book and from within the church. Chapters in this book will have asked what kind of preaching meets the specific hungers of our time, and later paragraphs of this chapter will ask about the marks of preaching in a revolutionary age.

II

Meanwhile we must inquire about the language of today's preaching. It cannot be slangy language. Some prayers and sermons were written in the beatnik language, and they had their place—for the beat movement.[5] The comfort concerning "mod" dress and "mod" jargon was that they are a present fashion, and that fashions pass. The New Testament is written in colloquial Greek, not in classic or literary Greek, but *koine* or vernacular Greek is not slang: it is the common speech of that time. That fact is wonderful, for literary Greek is only for the literary, whereas the word of Christ ("the common people heard him gladly"[6]) is for all of us. At Harvard during my tenure there was a strong professorial preference for the cadences and style of the King James Version, because that version pleased Harvard literati. Nevertheless, the New Testament was written in idiomatic Greek because God is more pleased with the language of Boston Common. But the staunchness of common speech is not "way-out" speech or jargon.

---

5. The beat movement consisted of American writers and musicians in the 1950s and 1960s who protested the flaws in postwar American culture.

6. Mark 12:37 (KJV).

Preaching to a Revolutionary Age (I): The Background of the Task

Preaching now must forswear all pietistic speech, for the reason that our age laughs at it when it does not despise it. Such phrases as "whereunto we are born," or even "unto Thee" belong to a store for antiques. What is wrong with "to Thee" instead of "unto Thee"? Increasingly our time addresses God as "You" or even "you." What verdict shall we reach? Human life insists on being awkward especially in this respect: we never succeed in gathering all the advantages of a course of action in one corral, while driving all the disadvantages into the wilderness there to die like the ancient scapegoat. The advantage of "You" is its rightful intimacy, since God has walked our streets in Christ; its disadvantage is that it savors of irreverence as again and again we confront God's transcendent mystery. The advantage of "Thee" is that it honors the mystery, and uses one pronoun for humans and another for God (since humans are not God); its disadvantage is that "Thee" has a "holy tone" and seems archaic. The other day I took part in John Wesley's liturgy for the service of the sacrament. It was not hard to guess the power of the rubric for his day, but in our day the words seemed "old world." Their cutting edge was blunted by time. Each preacher must now make her choice, and cleave to it or change camps as coming history may confirm or condemn her. But the "holy tone" is taboo in any event. A stained-glass voice is a comic pride. Why should anyone listen to it?

Emotional speech, with the tremolo stop pulled all the way out, is suspect, so suspect that the celestial police may make the arrest and lay charges, yes, and require bond. Our time thinks that such whipped-up emotionalism is phony: the ropes and pulleys are no longer backstage but in plain view. Those who gladly listen to this tickling of the emotions are not listening; they are indulging an emotional orgy, as in many a revival meeting. True emotion has its place: it gathers fire in honest preaching, but even then the commissioned preacher will hold it in control, for her appeal is to the glad and obedient will. The wrong in contrived emotion is that it is a subtle form of coercion; and no preaching should be coercive. For pulpit coercion is conceited (the preacher does not necessarily know better than the hearer), and tyrannical (for the preacher is trying to usurp the freedom of decision from the congregation), and silly (for few people

Chapter Fifteen

accept "good advice"). So pulpit language is neither an ultimatum from Olympus nor a sea of molasses.

What is diction for today's pulpit? Anglo-Saxon words in their simplicity are better than words with Greek and Latin roots. A few adjectives, each in its own power, are better than many; and the same rule holds for adverbs, for these two parts of speech easily become decoration. No fulsome pulpit oratory can improve "His will is our peace."[7] Diction that arrests us or heals does not engage unusual words: it is the unusual linking of usual words, as when Shakespeare says, "Parting is such sweet sorrow," or when Drinkwater tells us that though he does not think "that trees have wisdom in their windless silences,"[8] he still envies them. Pulpit language need not enlist dull clichés, such as, "All those with whom we come in contact." The preacher's lingo should not call attention to itself, but it need not lie down and die in trite phrases. It should pierce, as in the child's question, "How would they do a war if nobody came?";[9] or it should bless like a quiet sunrise: "The only sorrow is not to be a saint." The defective preacher wrestles with words. Serviceable or moving speech comes only from prior silence.

Language is not a side issue in the preacher's task, any more than a person's flesh and bones are a side issue in being human. In the Old Testament a curse or a blessing was believed to be so potent that it was like a spear thrust, the spear tipped with either poison or healing. The speech of a prayer prevailed even in the hidden realm of God's intention: "Take with you words and come before the Lord."[10] In the Gospels, Christ's warning regarding words stops us, not least in our present world, which is under a vast featherbed of words: "By your words you shall be justified, and by your words you shall be condemned."[11] How can we escape that

---

7. *The Divine Comedy of Dante Alighieri, Paradise*, Canto III (New York: P. F. Collier & Son Co., 1909), 297, in which "tranquillity" is the equivalent of "peace" in Buttrick's quoted English translation.

8. John Drinkwater, "Reciprocity," *Poems 1908–1919* (New York: Houghton Mifflin Co., 1919), 1.

9. A child once posed this question to Buttrick. He said it remained on his mind for days.

10. Hos 14:2 (GAB).

11. Matt 12:37 (GAB) "shall be"; (RSV) "will be."

judgment? Thousands of people every day "give a talk," and that is about all they can give. "That was a good talk, Reverend"; such a verdict is the preacher's death warrant: the preacher had tickled the ears, but maybe that morning nobody heard the word of God. "As for every word that a man shall speak, it shall be required of him at the judgment."[12] Idle words are words that do no work. Sermons are rife with idle words, and the eyes of Christ are on them. "Now you are clean," he said, "through the word I have spoken to you."[13] He meant the word of his lips as well as the word of his life. Words are of all means of communication the most flexible, the most moving, and the most instant in power.

Preaching to a revolutionary time cannot traffic in outworn phrases and pious clichés. The preacher stands on the boundary line between the church and an alienated world. She faces the world. She speaks in the idiom of the world. Yet not as the lying advertiser speaks, even though the advertiser seems to have stolen all the adjectives—to prostitute them to commercial clutching. Verbs and nouns are more moving than adjectives and, in any event, an alleged automobile "rebellion" is not much like a rebellion: it is more like a shrewd calculation of status in the middle class. Pulpit language must now be straightforward and clear, depending more on the rhythms of a sincere love for persons—in Christ—than on tricky or sensational words. So the preacher stands on that boundary line using the world's worthy idiom, and making it pulse with the Gospel (a speech that therefore will deal in quiet intensity rather than in noise and tumult), yet never forgetting that the dear canonical language is just behind the preacher's back. Pulpit language is thus a kind of dialogue between the idiom of the present world and the always-validated phrases of scripture. The following is a transcript of an actual conversation after a church service on Palm Sunday:

Theological professor: "You were preaching about the atonement?"

Preacher: "Yes, of course. What else?"

Theological professor: "But you used no theological terms?"

---

12. Matt 12:37 (GAB).
13. John 15:3 (GAB).

Chapter Fifteen

Preacher: "No, why should I? This is a college chapel. Students nowadays don't understand our language, and couldn't care less. But neither you nor they missed the theme."

To speak in the other person's tongue while keeping troth with the unshaken verities of the book is no easy task, but it may not honorably be dodged. It is an exercise in "hard love."

III

But who is equal to such a ministry? No one. Yet God is equal to the task of using our broken attempts for God's purpose: the apostle Paul by his own knowledge and consent was a man of poor appearance and clumsy speech, but his half-impromptu letters are now New Testament scripture. Two roads lead to a preacher's strength. One is pastoral fidelity. If a preacher really enters into people's joys and sorrows, she learns their language. Sometimes their speech commits mayhem on grammar, and at other times it is lurid with damns, but, even then, the preacher can issue her own "revised standard version" and keep the original color and vitality. Psychiatry brings healing, and thus wins our gratitude, but it is no substitute for perceptive pastoral care. Psychiatry can sometimes overcome psychotic guilt, but what of real guilt? It can help meet frustration, but what of the final frustration of death? The pastor and the psychiatrist are meant for each other's help. In any event a preacher learns the rightful speech of her time by compassionate involvement in its life.

The other road to effectiveness is creative silence and spoken prayer. We begin to understand in some small measure the deeps whence creativeness (genuine discovery) is born. Discipline is required, which, for the preacher, is the discipline of Bible study and the literature of contemporary life, plus those great books, which are always contemporary. But we now know that discipline is not enough: there must be other interests and the practice of silence. If a scientist is only a scientist, she may work sixteen hours a day, but she will make no discovery, perhaps least of all in science. Einstein had his cello and his loneliness, not without friendships, as well as his devotion to physics: otherwise he could not have found his way to the principle of relativity. What happens—it is still a mystery—is that the major interest in its interplay with the minor interests (which are not minor in importance) sends up sparks from the friction—provided the silence. Thus discovery. To state it otherwise: the silence gives the subconscious a chance to work in the interplay between different devotions, this or that "interest" being a conscious labor while the other "interests" are "below the threshold." This discovery is always on the boundary line in a traffic between the energies of the conscious mind and those of the subconscious mind.

How shall the preacher in our strange time find her themes? In discipline of study focused in the Bible. Not in that alone, but that plus her pastoral concern plus her involvement in the life of her world. Yet there is another plus: silence and prayer. That same unseen traffic will yield her also the new word for a new time. The sudden sentence will flash out, overleaping all the careful steps of ordered thought. That sentence will pierce the conventional mind, and even the armor of greedy prejudice. Prosy folk will then ask the preacher to "prove it" or to "tell what you mean," but the prosiness is too late: the spear of God has found its mark. In our glut of words, so safe, so drab, so grasping, who shall save us from the flood, unless there is a word from silence? Christ's silence constrained people to say that "he speaks with authority." One woman knew that he had read her secret heart: "See a man who told me all things that ever I did."[14]

---

14. John 4:29 (GAB).

CHAPTER SIXTEEN

Preaching to a Revolutionary Age (II): The Road and the Message

What does the preacher say in the confusion of a changing world? Some years ago he feared faithlessly that his function had been overwhelmed by a flood of publicity, but that fear proved false. *Radio* is no substitute for the brave word of Christ: it is advertising, much of it mendacious, with incidental music. *Television* is no substitute: with rare exceptions it is neither art nor truth; advertising stole our eyes as well as our ears, with programs calculated to offend nobody and to distract everybody, a mass of trivia for trivial minds. *Journalism* is no substitute: there are fine journals but they are exceptions, for most news outlets travel on an ellipse with two foci, sensation and conflict, which bedevil the public mind rather than inform it. Why should the preacher fear? There are healthy voices in school and college; they win our gratitude, but they are hobbled by a required silence in matters of faith, and by devotion to an idol called "Learning," an idol that is better than an idol only as it worships the creative mystery. Maybe the preacher is or could be, the only free person—at risk.

Yet the Gospel and the Bible are a "thing incredible" in our time. Maybe preaching will seem an impertinence unless groups in every church restudy the book. The Bible said long, long ago that God is not an indulgent Grandfather "up there"; there is nothing new in the protestations of constructive theology that we make God in our own image, for that warning is central in the scriptures. The book *Honest to God*[1] led some of us to ask, "Why all the shooting?" The Bible has its own audacious *doctrine of human nature*, which laughs at both Sartre's histrionic pessimism and chamber-of-commerce optimism. It has its own *doctrine of history*, which finds little in common with either Spengler's cyclicism or Darwin's evolution.[2] It has its own *doctrine of truth*, which looks for final hope to neither the concepts of philosophy nor to the alleged "laws" of science. It has its own *doctrine of death*—as a new and crucial birth, not as the mere stopping of a physical organism. All this has a strange "sound" in our time. Yet the preacher must speak his word. If it is "true" in the Bible sense of the term it will prevail. The chaos of our gods falling on one another and on themselves with destroying and suicidal swords, are themselves, in terrible reversion, tribute to the truth of the faith. Then what is the message from the pulpit?

The Gospel is itself revolutionary! There is no need to give it that character! It is a revolution in its very nature. Yes, there has perhaps been an alternation in the history of the faith, a systole and a diastole, as when a priestly era of law and liturgy in the Old Testament was succeeded by the thunder and lightning of the prophets. But that fact only underscores our contention. William Blake portrays Christ as

> Tiger, tiger, burning bright
> In the forests of the night[3]

but long before Blake the Bible portrayed God as an eagle deliberately tearing apart the human nest that the young human race might learn to

---

1. John H. T. Robinson, *Honest to God* (Philadelphia: Westminster Press, 1963). For over a decade Buttrick corresponded with Bishop Robinson, who was a guest in the Buttrick home.

2. Jean Paul Sartre (1905–1980), French existentialist philosopher; Oswald Spengler (1880–1936), German historian; Charles Darwin (1809–1882), English naturalist, biologist, and evolutionary scientist.

3. William Blake, "The Tiger," *The Oxford Book of English Verse: 1250–1900*, ed. Arthur Quiller-Couch (Oxford: Clarendon Press, 1912), 562–63.

fly,[4] not waddle round a silly farmyard of comfort and convention. Ours is not a priestly time. The nest is being torn. The early followers of Christ were slow to realize the deeps of his person, mostly because they were blinded by an accepted nationalistic doctrine of messiahship (as we are!), but at least they knew he was more than a priest. Yes, he was later understood rightly to be "a great High Priest," but their early guess was not on the wrong road: he was at least "one of the prophets."

Open the Gospels almost at random: you will find the revolution. There are lay councils here and there in the wider church who are "alarmed" at what they call "revolutionary tendencies" in the pulpit. They claim that Jesus "taught spiritual truths to individuals," whatever that unbelievable phrase may mean, and that he was not concerned with "wider issues." These people have not read the Gospels, or, if they have, they were wearing blindfolds. For Christ broke with the tradition of the ancient Torah: he, himself a layperson, dared to say, "You heard that it was said to those of ancient times but I say to you . . ."![5] He broke with the puritanism of the Pharisees, for that item can be read between the lines of the parable of the prodigals: one prodigal left home and went the pace; the other prodigal stayed home as a church person in self-righteousness. He broke with nationalism again and again, as for instance in the parable of the good Samaritan: the Jews almost hated the Samaritans, as some people now almost hate people of color. He broke with bibliolatry, for he countered the Sadducees who insisted that the Pentateuch should be accepted word by word, who therefore did not believe in any resurrection, and who downgraded the prophets. He broke with the whole cult of wealth, status, and prestige, saying to his followers, "It shall not be so among you."[6] He broke with the violence of the Zealots, who thought they could overcome the Roman Empire with a few fanatic swords, and told them they were inviting a slaughterhouse. He broke with the trade that pushed its booths into the precincts of the temple. He broke with the temple itself. All that

---

4. Deut 32:11: "Like an eagle that stirs up its nest, that flutters over its young, spreading out its wings, catching them, bearing them on its pinions" (RSV).

5. Matt 5:21-22 (NRSV). Buttrick had quoted the RSV, "You have heard that it was said to the men of old."

6. Matt 20:26 (KJV).

Chapter Sixteen

Christ opposed is still with us in hardly different form. What shall the preacher do? He must fling down the gage of Christ's revolution at the feet of a blind and tyrannical age. That is precisely what Christ did—as in the Beatitudes.

II

Therefore, the preacher today must preach to the whole person. A person is not merely individual, despite the reiterated plea of the wealthy who try to muzzle preachers. Every person is individual-social. A person cannot be a person except in the give and take of community, and cannot well serve the community except in terms of unique personhood. Everyone needs the community, as in a symphony orchestra, both to fulfill one's nature and to serve one's generation; and the community needs each person's individual gift. Christ spoke both to the individual and to the community. He warned his nation against betraying its responsibility under God, and said flatly that they were like a tree with luxurious leaf, and no fruit. He challenged neighboring rulers and the Roman governor, and therefore the empire crucified him. As for sexual liberation, he never condoned sexual infidelity either in the married or the unmarried, but made it clear that there were other sins that may be darker in the eyes of God, for instance, the hate of those who wished to stone the adulteress, and the sheer unconcern of those who strode over the beggar at their doorstep. How can anyone in right mind describe Jesus as a "teacher of spiritual truths to individuals"? He was not a "holy man" peddling platitudes to hermits! He was involved in the life of his time. Someone says that the preacher is not Jesus. True, and more than true. But the preacher can hardly take a road alien from that of his Lord.

Yet there is of course another side to this whole issue, a more important side, since the social term of our nature, though it is always "there," is the extension of our lonely self. The preacher's primary word *is* to the individual, and this of necessity. For human nature is a third kind of paradox: each of us is in time, yet always above time. This stance above time, as when the Bible says, "My days are swifter than a weaver's shuttle,"[7]

---

7. Job 7:6 (RSV).

is the locale both of our freedom and of our real creativeness. Only the individual has this selftranscendence; the crowd has little power to view its own life, and is too volatile and too easily swept by crowd passions to fulfill that role. The trouble with preachers who limit themselves to what is called the "social gospel" is their blindness to the other dimension of our life. Pain is often a starkly lonely affair. So is agony of mind. So is the business of viewing our pilgrimage while we go down the road. So is death itself, for at death each person is starkly the individual. This factor can suggest the manner of our preaching to the whole person. Let us try to mark off the "steps."

III

First, it cleaves to the Gospel. The preacher has little right to proclaim his own "slant" either in economics or politics. Suppose he believes in cooperatives rather than in our usually accepted "capitalism," he still should not be a protagonist of any "system." Recently I visited a Shaker fort where in other days a group of persons had all things in common, until the treasurer took flight down the Mississippi River with all the cash. That is to say, all systems will pass away, and each is vulnerable to human pride. A certain broadminded professor left his church and took training to join another church, simply because he got tired of sermons that offered a series of desultory and highly individual comments on each week's newspaper headlines. Yes, the preacher cannot ignore the social and the body dimension of our strange life on earth, but what he says should always be from a double devotion: it should return God's love directly as a witness to God's gift in Christ, and it should return it indirectly in love for people because God has first loved us. Therefore, it cannot proclaim any "isms." Thus, the preacher can oppose the war system, but only because war cannot be reconciled either with love for God or love for neighbor.

Next, real preaching begins with the individual, though remembering that the individual is set in the community of the church and in the wider fellowship of humankind. For creativity has its fountainhead in the power of the individual to view both one's own life and the life of the world, and because a new way in an ever-new world begins with the courage of one person. The brutality of the old gladiatorial show was challenged, and the misgiving of the crowd was aroused when one man thrust his body between the gladiator and his intended victim. The Christian faith began in one person! Yes, it began in his lowliness from which he viewed both his own God-ordained mission and the human flock for whom he died as "the good Shepherd."

> Jesus walked this lonesome valley;
> He had to walk it by himself.
> Oh, nobody else could walk it for him.[8]

This was true of Jesus in the deeper dimension than the merely human, yet it is true for each of us on our level. The next stanza of that haunting simple song begins, "We must walk the lonesome valley," but it should have begun, "I must walk," and then, "you" (singular and plural) "must walk." So this preaching to the totality of human life must ask, "What does the present Christ require in his love that you and I should do and say?" Only thus can the "you" singular broaden into "you," the congregation.

Next, effective preaching does not get trapped on one Sunday in the social realm, and next Sunday in the individual realm. If the preacher says in effect, "Today I shall discuss unemployment in the light of our faith," and on the following Sunday, "Today I shall speak about private prayer," the congregation is condemned to an unreal oscillation. For unemployment is also an individual affair, especially for the person unemployed and for the one who is the next-door neighbor; and private prayer is never fully private, for it must include intercession for the person living in the nearby ghetto or press-ganged by our modern wars. If we say of Jesus, according to a much-sung hymn (too much sung!), "He told me that I am His own," and if we claim that such a word is his only word, we should suspect that the conversation is not with Jesus, but with the adversary, for Jesus is "the Man for others,"[9] not simply in my selfishness the "Man

---

8. African American spiritual, public domain.

9. Dietrich Bonhoeffer, *Letters and Papers from Prison*, ed. Eberhard Bethge (New York: Collier Books, Macmillan Publishing Co., 1972), 382.

for me." There is no such oscillation in our daily life: the two terms fuse. Social concern comes to focus in the individual constraint, and that leads out and on inevitably to the society without whom we could not live at all. Thus preaching must run like electricity between two poles. Even the illustrations must shuttle between two terms, which in their mutuality are one realm. The *individual stress* is seen in the story of the waif who, when someone asked him in unconscious sadism, "Why doesn't God give you some shoes?," answered, "God told somebody, but somebody forgot."[10] The *social stress* is in that word that Angela Morgan heard from the cross: "I cannot come down until all men take me down."[11] So, the proclamation unites both terms of the paradox that composes our human lot.

Next, such preaching will live in a patient persistence, with accent on both adjective and noun; and it should begin where people live. In many a northern church the preacher can say of civil rights, "You and I know that this strife of color is wrong, and that to suppose God is centrally busy with pigmentation of the skin is a form of blasphemy; our secret thoughts are much truer than our public lethargy." That word would be just as true in a Mississippi church, but there it might be more effective to say, "You and I know that life cannot be worthily lived in this festering bitterness, so what shall we do?" The preacher is like the old-time shepherd who went before the flock. If he strides off by himself, however badly, he betrays the flock; if he stays "put" because the flock has no wish to move, he again is a betrayer, not least because that strategy leaves the field bare and condemns the flock to starvation. So, the appeal of the preacher is not, "You blind sinners!" It is rather, "Wouldn't you deeply like to walk this new road? It leads through pain—to life in Christ."

---

10. "Somebody Forgets" (from the Philadelphia Public Ledger), *Friends' Intelligencer*, vol. 59, 1902, p. 780.
"If God really loves you, why doesn't He take better care of you? Why doesn't He tell somebody to send you a pair of shoes, or else coal enough so that you can keep warm this winter?"
"I dare say He does tell somebody, and somebody forgets."

11. Buttrick frequently quoted poetry from memory. It appears that his recollection here differed from the actual verse of Angela Morgan's "God Prays," *Forward March* (New York: John Lane Co., 1918), 96–99, if that was in fact the poem he thought he was quoting. The verse reads, God speaking, "Till the people rise, my arm is weak; I cannot speak till the people speak; When men are dumb, my voice is dumb—I cannot come till my people come" (96).

"Finally, brothers and sisters" (though many a needed stress is here left unspoken), preaching to the whole of human life, and especially preaching to a rightful social concern, is both oblique and direct. Jesus was sometimes direct, though only when indignation blazed forth from love. When wicked persons abused a child, the wrath of Jesus was a darting flame: "It were better for that man that a millstone were hanged about his neck, and he were drowned in the deeps of the sea!"[12] There were two millstones then, a small one worked by hand and another so large that a horse or mule would turn it. In that anger of Christ, he spoke of the big millstone! Thus in an Alabama city, when white "men" flogged Negro children to bar their way to an integrated school, one minister spoke precisely as Jesus spoke, though with confession of his own share in the public sin. The news account had it that many of the congregation knelt at the chancel rail confessing their sin. What of the other ministers in that town? What of those in that one church who sat still and frowned—on a preacher "meddling in politics"? We can only commend these blind and cowardly critics to a cleansing by fire, yes, hell fire. But often the preaching of Jesus was by the searching of the oblique approach. Thus, his *modern* story of the good Samaritan might tell us that first a minister and then a choir leader passed by the wounded man on the other side of the road, for the same reason as in the original account: that they did not wish to miss church, and were sure that such a wish must always justify them; but a black person, a travelling salesman who professed no creed, "took pity." As in the case of the original hearers, we would be caught in the dramatic story, and only then realize that the fatal spear (fatal to our sorry hates) had pierced us. When shall the preacher be direct, and when oblique? Prayer and the occasion must teach him.

IV

Now we return to the momentous issue of language. Linguistic analysis is not a final faith, for we cannot long discuss a person's speech without asking about the nature of the person; but neither is this analysis a temporary aberration, especially since the high priest of the movement, Ludwig

---

12. Matt 18:6 (GAB).

Preaching to a Revolutionary Age (II): The Road and the Message

Wittgenstein,[13] has torn down the inner rigid walls. So, we add two comments to those earlier made about pulpit speech. *This first: pulpit rhetoric is existential.* It is not argument, for no one was ever argued into power and peace; and, besides, nobody likes to be worsted in an argument; it is a poor exchange if we win an argument and lose a friend. Such preaching is not an attempt to prove that Christian faith is "reasonable," for it is not "reasonable": the New Testament says it is a "scandal." In any event, real proof lives at deeper levels than those of the rational mind. Preaching is closer to drama than to a syllogism. When in *The Death of a Salesman* his sons say after the father's suicide that he tried to get by "on a smile and a shoestring," and when his wife tells us that "he never knew who he was," we know what is meant—beyond any argument. In fact, we nod and silently answer, "Don't we all?" Existential speech strikes at our very existence. It is addressed to our very life, to the one whom William Barrett calls *Irrational Man*[14] because the strange dilemma of human days cannot be caught in any neatly tied net of science or metaphysic. When Shakespeare says that every star sings in the music of the spheres, "Still quiring to the young-eyed cherubins," we see a sudden cleft in the mysterious sky; and when he says further, "Such harmony is in immortal souls,"[15] we *know* the hurt of buried music in our needlessly humdrum hearts: in this sense pulpit language is existential.

This next: preaching is the language of dialogue. It does not tell people what to believe but shows them what they already believe. A "feedback" after the service has its merits, provided we know its dangers. Searching minds find opportunity in such a conversation, but pedantic minds turn it into argumentation so that its true authority and glow are drained away. But whatever the merits or demerits of the "feedback," a sermon can still be a dialogue. It's true language is not that of Jove thundering from Olympus: only the sinner can preach. It does not throw yesterday's language at today's congregation. It does not traffic in platitudes spoken at

---

13. Ludwig Wittgenstein (1889–1951), Austrian philosopher of mind, linguistic analysis, and mathematics who taught at the University of Cambridge.

14. William Barrett, *Irrational Man: A Study in Existential Philosophy* (Garden City, NY: Doubleday Anchor Books, 1958).

15. William Shakespeare, *The Merchant of Venice*, act 5, sc. 1, lines 62–63.

a safe distance from the change and crisis of our present world. It stands with the hearer: "You and I have *known* have we not?" Then the preacher might instance the story of the dead speaking to one another from their graves in that little hilltop cemetery in Thornton Wilder's *Our Town*.[16] They ask one another if their neighbors come to lay flowers and weep, and make their comment: "It's just as if they were shut up in little boxes." That spear thrust is tipped with life. No need to ask the congregation if they believe. The issue has now struck to much deeper ground than the congregation's "but," and some prosy preacher's prosy "proofs." Preaching is genuine dialogue: the preacher speaks "out loud," the congregation replies in an uncoerced silence.

V

We have not left or lost the Gospel. It is always Gospel, a realistic *gladness* even in our revolutionary time. The planet is "subject to futility," not of itself but of God's deliberate act. Such is New Testament faith. But there is no pessimism, for the frustration itself is the birth pangs of a new life. Thus the eschatological hope, which is not a saccharine "otherworldliness" but a travail leading to an undreamed-of dimension both of form and spirit, a dimension more wonderful than this life as this life is compared with prenatal life. So the Gospel is neither a timebound pessimism nor a timebound optimism but a two-dimensional realism. The Gospel is never fooled into thinking that our fields and cities can live on themselves. It knows that life comes not from the ground alone, but from the mysterious sky. The preacher never pretends that mortal life can make our world perfect, for how can perfection belong to a finite existence? It never sells out to the proud pretension of an "ideology": it is not given to humans to draft a political creed for all for the coming ages. The preacher bears a brave witness and lifts a bright banner above the ebb and flow of the years. Thus life becomes sacramental. It prints the pattern of the sky, now

---

16. Thornton Wilder, *Our Town: A Play in Three Acts* (New York: Coward McCann, 1938).

opened, in Christ, on the stuff of earth. Thus the earth becomes foretaste of an awaited joy.

The Gospel is the shining mark for a revolutionary time. Without it the revolution will be well named: it will simply revolve to bring back the old stagnation. Thus the Russian Revolution, which hoped to deliver people from peonage in daily work, brought only a new servitude in which mind is the child of matter, history is a civil war, and physical labor is the only wealth. But the Gospel does not sell out to any reductionism such as that of science, and least of all to some dusty materialism. It speaks to us in our loneliness and in our comradeships; it speaks to our body as a treasure, and to our psyche. A friend and colleague posted a cartoon on the outside of his office door, so that any person going down the corridor might see it. It showed two goldfish discussing their condition. One said, "There is nothing beyond our pool." The other answered, "Then who keeps changing the water?" One world only? Not when its human creatures can say, "Time is swift"! Not when unseen mountains bring rain to our little village of time and space! Not when that mystery has broken through the mystery of sky to walk our village street, there to bear our griefs and overcome our death! The revolution in our time will be but another rabble, yes, and a bloodletting, without Christ for guide.

CHAPTER SEVENTEEN

Preaching to an Age Under Judgment: The Cross

Most of us don't know that we're under judgment. Then what of the preacher who does know? The college question, "How can a gallows long ago and far away save me?" is rarely asked. It has become a yawn: "Who cares?" A few inveterate optimists still trot out the military lie: "The situation is well in hand": they still believe that our hands can compass any task (especially commercial), and our minds solve any problem (especially scientific). But their numbers shrink as misgivings invade our "peace of mind." Self-interest has not brought public good. So mistrust now spreads. But it has not brought penitence. We may have failed, but we're not wrongdoers. If we are, "Who cares?" The preacher confronts that apathy.

I

The preacher can't use the word *sin* very much: it has become a censor's word. As for forgiveness, it is unsought because it is hardly understood. George Bernard Shaw called it "a beggar's refuge." He said, "We must pay our debts."[1] He did not explain how a person pays if the neighbor one has

---

1. George Bernard Shaw, *Major Barbara* (Fairfield, IA: 1st World Library—Literary Society, 2004 [1907]), 144. "UNDERSHAFT: Come try your last weapon. Pity and love broken in your hand: forgiveness is still left. CUSINS: No. Forgiveness is a beggar's refuge. I am with you there: we must pay our debts."

duped is dead. Whitman almost laughed at sin; he would rather live with the animals: they do not wake in the night and whine about their transgressions. Neither do they rob a bank or betray other cows,[2] much less write poems about Whitman. But our age turns more quickly to Emerson and Whitman than to tales of tragic fate in Melville or the tracing of guilt in Hawthorne.[3] As for the word *sin*, the modern preacher had better buy a book of synonyms, for pulpit language, always vital, is now crucial.

The word *sin* is out because we half-believe we have no freedom, or because we would like to believe it. Scientism (not science) turns everything including us into an object, and an object by definition is not free. Robots commit no crime. If God is, God is either a tyrant or a has-been; if God is not, "Who cares?" Our "massisms," the government for example, sweep us along like straws on a stream. Straws do no wrong. It is doubtful if we have argued ourselves into the notion that we are not free, the fear (or veiled hope) comes of frustration. It is more doubtful if we really believe we are fleshly robots, for no robot could say, "I am only a robot," unless a human so manufactured "it." To say, "I am not free," implies freedom or at least a memory of freedom—and the hope of freedom regained. Whatever our train of thought, we shall reassume freedom when the train stops. This the preacher should say lest we sink into an unreal world. If science should deny freedom, science itself seals its own doom.

The word *sin* is taboo because we have learned about psychotic guilt, and now try under that discovery to disclaim real guilt. A preacher should acknowledge the fact of psychotic guilt, and in pastoral counseling watch for it. If an attractive mother encourages visitors to say of her daughter, "She'll never be as beautiful as her mother!" (see the play *Lady in the Dark*[4]), the child may rebel, assert herself, secretly feel that she ought not to hate her mother, try to make amends by self-punishment, or tread some other

---

2. Walt Whitman, "A Song of Myself," *Leaves of Grass* (New York: Doubleday, 1997 [1855]), 57ff. A paraphrase of "I think I could turn and live awhile with the animals. They do not sweat and whine about their condition, They do not lie awake in the dark and weep for their sins, They do not make me sick discussing their duty to God, Not one is dissatisfied."

3. The nineteenth-century Transcendentalist, Ralph Waldo Emerson, as well as Anti-Transcendentalists, Herman Melville and Nathaniel Hawthorne.

4. A 1941 musical play from the book by Moss Hart, music by Kurt Weill, lyrics by Ira Gershwin.

half-compulsive road. But, even so, we should not shortchange realism. It is hardly enough to say of a drug peddler outside a high school, "He may have an inferiority complex." When psychiatrists flock to Park Avenue, is money involved or are they all psychotic? In the drama *J. B.*,[5] Archibald MacLeish protests this easy psychiatric "out," and calls it "this defiling innocence." In the term *psychotic guilt*, psychotic is only adjective; guilt is still the noun.

Sin is an alien word for another reason: too many pulpits have given the word a holier-than-thou cast. The visiting evangelist's first sermon is on "The Sins of Homeville." They are theft, drink, foul speech, and sex. They are not war, racism, and suburban pride. The student was asked about his preacher, and answered, "I'm as good as he." Translation: "He condemns and I hate self-righteousness." This kind of sermon goes counter to the word of Christ: "Don't judge censoriously lest you be so judged." Preachers are so judged: pictured as persons with secret vices. In most instances this charge is caricature. But the distortion would not be popular, as in the play titled *Rain*,[6] if pulpit censoriousness had not invited it. Yes, the accusation vents the critic's spleen, but the preacher's fulminations start the exchange. If the word *sin* is used, the preacher should say that only a sinner can preach, for only a sinner can know God's grace. Maybe the word *sin* should lie fallow.

II

But though the word is disbarred, the fact remains. Truth doesn't change with changing words. Therefore, people still confess their sins. Nowadays the confession is often oblique: it blames the "system" or the neighbors. At the Nuremburg trials[7] the culprits pleaded that they threw

---

5. Archibald MacLeish, *J. B.* (New York: Houghton, Mifflin, Harcourt, 1956). Also, in *Best American Plays: 1957–1963*, ed. John Gassner (New York: Crown Publishers, 1963), 589–633. A Pulitzer prize–winning play about the biblical figure Job. Archibald MacLeish and George Buttrick were good friends during Buttrick's Harvard years.

6. A 1922 play by John Colton and Clemence Randolph, based upon the W. Somerset Maugham short story "Miss Thompson," later retitled *Rain* and made into three films and an opera.

7. The post–World War II international military tribunals that prosecuted officials of the Nazi regime for the Holocaust and war crimes.

Chapter Seventeen

Jews into ovens because of military orders. But the men who issued the orders could have given better orders, and those ordered could have disobeyed orders, for "we must obey God rather than any human authority."[8] If we try to excise the word *God*, we must still say, "we must refuse obedience to brutal depravity." Then God has returned, "the nameless of a thousand names." This blaming the system has its truth, for evil inheres in systems, and the ones who control the power of systems are usually corrupted by it—corrupted and made blind. But individual responsibility is not canceled. To declaim against the marriage system hardly absolves married people. If we trip over the sidewalk, we make little sense if we cry, "Away with feet and sidewalks!" So our often-justified anger over policies and practices, however justified, is yet the oblique confession of our guilt.

Sometimes confession is not oblique: it is direct and poignant even in our don't-care world. The sensitive preacher hears confessions, hopefully not to betray the confidence. She won't if she *is* sensitive. She may hear a widow say, "How shamefully I failed him, and now he's dead." The sensitive preacher will not then say, "Oh no, I'm sure you were always kind." No, she will say, "Don't we all?" She may hear a Viet veteran say, "I shall never blot that picture from my mind." A coed may say of some sex adventure, "It seemed so beautiful at the time." How shall our preacher answer? Not by condemning. Rather, say to the coed, "Maybe it was beautiful—in some ways." To the soldier, "Perhaps you have been spared to help erase such pictures from all history." The truly sensitive preacher knows that such counselees are the salt of the earth. Shaw's "we must pay our debts" is now revealed as shallow as it is brutal. But, then, Shaw was sometimes a gadfly though he could have been an eagle. Sin remains (by whatever name) as a prime fact, and pardon as a prime need.

Actually, when the preacher is silent about guilt and judgment, the person of letters climbs the pulpit. Some reader suggested to the author of *The Lord of the Flies*[9] that the naval vessel, finding the group of boys marooned on a far island, returned them "to the amenities of life," so that in their homeland their nasty violence was cured. The author demurred because the naval vessel was engaged in warfare not unlike the brutality

---

8. Acts 5:29 (NRSV).
9. William Golding, *The Lord of the Flies* (New York: Capricorn Books, 1954).

of the island gang. Then what was Golding writing about? Golding replied, "Original sin."[10] Albert Camus's *The Fall* is a modern version of the doctrine of the fall of humanity, though (unlike the New Testament) the book has no sunrise. Allen Tate is even more forthright: civilization is a facade to hide the abyss of evil, though again there is no hope.[11] Robert Penn Warren tells of a man discovering that his ancestor had hacked a black man to death: that crime was in his own blood! Then what of his inherited Jeffersonian faith? Again, there is no redemption, but this instead: "There's no forgiveness for our being human."[12] The poem speaks also of "the immitigable ferocity of self."[13] The revivalist holding his "crusade" in Homeville lives in a kindergarten world. He has hardly glimpsed the enormity, the ravening dread and devastation of evil in us—and mysteriously in the constitution of our mortal world. Sin is our foe, for there is treachery in every camp. The word *sin* is of doubtful worth, not least because it has become the tiny ploy of the revivalist in Homeville. But the *fact* is such a fell shadow that no human power alone can withstand it.

The Bible knows about psychotic guilt: "You fathers must not goad your children to resentment."[14] It knows that the prevailing culture can blind us,

---

10. It is not known what reader Buttrick was referring to when Golding responded with the words "original sin." In a publicity questionnaire for the book, Golding said, "The theme is an attempt to trace the defects of society to the defects of human nature. The moral is that the shape of a society must depend on the ethical nature of the individual and not on any political system however apparently logical or respectable. The whole book is symbolic in nature except the rescue in the end where adult life appears, dignified and capable, but in reality enmeshed in the same evil as the symbolic life of the children on the island. The officer, having interrupted a man-hunt, prepares to take the children off the island in a cruiser which will presently be hunting its enemy in the same implacable way. And who will rescue the adult and his cruiser?" (*The Lord of the Flies*, 189).

11. Allen Tate (1899–1979), southern American writer belonging to the literati called the Fugitives, which included John Crowe Ransom (1888–1974), Donald Davidson (1893–1963), and Robert Penn Warren (1905–1989), who published their works in the journal *The Fugitive* (1922–1925) at Vanderbilt University.

12. Robert Penn Warren, *Brother to Dragons: A Tale in Verse and Voices* (New York: Random House, 1953). Thomas Jefferson's nephew hacked to pieces the body of a slave and threw the pieces into the fire in front of other slaves. In the poem, Jefferson declares, "There is no forgiveness for our being human. It is the inexpungable error."

13. Warren, *Brother to Dragons*, 47.

14. Eph 6:4 (NEB).

for it says of the younger prodigal, "when he came to himself": when the grip of the mores was broken. It knows that evil can and does erupt from the subconscious, for it tells us that we fight not "flesh and blood" only, but hidden "principalities and powers." It knows our fear that evil may overwhelm us: "God keeps faith, and will not allow you to be tempted above your strength."[15] But it refuses to blink at the enormity of evil, and it refuses to yield the fact of human responsibility. We are guilty people, not defective robots. Then it redefines "sin," and gives us a new and startling scale of values. The woman taken in adultery was not thereby brought to sainthood, but those who proposed to stone her had the greater guilt.

What is this redefinition? The "Jesus freaks"[16] see only a small side of the human dilemma, for they are blind to our corrupted systems and to our dangerous call to grapple with them. The Age of Aquarius praises or blames the stars, so that persons become only marionets dancing on celestial strings. "Sin" is our refusal to obey God. If the name God is a blank or a blur, "sin" is the pride by which a person tries to be the center of a world, which that person never made. "Sin" is the bully on the world street. "Sin" is the money itch. "Sin" is the ambition that seeks front stage, center, spotlight. "Sin" is therefore treating our neighbor as if she didn't have a name: it is using her as a stepping stone to our prestige or stealing her birthright. To love God *only* leads on to a dead pietism; to love humanity *only* leads on to a landlocked humanism. So "sin" is the denial of love—love beyond, love within, love next door. So what shall the preacher say? The preacher lives in Homeville while revivalists come and go.

III

So then, to the wonder of redemption! Where else is it heard or seen except in the amazing grace of Christ? Our proposed self-healings are tragicomic. Computers? Ask them to mend a broken heart! Education?

---

15. 1 Cor 10:13 (GAB).

16. Or better known as "Jesus People," which was an evangelical witnessing and coffeehouse movement (that eventually spun off new denominations) reacting to the materialism among evangelicals and mainline Protestants, as well as the hedonism among free-love hippies.

What kind? "Reading, writing and 'rithmetic" (with the first two forgotten, and the third made dedicate to money and physical power) educate both Dr. Jekyll and Mr. Hyde! Evolution? If it applies to people, they can wreck it, and they do; and evolution itself is held in entropy, the slow cooling of the planet.[17]

Harvey Cox is right in his contention that God has given us responsibility for this planet and freedom to act, not expecting God to nudge our arm every moment, but Cox forgets that we all live in a nexus of past irresponsibility.[18] Our home remedies are only bottles of polluted water. The tree of evil has roots as far back as the creation and branches as wide as our world. Our tree surgery is only a superficial daubing of tar. The Son of God must be nailed to the tree before it can grow in life and beauty. Thus, the preacher's word is "grace so amazing, so divine" that we can hardly believe or bear its gentle power.

If we had eyes, we would see that day by day we live in what theology calls "general grace." How does truth endure in our flood of lies, or love in the blood and burnings of our wars? Not by our small banners. We aid and abet the flood. Yes, a personal constraint is laid on each of us, but who empowers the constraint? Meanwhile our checkered human love—the photographs in our living room—is a broken paradigm of God's love. Jesus is not "too good to be true": he is too good to be untrue. But that is to anticipate. We here plead that we live in a helping order, and that this "vast treasure of content"[19] is not our contriving, but sheer gift.

The Old Testament therefore acknowledges pardon. "In thee is forgiveness and therefore thou art revered."[20] We find no such assurances in the Oriental faiths. Hinduism offers only the wheel of recompense in endless reincarnation. The glib similitudes of "comparative religion" are often blind to the startling differences. Yes, the people of the covenant clutched at favor when God was calling them to mission, but always there was a

---

17. Had Buttrick lived until 2020, he might have said, "rapid overheating of the planet."

18. Referring to Harvey Cox's *The Secular City* (New York: The MacMillan Company, 1963). Buttrick lectured publicly on the book.

19. From James Whitcomb Riley's poem, "The Perfect Prayer."

20. Ps 130:4 (NEB).

faithful remnant; and when *they* were weak in the prevailing malaise, the covenant was renewed in the blood of one person. Now we have come to *special* grace. For general grace, despite the bland universals of philosophy and the plausible "laws" of science, always sets in at single points.

IV

This proclaiming (not declaiming) of special grace in Christ is the spearpoint of every sermon, the spear being tipped with healing. The preacher need not fear this particularism. History is ruled by events. But if events are not ruled by one Event, history is a meaningless succession, a game of scrabble with no letters making any word, and no word making any sentence. So, in the world, which kids itself that circumscribed science is "truth" and where students seek vainly a "philosophy of life," the preacher cleaves to the Event, crying, "Behold the Man!"[21]

The Event is a fourfold event. We could as easily "work backward" from the fourth to the first, for the four flow into each other, but we here follow chronology.

First event: the life of Christ. There could have been no special grace if Jesus had not lived our life. There is no laser-beam salvation. A visiting angel would have set our teeth on edge and mocked our tragic need. Isn't there a story of a school teacher, convinced that someone in the class was a thief, telling the students that they would lock doors and windows and wait for the confession? And of Mary, the last student to be guessed guilty, making confession? "Not *you*, Mary!" exclaimed the teacher. "No, but someone must raise a hand." Yes, indeed. But what hand is clean enough to carry the burden of the group? Not *our* hand. So we confront at once the paradox of Christ—in a world of paradox. How can we be genuinely free, and yet under sovereignty? But we are! Is Christ the bridge between our power to view our human days and at the same time live them? But we anticipate: salvation comes only through the One sharing our pilgrimage and paying the price, yet never swerving from holy love. The death of a gangster would bring small catharsis in our redemption.

---

21. John 19:5 (NEB).

Second event: the death of Christ. There could have been no healing if Christ had not died our death and his death. Why? For all kinds of deep "reasons." This: only as Jesus dies can he share our life. And this: only as he dies can he offer God an unbribed devotion. And this: death reveals things that life cannot bring, a fact by which we surmise that death is not dead. Then what of the cross of the bridge man? Why is it the despair of artists, yet a magnet that ever draws them? One artist whom we know tied a young man by ropes to an actual cross, hoping thus to give his picture physical realism. The trouble was that the young man was not Jesus. Why has Bach turned the cross to music as in the *Saint Matthew Passion*? Why does the New Testament again and again link sin and the cross? Why is the shadow of an empty cross now flung over our planet? Logic has no answer. How could it when logic itself rests back on axioms, which it must accept or die? There is something axiomatic about the cross. When we look at it, we become aware that someone on the other side is looking through it at us. Should we say that Jesus, revealing God to humans, representing humans to God, thereby grapples with ancient wrong and modern treachery and so dies? The question pierces to the roots of our strange life. How could a now-empty cross, a "funny little gallows," cross the sea and the long years, tread the church aisle when we weren't looking, and from the chancel rule our worship? Miracles waylay us, this miracle as focus, but usually we do not see or feel.[22]

Third event: the resurrection of Christ. The answer to our questions just asked is the resurrection. That light has flung far and wide the shadow of the cross, and made it an empty cross rather than a crucifix. That event has given us the massive doctrines of atonement. For if God raised Christ from the dead (*raised* is a more characteristic New Testament word than is *rose*), then God was in Christ's dying. Doing what? Bearing our sins as only God can, and bearing them away. The words that symbolize these doctrines, such as *sacrifice, ransom, expiation, reconciliation,* or *justification,* are all symbolic pictures or metaphors. That fact does not make them

---

22. Editorial note: Human sight and feeling fail to behold the miraculous manner of God's incarnation and redemption by means of an executioner's cross. The cross "waylays" us, that is, takes us by surprise since the suffering and death of the Son of God as a political prisoner scandalizes our triumphalist notions of God's actions in history.

false. It enhances their verity, for word pictures are far more effective carriers of truth than concepts or laws. Each metaphor pierces us; each falls short. For who can fulfill Milton's resolve to "justify the ways of God to men"?[23] The resurrection interprets not only the cross but also the shared life, for now the words of Jesus are not simply that: they have the glad authority of One who was raised from the dead. Without the resurrection, Calvary would have been the final despair: the best would have perished at the mercy of the worst.

Fourth event: the now-present Christ through the gift of the Holy Spirit, without whom even the resurrection (and Christ's life and the death) would have been locked in history. But the Presence makes contemporary the whole Event. The Spirit broods over the words and happenings of Christ's life, set within the great ongoing story of the Bible, and is the real and focal inspiration of the scriptures. The Spirit brings home the judgment and the healing of Calvary. The Spirit validates the resurrection. The Spirit moves in the life of the hearer and gives the preacher her power. How could Christ rule the centuries? How could the early church survive the seductions of pagan temples, the might of the Roman Empire, the brassy invasion of trade, and the sheer inertia of the crowd? Had we lived in that time we wouldn't have given a nickel for the church's chance. How can Christ return, poorly in *Jesus Christ Superstar*, better in *Godspell*, to the drama of our era? By the gift and grace of the Spirit, our "advocate," our "justifier," our "intercessor," and our daily shield and sun. What a message to proclaim! It is beyond compare! It has no rival in its piercing effect, its bracing light, its pertinence of glory! As the preacher broods on the Event, he will cry with Paul, "For to me to live is Christ"![24] Then once more the preacher's words will have power.

No term in one Event may be pushed into the margin. Liberalism focused on his life and word, and so drifted into theological shallows. Fundamentalism emphasized his cross and so passed through stress on "sin" into censoriousness and social unconcern. The "celebration" movement[25]

---

23. John Milton, *Paradise Lost*, book I, line 26.
24. Phil 1:21 (KJV).
25. The Jesus movement of the 1960s and 1970s.

may easily forget a stark tree without which the resurrection would have been an empty light. The contemporary "spiritualist" cults, marked by glossolalia ("tongues") and "healings" may forget everything that preceded Pentecost, and settle for an ebullience and a self-indulgence instead of a whole Gospel. The total Event is just that: an Event, not a theory. It flames in the midst of our human story with a quiet yet undying light, illuminating and interpreting the past, making a pathway for all coming time. Christ in his life makes common cause with our life. Christ in his death grapples with the fell foe, and so deals radically with our need. Christ in his resurrection conquers, and so God validates his Word. Christ in his presence brings the whole Event into every home and culture in every generation. There is now one question only for every sermon and every church: "What is the will of Christ?"

V

Someone says, "But this is still a faith"? Of course, for every endeavor, bright or blundering, travels by faith, for our life is always a thrust into an unknown future. Consider the incredible faith of science: "We will immure ourselves in our laboratory, and *trust* that we make good use of our discoveries." Was any faith so naive about human nature? Consider the still darker faith of politics: "The balance of power will save us, though weapons more and more threaten the extinction of the race." Consider the blind faith of commerce: "Technology will lead us to the golden age." Compare the Gospel with all this nonsense. Does someone persist, "You are attributing meaning to the Event?" Not attributing: for the Event itself (Christ himself) beckons meaning, and to that beckoning we assent—at risk and in joy.

So let the preacher say to a don't-care world: "You can't stand anywhere, or everywhere, or nowhere: you must stand somewhere." Covertly or deliberately each of us chooses where to stand. The choice becomes open whenever we recite the creed, which is not primarily an excursion into theology, though that is involved, but a banner under which a person pledges his and her life. It breaks clean through the protest of a Camus or the bafflement of a Kafka. It brings all our days under the saving name.

Chapter Seventeen

The sunset: for nothing is created without Christ. The bank account: for we cannot serve God and cash. Sorrow: be patient: it shall yet become the pain-joy of a woman in childbirth. Persecution: away with self-pity: the persecuted are gathered into the bright company of the prophets now met around a cross. So the pilgrim goes her glad way, her strength always stronger than her burden. What a Gospel! The church is not the company of the righteous, still less of the self-righteous: it is the new family of the forgiven sinners, the gathering of the grateful, the followers of the name.

VI

But isn't the preacher offering "cheap grace"? The answer depends on the meaning of "cheap." If it means "of little worth," the grace of God is godlike, not trivial: it is as costly as the cross, and as profound as the resurrection. If the word means that the preacher and her "converts" can trick God to obtain grace at bargain rates, no, God is never mocked. If the word means that men and women can claim God's forgiveness and then presume on it, the answer is still no, for the presumption is soon powerless against God's holy love. If the word means that we can half-believe the Gospel, and then revert to our unbelieving life, while still claiming the name, yes, but only for a while. Is this a common malaise? Yes, but the half-belief soon dissipates, and the last state of the half-cured guilt is worse than the first. This malaise has settled on the church. It has been made the refuge of semi-believers. The revivalist claims, "Changed people will change the world." But it simply doesn't happen: the claim is proved false. The "converts" become the enemies of change. Converted from what, to what?

When grace is offered in Christ, one response, of two, is that we love God with an undivided heart. Therefore worship, which is the *direct* answer to God's love. If we do not worship God, centrally in Christ, we shall not cease to worship, for we are worshipping creatures. We shall worship "the American way," which many try to equate with the kingdom of God on earth, or we shall engage in some other form of self-worship. The sermon dies except in the context of worship. Worship is centrally thanksgiving for God's incredible gift in Christ, but that involves renewed confession and intercession and commitment. Worship is *willed* worship: the offering of self in answer to God's self-offering. Worship is therefore work; it is not a clutching at "a mountain-top experience." Such clutching leads only to a sauna bath in the valley. There is nothing "cheap" about genuine worship. Incidentally, each new age "comes on" new forms of worship. But alternative forms of worship are gain only as each are true to the needs and yearnings of our human nature, and to the claims of the Gospel.

The other response? We try to love our neighbors after the manner of that forgiveness that God has already shown both them and us. Love by nature is love shared. It concerns our group life, as well as individuals. It is both neighborly and political—in the original meaning of that latter word (*polis* = city). So preacher and people eschew a busyness with many wheels spinning out of gear. By word and act, deed of lips and deed of hands, they undergird the sorrow of the person next door and protest the monstrous iniquity of modern war. So to live is the *indirect response* to God's love toward us. The grace of God saves us from more than private transgression (if transgression can ever be private), and if we try to capsule grace in individualistic entities it will end in a fictional peace. The proud structures of our common life blind us and then infect us—and harden us. Structures in science, business, and government become like stone fortresses. Compassion ebbs. Then the saved persons, the *really* saved persons, are broken at the base of the wall—and are glad. They are now members of the broken body of Christ, and with their Lord conquer in the dying.

Thus the preacher's word to a world under judgment. No other person has any word of hope except by covert borrowing from the Gospel. A mother dropped indelible ink on a valuable silk handkerchief. An artist came, darkened the blot so that it became the hiding place in the trunk of a tree. Then he drew leaves on the tree, and children playing. The handkerchief now was far more precious than at first. That mother was far too wise to point the moral. The grace of God overwhelms all morals, for it is a gift to the unrighteous. She said only, "Isn't it wonderful that things can be so?"[26] If the preacher is silent or inept, what other voice can speak that word? What other word is really worth the speaking? "Isn't it wonderful that things can be so?" Amazing grace!

---

26. A widely circulated story about John Ruskin, nineteenth-century British artist, critic, and social reformer.

CHAPTER EIGHTEEN

Preaching to a Death-Filled World: Resurrection

Our ancestors preached about judgment, heaven, and hell. Such preaching is not often heard in our time. When it is heard, it seems archaic, and is either laughed out of court or condemned as "otherworldliness." Our skeptical and pluralistic society believes in "one world at a time," despite the fact that here and now each of us lives in two worlds at the same time. So our planet is a little village set in arid fields: there are no streams flowing from unseen mountains. Indeed, there is no sky. That's why there is no light except that which shines despite us, unbeckoned and denied. Meanwhile our earth is filled with death, and we propose that God is dead. We yearn for life. We are "the Pepsi generation," trying to convince ourselves that pep comes from a soft drink or a hard drink. Was death ever so wholesale as in the twentieth century? Our roads are filled with death: safety councils plead with us in vain to stop the expressway slaughter. Our wars leave whole lands red with human blood, which we try to justify by tired slogans and cruel habit. Meanwhile everyone must die. Maybe our ancestors were nearer truth than we! How shall the Christian pulpit address a death-filled age?

Chapter Eighteen

I

We can see why the pulpit's eschatological dimension is now almost lost.[1] One factor is a rightful revolt against a false otherworldliness. Our present life is not a "vale of tears," even though it is finite and therefore "subject to vanity."[2] This world is a goodly valley, though we can profane it, for God in the creation "looked on it and behold it was very good."[3] We should rejoice in it, singing in a hymn too rarely sung, "Glad that I live am I."[4] Our science, education, art, daily work, and friendships are excellent gifts. Jesus thought that the world of nature and the world of persons were both worth his coming and his death. If the pulpit becomes morbid or even ungrateful, the world about us rightly refuses to listen.

Another reason: our preaching about heaven and hell has often been a comic or tragic selfishness. Hell has been pictured as a sadistic hell that blasphemes both God and humanity. Heaven has been pictured as a candy heaven for "good little boys and girls," thus turning God into a maiden aunt who has little more to give than sweets. Mark the sheer egocentric pride of such a hymn as

> O that will be
> glory for me,[5]

with "me" sung in cloying reiteration. The picture of the "saints" standing on a balcony enjoying the sight of "sinners" being fried in the eternal fire no longer decorates the narthex of our churches, though I saw it in one church, but the unconscious sadism dies hard. Not even we in our mixed good and evil would so deal with our children either in their supposed goodness or in their known evil. We would not condemn them to eternal

---

1. The dimension that is beyond the realm of space and time yet impinging upon it.
2. Rom 8:20 (KJV).
3. Gen 1:31 (GAB).
4. Composed in 1909 by Lizette Woodworth Reese (1856–1935), Baltimore, Maryland, poet and teacher.
5. "O That Will Be Glory," composed by Charles H. Gabriel (1856–1932), native of Iowa who composed thousands of songs under various pseudonyms.

torment for time-bound transgressions. The world refuses and ridicules this candy-heaven and sadistic hell, and the world is right.

Another reason why life-after-death preaching has almost disappeared is this: we have believed we could contrive our own heaven. The church itself has been seduced by this false optimism. Read the news. Medical science proposes to conquer death by freezing and reviving the corpse. Biological and chemical science hails the day when soon human nature can be remade into a sure excellence—without any regard for human freedom. Human brain and skill can quench any hell here or hereafter, and fashion in this world a better heaven than the Bible portrays. The hope of Auguste Comte[6] persists: theology is superstition, philosophy is abstraction, but science is the highroad to the golden age. The church in its semiconscious accommodation to the world is smeared with this sacrilegious human pride. There seems little room for any preaching on the life beyond this life.

Another reason, the last we shall mention though there are many more, is our "death wish" to which also the church has half consented. Freud[7] has shown, with scant room for cavil, that human beings sometimes want to die even though they fear death, or that they wish at least to "go back into the womb." Afraid to meet the future, they try to retreat into the past, though the past has gone, never to return. The Birch Society is plainly paranoid: President Eisenhower was to them a communist, though he was actually a conservative, and the fluoridation of our water supply was a communist plot to poison us! These frightened folks want to run home to mother, even though the human pilgrimage is always passing a new point of no return. Why should such people think on destiny? They covet no future. They wish to get buried in the past. They seek only escape. The great adventure of Christian faith makes too great demands, and current preaching caters too often to their faintheartedness.

---

6. Auguste Comte (1798–1857), French philosopher of scientific positivism.
7. Sigmund Freud (1856–1939), Austrian neurologist and father of psychoanalysis.

II

But the mood now changes: our trust in our own proud powers is daily confounded. We have multiplied death instead of conquering it. Our brazen attempt to be our own god has made a hell on earth. Our only heaven now is a fraudulent refuge through drink and drugs. Many people spoof themselves that two world wars were merely passing clouds, and that the blight of our cities is only the seeming confusion that attends a new and glorious home for humankind: they, like John Dewey,[8] still believe that deliverance comes through education, democracy, and science. But increasing numbers wonder and wonder. Some even ask how a finite world can be anything else but finite. It can be made a more homelike inn for wayfarers who are always on pilgrimage, but (they wonder) if it can ever be made perfect. Perhaps, they surmise, it is only a prenatal world, and then the surmise rekindles a hope that can be fulfilled only beyond this world.

Then conscience awakens. Suppose there could be perfection here, what of those who have been killed in accident and war? Have we any right to forget them? Has God any right to use them as manure to fertilize the fields of earth for those who follow them? Ivan, in *The Brothers Karamazov*,[9] roundly declared that God has no right so to treat even one idiot child. Ivan spoke from sound and compassionate instinct; his fault was a demand from mortal mind to comprehend the eternal wisdom. Perhaps this pricking of conscience is the reason why we try to justify capital punishment: we think that if the culprit is hurried off to the electric chair, we are somehow acquitted of our complicity in his crime. At any rate, a belief in the perfectibility of this planet hardly absolves us (or God) for unconcern for those who have died in the long imperfect journey of our human races. The hope of the hereafter is called "selfish" in our time.

---

8. John Dewey (1859–1952), American pragmatist philosopher and psychologist.

9. Fyodor Dostoevsky, *The Brothers Karamazov*, abridged by Edmund Fuller (New York: Dell Publishing Co., 1956 [1880]).

Actually it is callously selfish not to hope. Is a child dying of leukemia to be cast "as rubbish to the void"?[10]

A further fact contributes to the shift in mood: the atomic bomb. *We* build the *perfect* society? There is perhaps more cruelty to the square inch nowadays than our planet has ever known, and nuclear war may write *finis* to all history. By some freak of the cosmos a strange race of parentless bipeds inhabited for a few years a pinpoint of land in a remote system of a remote galaxy, and in a puff of smoke suddenly vanished. Humanism must now face that prospect. Of course, that same prospect in miniature always confronts each of us. We are born to go to school, work, marry, beget children, and then, just as we have gathered some small measure of wisdom and goodwill, we die. If there is nothing else to say, the joys are perhaps worth the journey, even though they are no longer in any memory, but we shall wonder and wonder if the whole show is better than a mockery. Contemporary fashions, frenzied dancing, death-speed on our highways, the monstrous cruelty of our wars are not unlinked to the fact that mortal life has become a prison. A Unitarian minister argued that our world is in a mess because the church has set humans to mooning about heaven, thus distracting them from the rightful tasks of earth. He does not know what the evangelical church preaches.[11] I have not heard a sermon on heaven and hell in decades! Our pulpits are stricken by a disease called "this world only." If our present life is only a puff of smoke, why engage in any present tasks? Camus[12] was honest enough to propose suicide as the only sensible option.

---

10. Alfred Lord Tennyson, "In Memoriam," LIV, *The Poems and Plays of Alfred Lord Tennyson* (New York: The Modern Library, Random House, 1938), 312. "O, yet we trust that somehow good Will be the final goal of ill, That nothing walks with aimless feet; That no one life shall be destroy'd, Or cast as rubbish to the void."

11. For a discussion of the meaning of *evangelical* as Buttrick employed the term, see the introduction. Here he is referring to the "evangelical Church" as those denominations stemming from the Protestant Reformation for which the christocentric and biblical "evangel" (Gospel) is authoritative for preaching, witness, and mission, as distinct from Roman Catholicism on the one hand, and, on the other, "evangelical" as construed within circles of ecclesiastical-cultural fundamentalism with which Buttrick did not concur.

12. Albert Camus (1913–1960), French philosopher, novelist, playwright, and essayist.

Chapter Eighteen

III

Then how shall we preach to a death-filled age? Certainly we shall not threaten people with a sadistic hell, though there is a place in preaching (as in medicine) for warning; and we shall not bribe people with a candy heaven, and we shall neither disparage this life nor distract people from its brave witness and rightful labor. We shall say that this life is precious and filled with promise. Old-time preachers knew that this world is not perfectible, a fact we try to dodge, but they still had no warrant to brand it "a vale of tears." Here we have joys in abundance, and could have more but for our atomized selfishness. Even if our daily work is dull, our avocation can be exciting; and the amenities of life are called such only by our shabby ingratitude: they are treasures beyond price. What of home, and the friendships that cluster round it? What of the great hearts of our race? What of zest of body in both life and love? What of white candlelight vigils of the spirit? What of the fact and faith of Christ? What of the adoration of the mystery? The Bible glories in earth and flesh: only a morbid gnosticism[13] discounts them. The Apostles' Creed bids us believe in "the resurrection of the body." Resurrection in that context does not mean the

---

13. Buttrick disavows gnosticism's denigration of the earthly body, along with its radical dualism positing that the lower, material world is essentially evil in contrast to the upper, heavenly world that is purely good. The *Dictionary of Philosophy and Religion: Eastern and Western Thought* (New Jersey: Humanities Press, 1980) defines gnosticism as "a philosophic-religious movement related to the mystery religions and directed toward personal salvation [and] like the mystery religions, claimed an esoteric wisdom, sharply distinguishing between the uninitiated and the initiated [and] stood in competition with Christianity, reaching its highest point in the latter part of the 2nd century A.D." (192). Conrad Henry Moehlman wrote, "The total trend, designated Gnosticism, has become a syncretistic whirlpool with one eddy the orientalization of the Graeco-Roman civilization and the other the hellenization of the Orient. Christian gnosticism tended toward repudiation of the O.T. [Old Testament] and made Jesus an appearance and his death only apparent. In gnosticism the same god could not be both creator and judge and redeemer." See *Encyclopedia of Religion*, ed. Virginius Firm (Paterson, NJ: Littlefield, Adams & Co., 1959), 300–301. Elaine Pagels wrote, "The conviction—that whoever explores human experience simultaneously discovers divine reality—is one of the elements that marks gnosticism as a distinctly religious movement." See Elaine Pagels, *The Gnostic Gospels* (New York: Vintage Books, A Division of Random House, 1979), 134. Buttrick claimed that biblical Christianity avows that self-knowledge and self-discovery are insufficient and incapable of transforming and redeeming human sin and evil, which is accomplished by the actions of God in history, consummated within and beyond history through the sacrificial and atoning death and resurrection of Jesus Christ.

renewal of the bones or the revival of the flesh. It means what it says: the body also is worthy of a new and wonderful form beyond death, the body and the sky and fields and cities in which we now dwell. This our preaching should say. Otherwise it is condemned.

Next: we should say that our present world is already two-dimensional. We do not and cannot live in "one world at a time," for here and now we always live in two worlds at a time. This we know from our ordinary language. For we say, "Time is swift. Only yesterday I was young, but now our children have their children." How can we so speak? Because there is in our nature a vantage point above the hurrying years. The word *finite*, the acknowledgement of our limitations, implies the word *infinite*. Should we not say that the word *earth* implies "heaven"? The conversations we hold with ourselves are more crucial than those we hold with our neighbors: "Why art thou cast down, O my soul?"[14] Thus the discursive person and the steadfast person are always in colloquy. The one says, "I can just make it across the road between the traffic"; the other answers, "Why risk it? You might get killed." The one says, "My lust must be satisfied"; the other, "You have no right to 'use' a person: a person is not a thing." So Jesus spoke: "But if you don't forgive others" (on earth), "neither will your Father forgive your sins" (in heaven).[15] "Those who want to save their" (discursive) "life will lose it" (their other life).[16] The cult of "one world at a time" is a thin and thoughtless cult: it leaves a person with neither soil in which to sow his seed nor sky for his uplifted face. This the Christian pulpit must say. What joy to say it! Christ did not *create* our sense of the hereafter, for that sense is always mixed with our human clay: he brought it to light and life.

Then we can say, God is God. We cannot think of earth without thinking of heaven. We cannot say "time," without longing for eternity. To say, "God is dead," is to sell out to a flat contradiction in terms, for God (the infinite and unconditioned by whom alone we know our time-bound and seemingly forsaken life) and death are irreconcilable. Jesus, with his "Have faith in God," was not being blind or stubborn or naive. He was telling

---

14. Ps 42:5; 43:5 (KJV).
15. Matt 6:15 (CEB).
16. Matt 16:25 (NRSV).

us that we could not doubt without a prior and inescapable faith. He was bidding us cleave to God lest life dissolve in madness and chaos. We understand why mortal life is promise: it is always being drawn back into its creative source. Thus, its order conquers the threat of disorder, granted our faith. Its iron filings fall into final pattern under the divine life-magnet. Always we are thrust into the future, while remembering the past. Thus we are whole but always incomplete. Thus time and space are a continuum, because time gives space its endurance, but the continuum is always prophetic, because time is always hurrying home. Therefore the wisdom of the Bible: "Here we have no abiding city but seek one which is to come."[17] Therefore the comment of Jesus on the whole faith in resurrection: "You do not know the power of God."[18] Since God is God, God cannot be a tinpot monarch ruling over a series of graveyards: God is God, the unconditioned, the ground of creation. These comments are better than logic: they are axiom by which all people live, in conscious or unconscious mind.

But however much we are grateful for this life, it is by nature frustrated. It is not perfectible. It is "subject to bondage."[19] It was so created. Much can be done to make the planet a place of beauty and goodwill, but there are always limits. For one thing, our human constitution is such that we can never escape a measure of anxiety: we are on the road of death, and we see ourselves on that pilgrimage. If we died as cows die, we might be no wiser. But we know we must die. So anxiety besets us, and the anxiety draws us into self-concern, and self-concern is idolatry, and idolatry leads to fantasy and disaster. Heidegger speaks therefore about the "stigma of finitude,"[20] a phrase parallel to the biblical doctrine of a "fallen world."

---

17. Heb 13:14 (KJV, alt).

18. Mark 12:24 (NEB).

19. See Romans 8:20-21, "For the creation was subjected to futility in hope that the creation itself will be set free from its bondage to decay" (NRSV).

20. Martin Heidegger (1889–1996), "Being and Time [Sein und Zeit]," *Existence and Being*, intro. by Werner Brock (Chicago: Henry Regnery Company 1949), 52–106. Heidegger examined the ontological aspects of finitude as constitutive of human existence, stating that "death is imminent every moment. Death is thus defined as the innermost and irrelative potentiality of Being, certain and indefinite as to its 'when' and not to be overcome" (60). Paul Tillich (1886–1965) used the phrase *stigma of finitude* to characterize "the threat of non-being" as "the negative side of revelation. Without it the mystery would not be mystery." *Systematic*

For another thing, our freedom *is* freedom, genuine, though limited; and freedom can always be abused. The freedom, of course, is always within our *human* limits: we cannot trample on our neighbors and expect to be loved. The freedom is always within *natural* limits: we cannot grow lollipops on cabbage stalks, or pitch a tent on the sun, or fly to China using the breaststroke. Besides, the final limit is death itself. The body is joy, but the body is at last given to corruption, and the whole world is doomed to transience.

So what do we preach? The resurrection of Christ as pledge that the very body "of our lowliness shall be changed into His body of glory."[21] We need not fear to proclaim that Event without which history has no meaning and life's corruption no articulate promise.[22] All the questions raised by our scientific time regarding the resurrection were answered by his first disciples. They answered the psychological charge of "illusion," for they said, "Why stand we in jeopardy every hour?,"[23] meaning, "Wouldn't we be arrant fools to die for a trick of consciousness?" They answered the skeptic charge that the resurrection was a deliberate fiction to bolster a Pauline cult: "If Christ be not risen we are found false witnesses of God,"[24] meaning that by such mendacity they would be worthy only of final damnation. They themselves were truthful people in their daily life—in a world of lies. They worshipped Jesus as "the truth." They bade each other, "Speak truth to all people."[25] Then came the church—with endless hallelujahs for him who conquered death. Then came the New

---

Theology, vol. 1 (Digswell Place, UK: James Nisbet & Co., 1953), 122, 129. Buttrick read Heidegger and Tillich extensively. Tillich was Buttrick's faculty colleague and friend at both Union Theological Seminary (NY) and Harvard Divinity School. Buttrick unconsciously attributed Tillich's "stigma of finitude" to Heidegger, a fact that Buttrick's wife, Agnes, doubtlessly would have caught had she, per her customary practice for all of his books, edited these lectures for footnotes and bibliography.

21. Phil 3:21 (GAB).

22. Buttrick lectured widely on the subject of his book, *Christ and History* (New York: Abingdon Press, 1963).

23. 1 Cor 15:30 (KJV).

24. 1 Cor 15:14-15 (KJV).

25. Eph 4:25 (GAB). "Let all of us speak the truth to our neighbors, for we are members of one another" (NRSV).

Testament without one *in memoriam* sigh. Then came architecture, art, and music for Christ's diadem. Then came great theologies of the cross, which without Easter would have been bleak and final tragedy. Then came saints and martyrs, and the sense of a presence strong enough to overcome even the dark defections of the church. The evidence is not scientific: it is vital. This faith is never coerced: it is beckoned and invited to prove itself by glad abandon.

The resurrection to be preached gathers in not only each of us but all of us and all history. Christ ushered in a new age, not to condemn the old age but to fulfill it. The mind of the Hebrews was moving from belief in Sheol, the shadowy, feeble land of the dead, to a belief in personal resurrection; and Christ aligned himself with the Pharisees in the new and vivid hope against the Sadducees who would not change even a letter of the Mosaic Pentateuchal law. Surely it is not without pertinence that Christ believed in resurrection. What is more important is this: the New Testament, taking its cue from Christ, is sure that the pre-Christian years are brought to fulfillment by the Easter fact. The word is, "that they without us cannot be made perfect."[26] Each generation brings its predecessors nearer to the total and appointed destiny in Christ, so that at last all history is fulfilled in Christ. The cave of this world opens on ranges and ranges, vistas and vistas of life, because in Christ all things in heaven and earth "cohere."[27] The music of all the spheres finds its Amen in him. In him Ivan's idiot child comes to newness of life. In him preaching is focused in his resurrection.

V

What else in preaching to a death-filled time? We have no blueprint of heaven or hell, for that is nowhere given in the New Testament. Would we understand if it were given? A person born deaf can hardly comprehend the Ninth Symphony. Besides, the Gospel does not distract us from the present tasks. But through Jesus we know enough of the hereafter to

---

26. Heb 11:40, translated "*should* not" (KJV, RSV), "*would* not" (NRSV, CEB "wouldn't").

27. See Col 1:15-17. "By him all things *consist*" (v. 17, KJV), "*hold together*" (NRSV).

proclaim its message to our present life. We can say and should say that at death there is no Rip van Winkle sleep. We are born at once into the next life, taking with us nothing that we have and everything that we are. Rip's waking was a pathos, for while he slept the world moved on, and he woke to bafflement and loss.[28] Surely such a waking is not according to the mind of Christ. That verdict seems to be implied in his words to the dying thief: "This day you shall be with me in paradise."[29] The Roman Church, defending the doctrine of purgatory, proposes that Christ actually spoke as follows: "I am saying to you today that (sometime) you shall be with me in Paradise."[30] But such a translation strains the Greek idiom to the breaking point. "Paradise" comes from the Persian (a fact that should not surprise us, for there were Persian monastic orders in the wilderness beyond Jordan alongside such Jewish groups as the Qumran sect), and means a "flowering garden." The ugliness of this present life shall be cancelled. Meanwhile no sound theology will deny the need of our purgation.[31] Who is fit either for highest heaven or deepest hell?

We proclaim also the fact of judgment, for it is central in the Gospel. Every crisis is judgment. That is the core meaning of the word as it comes

---

28. Washington Irving (1783–1859), *Rip Van Winkle*, pictures and decorations by N. C. Wyeth (Philadelphia: David McKay Company, 1921 [1819]).

29. Luke 23:43 (GAB).

30. For Luke, "today" (Gk., *sēmeron*) consistently means "now, before the day is over," appearing nine times in his Gospel, e.g., Luke 4:21 ("Today this scripture has been fulfilled in your hearing") and 22:61 ("Before the cock crows today, you will deny me three times") (NRSV). The contested interpretation of 23:43 ("Today you will be with me in Paradise" [NRSV]) has hinged upon the placement of the comma, before or after the word "today." Subsequent to the oral and written transmission of the underlying Aramaic, early Greek translations contained little to no punctuation. Yet, some would point to the Curetonian Syriac version of the Lucan Gospel (late second, early third century) containing a textual *variant* in word order, thereby joining "today" to "I say to you" instead of to "you will be with me." For Buttrick, the Syriac (and ostensibly Roman Catholic) interpretation of the passage "strains the Greek idiom ['Truly, I say to you'] to the breaking-point" of an unwarranted interpolation. Buttrick emphasized the universally accepted translation by rendering "today" as "this day." Even the French Catholic *Jerusalem Bible* (1956), which Buttrick recommended to students, translated the Greek into French as *dès aujourd'hui tu seras avec moi dans le Paradis* ("from today you will be with me in paradise"). Buttrick wrote, "Protestantism has suffered because, in proper recoil from arbitrary theories of purgatory, it has erased from prayer the memory and mention of the 'communion of saints.'" See *Prayer* (New York: Abingdon-Cokesbury Press, 1942), 276.

31. Cleansing.

directly from the Greek. As instance, the Vietnamese war uncovers and judges the predatory nature of what we call civilization. In T. S. Eliot's *The Cocktail Party*,[32] the death of Celia, who went in love to serve an African tribe and was crucified "near an anthill," made a crisis of decision for everyone in her home circle of friends. So by any fair assumption the crisis of death will be judgment. Perhaps that is why when someone dies, we say, "Poor Jim." Maybe he isn't poor; maybe he has been welcomed into "eternal habitations." What we mean is that his earthly chance has ended, and that his record cannot now be changed. He must stand before the throne as he is. Perhaps we really mean, "Poor me," and that Christ may meet us in the hereafter and ask, "Why did you give me that kind of answer in your earthly life?" Suppose we have sold out to things and the masses!

Why should preaching avoid the issue of heaven and hell? The New Testament knows nothing of a sadistic hell or a candy heaven. Such a phrase as that in the King James Version as "everlasting damnation"[33] is a serious mistranslation. "Everlasting" points to the fact that New Testament folk regarded time as moving in successive ages, and that for the Christian time is now BC and AD.[34] "Damnation" should be translated

---

32. T. S. Eliot (1888–1965), *The Cocktail Party* (New York: Harcourt, Brace and Company, 1950).

33. See, e.g., Mark 3:29 (KJV), "eternal damnation."

34. Buttrick concurred with the demarcation of history denoted as "BC" and "AD" in consequence of the central and pivotal Christ event. See George A. Buttrick, *Christ and History* (Nashville: Abingdon Press, 1963), in which he wrote: "If every historian takes some stance, the main question is, what stance?" (32). "Historical records are not to be treated as if they were letters by which historians may play a game of scrabble, each making what words he chooses. But though we must be 'true to the facts,' no man can escape interpretation of the facts. What interpretation? The calendar shows the Christian stance: Christ has split history into before and after" (33). "The faith of a follower of Christ holds that Christ is the focus of history, even as he [Christ] has split the calendar of history into before and after; that he [Christ] is the stance from which the panorama should be viewed, and the spirit in which it should be viewed" (43). "History newly poses the old question: 'Then what shall I do with Jesus who is called Christ?'" [Pilate's question to the chief priests and elders, Matt 27:22 (RSV)] "What event is focal, so that all events may be construed in its light? One Man has split history into before and after, a fact which does not coerce, but which surely beckons. Who in our human story can lead the tragedy of history into joy beyond tragedy? Where shall we find tidings of that Mystery in Whom all history is held? These are the questions. Are they not but different versions of the question about Christ?" (157).

"condemnation." Thus, we could say, "These shall go into the darkness of the old era, and these into the light of the new kingdom." Surely such preaching has its place. That is what Christ himself said. When we follow him, we know his heaven; when we betray him, we invite the hell of loneliness and war. If that is true now, why should we insult the intelligence of a congregation by proposing that there is no hell or heaven in the hereafter? The worldling's jibe that our faith is an affair of (Sunday school) "rewards" makes small sense. In New Testament faith the "rewards" are not mercenary, and the penalties are not punitive. Besides, the hereafter would be a topsy-turvy world if the issues of this life were unpredictably accidental or amoral.

We should not pretend to know the specifics of the hereafter either in time or in space. Time and space are categories of *this* world. The New Testament does not satisfy our curiosity in these regards. If it did, both its language and its meaning would elude us. There are parables and pictures, but no this-world dogmatics. There "they neither marry nor are given in marriage."[35] Such a dictum does not mean that human love ceases: it means that it is transmuted into a higher love, and that the "time" and "space" of the hereafter are beyond our present ken. But words such as *darkness* and *condemnation* have their warning, just as "light" and "life" have their welcome. The suburban home is filled with light, but if it is careless of folk who climb the dark staircase of a black slum, it shall hereafter know that Christ is no stranger to the *Third Floor Back*,[36] and understand his warning that "the last shall be first." Meanwhile who among us can claim righteousness? The story of Dives in the hereafter is not a chunk of theological dogma, but it may well be a more vital truth.[37] Always our mortal life is a thrust into the future. Why should it move into a Sartrean "nothing"?[38] That fiat verdict is a sheer act of faith—or of unfaith, with far less warrant and beckoning than Christian faith. For the blind and

---

35. Matt 22:30 (RSV).

36. Jerome K. Jerome, *Passing of the Third Floor Back*, a play (New York: Grosset & Dunlap, 1908 [1904]).

37. Luke 16:19-31, the parable of the rich man and Lazarus. Latin *Dives* = rich.

38. Jean Paul Sartre, *Being and Nothingness* (New York: Philosophical Library, 1956 [French, 1943]).

unbrotherly the future is a purgation of darkness; for those who love God and humanity through Christ the future is "with him."

VI

Only by the preaching of the hereafter can we avoid being callous in a callous world, the unconcern for those who die before their time. Only so can we do justice to the promise and ongoingness, which are the inalienable marks of our humanness. Zona Gale has a tiny parable of two tadpoles in a roadside pond. One thrust his nose above water, glanced around, and then dove to report to his companion, "There's a vast, terrifying, wonderful world round this pool, and it could destroy us utterly if it wished." The other replied, "You're a fool, and, besides, that's otherworldliness."[39] We know we are of the pool, and we are aware of that other world, and we know that, like a tadpole, we must soon change our nature and see that beckoning country.

Only by such a message can we be true to Christ's convictions and the meaning of his resurrection. He spoke of the eschaton.[40] The Gospel is not Gospel without its eschatological thrust. In the debate in his time about the hereafter he clearly aligned himself with the Pharisees, who believed in personal resurrection, against the Sadducees, who tried to cling to the old notion of a shadowy Sheol. As for his own return from death, the whole New Testament is bathed in that light. Without that joy both Gospels and Epistles would become nonsense. That faith does not distract us from present tasks, but it summons us to the cruciality of this present world. The struggle for civil rights would be worse than transience if the dark tar of death were flung over all our works. But if the word hereafter is this, "What about your black neighbors?," the issue takes another turn—*the* turn. These mortal days are not a cheap mockery or a sneering transience.

---

39. Zona Gale (1874–1938), American novelist, playwright, and first woman to be the recipient of the Pulitzer Prize in drama. Quotation from *We Believe in Prayer*, ed. Sidney Strong (New York: Coward-McCann, 1930), 34.

40. From Gr. *eschatos*, last things, end of time.

Only such preaching can keep faith with God, for if we have "hope in this world only"[41] his nature is under (his own) judgment. Is God a tinpot monarch ruling only an ever expanding graveyard? We would shrink from flinging that insult even at a sorry kind of neighbor! Our very finitude, our awareness of limits, tells of an infinite realm beyond the fence. In lack of that double consciousness our self-consciousness might vanish. Life itself might cease to be life: it might shrivel into thinghood while waiting its sure doom in a time-bound prison. Actually, every person believes in a hereafter. He may insist that he doesn't, but some off-guard moment will reveal his faith. That is what happened to a famous atheist, Robert Ingersoll, at his brother's grave. All his days he had made mock of the faith of the churches. But at that last sad moment he began to speak about a "star" in the night, and about "the rustle of a wing."[42] Some people suppress the hope in noble fear that they may be distracted from present courage. Others just suppress the hope—in fear that it cannot bear examination. But all people believe. They cannot help it, for it is an inescapable part of being mortal. Therefore, the most unbelieving bring flowers to a grave. Faith in Christ brings that belief to life, and gives it a personal focus in him. Therefore, the pulpit should say in comfort and judgment, in warning and glad hope, "Now is Christ risen from the dead, and become the firstfruits"[43] of that world where "beyond these voices there is peace."[44]

---

41. 1 Cor 15:19 (GAB paraphrase). "If for this life only we have hoped in Christ" (RSV).

42. Robert Ingersoll (1833–1899), son of a controversial abolitionist Congregational minister, lawyer, Civil War soldier, Republican politician, friend of Walt Whitman, humanist and renowned orator, who espoused his agnosticism partly due to childhood experiences of the severities of Calvinist Christianity. At his brother Ebon's graveside he said, "Life is a narrow vale between the cold and barren peaks of two eternities. We strive in vain to look beyond the heights. We cry aloud, and the only answer is the echo of our wailing cry. From the voiceless lips of the unreplying dead there comes no word; but in the night of death hope sees a star and listening love can hear the rustle of a wing." *The Works of Robert G. Ingersoll*, vol. 12, ed. Clinton Farrell (New York: C. P. Farrell, 1900), 391.

43. 1 Cor 15:20 (KJV).

44. Alfred Lord Tennyson, "Idylls of the King: Guinevere," *The Poems and Plays of Alfred Lord Tennyson* (New York: The Modern Library, Random House, 1938), 652, line 692.

Chronology of the Life of George Arthur Buttrick

March 23, 1892–January 23, 1980

1892 Born Mar 23, Seaham Harbour, Northumberland, England, as the only son and middle child between sisters Minette and Maud, to the Rev. Tom Buttrick (1861–1941), Primitive Methodist pastor, and Jessie Amelia (Lambert) Buttrick (1858–1948), an Anglican Scot

1909 University of Manchester matriculation exams in English literature (higher standard), English history (higher standard), mathematics, French, chemistry, and geography (July)

1912 Received into the fellowship of Albion Congregational Church of Hull, England (April); preached the morning sermon as student pastor (Sept 15), continuing as successor to the Rev. John Gardner, pastor

1913 Commencement exit dinner (July 13), Lancashire Independent College, Manchester

1915 Conscientious objector, World War I; YMCA chaplain's assistant, British regiment, European theatre for ten days until wounded and discharged; final exams in philosophy at University of Manchester (June 2-7); received Bachelor of Arts with honors in philosophy from University of Manchester (July); sailed to the United States from Liverpool on the SS *St. Paul*, arriving at Ellis Island (July 11) to visit his fiancée, Agnes Gardner, daughter of the Rev. John Gardner, pastor, New England Congregational Church, Chicago, IL; ordained and installed as minister of First Union Congregational Church, Quincy, IL (Nov 26)

Chronology of the Life of George Arthur Buttrick

1916 Married to Agnes Gardner at New England Congregational Church, Chicago (July 1)

1919–1921 Senior pastor of the Congregational Church, Rutland, VT; birth of first son, John Arthur Buttrick (1919); summer sermons and lectures at the Moody Northfield (MA) Conferences for Women (throughout the 1920s and early 1930s), published in *The Record of Christian Work*

1921–1927 Senior pastor of Old First Presbyterian Church, Buffalo, NY

1923 Naturalized as a US citizen, US District Court, Buffalo, NY (May 3); birth of second son, George Robert Buttrick; one of five upstate New York Presbyterian ministers to organize the formulation of the Auburn Affirmation (1924) for safeguarding "the unity and liberty" of the Presbyterian Church, in successful opposition to the fundamentalists who sought judicial control of the denomination

1927–1954 Senior pastor of New York City's Madison Avenue Presbyterian Church; first sermon, "Christ Our Confidence" (Apr 7); associate professor of pastoral theology at Union Theological Seminary, NY; birth of third son, David Gardner Buttrick (1927)

1928 Preached at churches in England and Scotland (July); *The Parable of Jesus* from sermons and lectures including those at the Moody Northfield Conferences appearing in *The Record of Christian Work*

1931 *Jesus Came Preaching* from the Lyman Beecher Lectures at Yale Divinity School

1934 *The Christian Fact and Modern Doubt* from the Merrick Lectures at Ohio Western University and the Earl Lectures at the Pacific School of Religion

1936 Preached in Protestant churches across the United States during the National Preaching Mission

1939 President, the Federal Council of Churches of Christ in America (1939–1940); "Preaching the Whole Gospel" from his Yale Lyman Beecher Lecture (Apr 8) in *Preaching in These Times* (1940); the Federal Council of Churches presidential radio address to the nation (Sept 8); "peace visit," accompanied by Rabbi Cyrus Adler, president of Jewish Theological Seminary, to President Franklin Roosevelt at the White House (Dec 27) to discuss ending the burgeoning World War II and establish an enduring peace, proposing a US peace delegation to Japan

1942 *Prayer,* the Religious Book Club's January selection, from the Ministers' Week Lectures at the Candler School of Theology, the Ayer Lectures at Colgate-

Chronology of the Life of George Arthur Buttrick

Rochester Divinity School, and the Cole Lectures at the School of Religion of Vanderbilt University

1946 *Christ and Man's Dilemma*, in response to the dropping of the atomic bomb on Japan, from the Summer School Lectures at Union Theological Seminary, NY, the Rockwell Lectures at the Rice Institute of Houston, and the John C. Shaffer Lectures at Northwestern University

1947 Summer in England

1950 Addressed the White House Conference on Children and the World

1951 World tour as the Presbyterian Church's Foreign Mission Board Joseph Cook Lecturer to the Orient, Middle East, and Europe (Sept–Dec); *So We Believe, So We Pray* from lectures at the Ministers' Conference of Texas Christian University, the Ministers' Convocation of the Southern California Council of Churches at the University of Southern California, and the Ministers' Conference of Union Theological Seminary, NY; general editor, *The Interpreter's Bible* (1951–1957)

1952 World tour as the Presbyterian Church's Foreign Mission Board Joseph Cook Lecturer to the Orient, Middle East, and Europe (Jan–Feb); named Churchman of the Year by the Editorial Advisory Board of *Church Management*; published *Faith and Education* from lectures at Austin College

1954–1960 Minister of Harvard University's Memorial Church, Preacher to the University and Plummer Professor of Christian Morals; Plummer Professor Emeritus (1960–1980)

1957 Fellow, American Academy of Arts and Sciences

1959 *Sermons Preached in a University Church* from sermons delivered at Memorial Church

1960–1961 Harry Emerson Fosdick Visiting Professor, Union Theological Seminary, NY; *Biblical Thought and the Secular University* from the Rockwell Lectures at the Rice Institute of Houston

1961–1969 Professor of Preaching, Garrett Theological Seminary, Evanston, IL

1962 Editor, *The Interpreter's Dictionary of the Bible*

1963 Debated Arnold Toynbee on the interpretation of history at Grinnell College, IA; *Christ and History* from the Auburn Lectures at Union Theological Seminary, NY, the Rall Lectures at Garrett Theological Seminary, the William

Belden Noble Lectures at Harvard University, and lectures at Baldwin Wallace College and Colgate-Rochester Seminary

1965 Received Chicago Bible Society's Gutenberg Award for editorship of *The Interpreter's Bible*

1966 *God, Pain, and Evil* from the Earl Lectures at the Pacific School of Religion, the Emory Lectures at Emory University, and the Lowell Lectures at the Lowell Institute of Boston

1968 *The Beatitudes*

1970–1971 Professor of pastoral theology, Vanderbilt Divinity School; *The Power of Prayer Today* (1970)

1972–1978 Roble Lecturer in Christian Preaching at Southern Baptist Theological Seminary and Visiting Lecturer in Homiletics, Louisville Presbyterian Theological Seminary

1973 *To God Be the Glory*, Theodore Gill, ed. (Festschrift honoring Buttrick)

1976 Editor, *The Interpreter's Dictionary of the Bible, Supplementary Volume*

1980 Died in Louisville, KY (January 23), interred in Charlevoix, MI; memorial services at Highland Presbyterian Church, Louisville; Madison Avenue Presbyterian Church, NYC; Memorial Church, Harvard University

Across the Years Buttrick traveled widely throughout the United States and abroad, preaching and lecturing for churches, colleges, universities, seminaries, ministerial conferences, and ecclesiastical assemblies. He received honorary doctorates from Hamilton College (1927), Middlebury College (1930), Yale University (1932), Miami University of Ohio (1934), Albright College (1940), Bethany College (1940), Princeton University (1940), Columbia University (1944), Harvard University (1960), Grinnell College (1963), Northwestern University (1963), Bucknell University (1965), College of Wooster (1967), and Davidson College (1970)

Index

Page numbers for definitions in boldface, figures in italics; period separates roman numeral page numbers from footnote numbers.

Agnew, Spiro, 99, 145
Alston, Wallace McPherson, Jr., 140n20
Altizer, Thomas J. J., 61n9
anxiety, 23, 117, 200; Age of, 134
Apostle's Creed, The, 6, 198
Arnold, Matthew, 119–20
atomic bomb, li, 156, 197, 211
Auden, A. H., 134–35; "It," 146

Bach, Johann Sebastian, *Saint Matthew Passion*, 187
Baptists:
    Anabaptists, 123
    Tennessee, 44
Barrett, William, 175
Barrie, J. M., 69
Barth, Karl, xiv, 5, 52, 54, 55n17;
    The Epistle to the Romans, 54
Bauer, David R., 70
Baumer, Frank L., 135
Beatitudes, the, 7n10, 170;
    The Beatitudes (Buttrick), 212
Beecher Lectures, Lyman, xxiv.n2, xxv, 210
Beethoven, Ludwig van:
    Fourth Symphony, 8

Ninth Symphony, 202
Berdyaev, Nikolai Alexandrovich, 82
Bible, commentaries, 73
bibliolatry, 142, 169
Blake, William, 5, 168
Bonhoeffer, Dietrich:
    and Christ as "the Man for others," 141, 172n91;
    and "worldly Christianity," 55;
    and "worldly faith," 148
Bornkamm, Gunther, 51
Boyd, Malcolm, 52
Bradford, Gamaliel, 33
Briand, Gabriel, 7
Brooke, Rupert, xiv, xxxvi
Brooks, Phillips, 107
Brown, Raymond E., 51, 74
Browning, Robert, 9n19, 10n20, 157–58
Bryce, Lord James, 77
Buddhism, 45, 147
Buechner, Frederick, 69
Bultmann, Rudolf, 15
Bushnell, Horace, 107
Buttrick, Agnes (Gardner), xxvi, xxxii, xxxiv.n45, 209, 210

213

Index

Buttrick, David Gardner, xix, xxvi.
    nn7–11, xxvii.n13nn15–16,
    xxix.nn22–24, xxx.nn26–28,
    xxxi, xxxii.n33, xxxiii.nn39–40,
    xxxiv.n43, xlv.n89, xlviii.n94,
    lxi, 97n22, xlv.nn89–90
Buttrick, George Arthur:
    Albion Congregational Church,
        Hull, England, xxxi, lxiii, 209;
    Auburn Affirmation, 125n5,
        210;
    birthplace, xxv, 209;
    books, front matter, 210–12;
    calling as preacher, xxx;
    children, xxvi.n8;
    Churchman of the Year, 211;
    Cong. Ch., Rutland, VT, xxxii,
        210;
    conscientious objector, pacifist,
        xxvi, xxxii–xxxv, xlix, lii–liii,
        98n23, 144n5, 209;
    daily calendar, xliv–xlviii;
    death, lxiv, 212;
    drawings, xxi;
    Federal Council of Churches,
        president, xlix, 210;
    First Union Cong. Ch., Quincy,
        IL, xxxii.n35, 209;
    Gutenberg Award (Chicago Bible
        Society), 212;
    Harvard University years, liv–lx;
    honorary doctorates, 212;
    interview with Charles Davidson,
        xxxiii.n41, xxxiv.n45, li.n105,
        lii.nn108–9;
    Joseph Cook Lecturer (world
        tour), liv, 211;
    love, as agape, eros, philia, 7–8;
    love notes from Agnes Buttrick,
        lxiii–lxiv;
    Madison Ave. Pres. Ch., NYC,
        210 (see main entry);
    marriage to Agnes Gardner, 210;
    Moody Northfield (MA) confer-
        ences, 210;
    mysticism, his, xlviii;
    national preaching missions, xliv,
        114, 210;
    Old First Pres. Ch., Buffalo, NY,
        xxx.n28, xxxii, 125, 210;
    outside engagements, xliv;
    parents, xxv, xxxi, xxxiii, 209;
    Primitive Methodist beginnings,
        xxv;
    school notebooks, xx;
    sermon worksheet, xl, 75, *79 fig.*;
    SS St. Paul, xxxiv–xxxv, 209;
    university exams, xxxiv–xxxv,
        209;
    US citizenship, 210;
    YMCA chaplain's assistant
        (WWI), xxxiii, 209
Buttrick, Jessie Amelia (Lambert),
    xxxi, 209
Buttrick, John Arthur, xxvi.n8,
    xxxii.n33, 210
Buttrick, Tom, xxxiii, 209

Calvin, John, xl, 127n10
Calvinism, 207n52
Camus, Albert, xiv, lvii, 137, 138,
    139;
    The Fall, 183
capitalism, xxiv, 128, 171
Carlyle, Thomas, 159n4
Carnegie, Dale, 4n4
Cartesian fallacy, 87, 88
Chalmers, Thomas, 102
Chardin, Pierre Teilhard de, 9

214

Index

Christianity:
  competitors of, lvii;
  and gnosticism, 198;
  at Harvard, lvi–lvii;
  "worldly" (Bonhoeffer), 55
Christian Science, 19
Christology (and christological), xvi, xlviii, liii, 9n17, 119n13
chronos, and *kairos*, 121, 155
church: inclusive fellowship, xxiv;
  home of preaching, 154–55
Clark, Adam, 69
Cleopatra, 55
Coffin, Henry Sloan, 60, 80–81, 102
communism, 53, 92n10, 115, 128, 144, 195
Comte, August, lvii, 195
Congregationalism, xxxi, lxiii, 209–10
conscientious objection, xxxii, xxxiii, 144n5
conservatives, xv, 122, 125, 127;
  unconservative, 127
Conwell, Russell, 95n16
Cosby, Frances J., 19n18
Cowper, William, 128n13
Cox, Harvey, 144, 148, 185
criticism:
  biblical, 50;
  form, 5;
  higher and lower, xxxix.n61, 51;
  historical, 15n8
crusaders, the, 36

Danker, Frederick W., 70
Dante (Alighieri), 35, 162n7
Darwin, Charles, 168
Davis, John D., 71

Dennis the Menace, 93
Dewey, John, 196
Dickens, Charles, 88
Dixon, Jeanne, 56, 146
Dostoevsky, Fyodor, 72, 196n9
Dummelow, J. R., 73

economics, xv, lix, 40, 46, 122, 155, 171
education, lix, 24, 30, 135, 155, 184–85, 194, 196;
  Christian, 130–31
Edwards, Jonathan, 107
Eisenhower, President Dwight, 195
Eliot, T. S., 99, 204
Emerson, Ralph Waldo, 57, 180
empire, xliii, 134, 137, 149;
  British, xxiv, xxxiii;
  Roman, lvii, 9, 28, 150, 169–70, 122, 188
Enlightenment, Age of, 134
eschatology, 13, 127, 176, 194, 206
Essenes, the, 6
evangelical, 184n16, 197;
  evangelism, 19, 118, 153;
  revivalism, the enemy of, 19
evil, 4n4, 7, 8, 45, 95, 149n21;
  natural evil, 9;
  and subconscious, 184;
  in systems, 182–84;
  tree of, 185
evolution, 9, 168, 185
expiation (vs. propitiation), 10, 11, 187

Farmer, Herbert, 33–34
Federal Council of Churches of Christ, xlix, 210
First Reformed Church, Albany, NY, 37

Index

Fitzmeyer, Jack, 70
Fletcher, Joseph, 52
Ford, Henry (and motor company), xxxvi–xxxvii
Fosdick, Harry Emerson, xxxviii. n55, xlv, lx, 59, 80, 102, 107, 113, 211
freedom, xxx, 18, 157, 171, 180, 195;
   individual, 129;
   the preacher's, 33, 55, 115;
   and wars, 144
Freud, Sigmund, lvii, 10, 195;
   Freudian doctrine, 145
Frost, Robert, 153n29
Fry, Christopher, 93
fundamentalism, 125n5, 188, 210

Gagarin, Yuri, 92
Gale, Zona, 206
Gardner, John, xxxii, xxxiv.n45, 209
Garrett-Evangelical Theological Seminary (Garrett Biblical Seminary), lx, 211
Gershwin, Ira, *Lady in the Dark*, 180
glossolalia ("speaking in tongues"), 20, 189
gnosticism, 123, 198
God, death of (theology), 61, 138, 199;
   grace of, liii, 5, 190–91; movement, 18
Godspell, 188
Golding, William, 182–83; *Lord of the Flies*, 182
Gore, Charles, 73
gospel:
   of God, 26;
   individual and social, 44, 121–31, 150–52, 170–74;
   preaching of, 3–24;
   as revolutionary, 168–70
Gospel of John (Fourth Gospel), 39, 51, 74, 82, 127n10
Gospels, the (versions), 10, 15, 16, 203n30, 204
grace: amazing, 184, 191;
   "cheap grace," 127, 190;
   of Christ, 36, 42, 84, 126, 137, 184, 185;
   "fruit of the Spirit," 23;
   of God, liii, 5, 63, 135, 181, 190–91;
   general grace, 185–86;
   special grace, 186
Graham, Billy, xv, 21, 122, 150

Hall, Thor, 30, 46n23
Hamilton, William, 61n9
Hamlet, 60, 75
Hampden-Sydney College, xix.n2
Hampton Institute (Virginia), xlii–xliii
Harvard Memorial Church, lvi, lx, 211, 212
Hastings, James, 71n14
Hawthorne, Nathaniel, 180
Heidegger, Martin, 40, 200–201
Henry, Matthew, 12n26
Heraclitus, 133n1
history:
   and Christ Event, 4;
   as Dialogue, liii;
   and progress, 9;
   and resurrection, 9, 16
Hitler, Adolf, xliv–xlv, 122
Holy Spirit, 5, 12, 14, 20, 21–23,

26n4, 27–28, 35–36, 45–46, 50–51, 61, 70, 91, 94, 107, 108, 124, 127, 141, 143, 152, 153, 188;
"indwelling Presence," 20;
the preacher's advocate, 28;
fortifier (strengthener), 22, 28;
and interpreter, 28
homiletics, the new, lxi, 44
Horney, Karen, 117
humanism, lviii, 96, 184, 197

IBM (International Business Machines), 40
idolatry, 200
incarnation (Christ's), 13, 34, 141, 153, 159, 187n22
individualism, 107, 117, 129, 156
Ingersoll, Robert, 207
inspiration: biblical, 50–51, 60; and the Holy Spirit, 70, 188; and literalism, 158
Interpreter's Bible, The (and *Dictionary of*), lviii, 71nn13–14, 74, 211–12
Ionesco, Eugène, 75, 95
Irving, Washington, 203n28

Jefferson, Thomas, 183
Jerome, Jerome K., 205n36
Jesuitism, 137n7;
Jesuitical persecution, 137
Jesus Christ:
church as body of, 20, 56, 112, 119n13, 128, 159, 191;
as Event, liii, 3ff, 13–24, 186–89, 204n34;
focus and meaning of history, liii, 201, 204n34;
and greedy trade, rampant militarism, blind nationalistic pride," 19;
historical (Jesus), the, xl–xli, 27;
"holy man" peddling platitudes, 170;
"I live by his presence" (Buttrick),18;
miracles (and his), xl, 14, 46, 64, 149n21, 187;
"more real to me than I am to myself" (Buttrick), xvi, xlviii, 18;
preacher's authority, xxxviii–xxxix, xliii, xlviii, 35, 188;
sinlessness, his, 7;
"Superstar" (musical), 18;
teacher of spiritual truths, 170;
as vague ideal, lii
John Birch Society, 113, 195
Jones, E. Stanley, 102
Jowett, John Henry, 114

Kafka, Franz, 138, 189
kairos. See *chronos*.
Khrushchev, Nikita, 92
Kierkegaard, Søren, 148
King, Martin Luther, Jr., 150
kingdom of God, xxix, liii, 14, 26, 27, 29, 35, 81, 99, 190, 205;
and the purpose of preaching, 36
Kipling, Rudyard, 35, 83, 106
Koestler, Arthur, 82, 135
Küng, Hans, 52

Lang, Andrew (the Wigtown martyrdom), 22n27
Lear, King, 65–66, 114
Lenin, Vladimir, xv, 46, 122
Levelers (England), 123
Lewis, C. S., 13n1, 119n12

Index

liberalism, 188;
   liberal minds, 125
Life Magazine (and Buttrick), 97
Lincoln, Abraham, 112, 153
Longfellow, Henry Wadsworth, 152n27
Lourdes, and Lady of, 66
Luce, Henry, 97n22
Luther, Martin (and "pernicious dramatics"), 29
lynchings (Alabama), xli–xlii

MacArthur, General Douglas, 32
Macbeth, 106;
   Lady Macbeth, 75, 106
Maclaren, Alexander, 73
MacLeish, Archibald (*J.B.*), 181
Madison Avenue Presbyterian Church (NYC), xvii, xxiii, lv.n116, 60n4, 69n9, 97n22, 102n10, 210
Manchester (Eng.), Lancashire Independent Theological College, xxx, xxxi, 209;
   University of, 209
Marty, Martin, 52
Marx, Karl, 53
Masefield, John, 57–58, 81
Maugham, Somerset, 181n6
Maurus, Rhabanus, 36n33
McLuhan, Marshal, 30
Melville, Herman, 180
Millais, John Everett ("The Martyr of Solway"), 22n27
Miller, Arthur, 146n8;
   Death of a Salesman, 146, 175
Milton, John, 29, 188
Moffatt, James, 73
Morgan, Angela, 173

Morgan, William de, 31
Moseley, Donald, MD, lxiii
Munkácsy, Mihály, 69–69
My Lai (massacre in Vietnam), 98
mysticism, xliii, 26, 45, 147;
   Christian mysticism, 45, 147

National Council of Churches of Christ, 78
National Preaching Mission, xxxviii, 114, 210
New English Bible, The, 62, 70–71;
   and other translations, 71n11
New Yorker, The, 54, 94
Nicodemus, the legend of (Volto Santo), 23, 39, 40
Niebuhr, Reinhold, xlix, lii, 8, 54;
   Faith and History, liii, 54
Nixon, President Richard, xv, 13, 18, 122
Nuremburg trials, 181–82

Orchard, W. E., 60
original sin, 10, 183

Pannenberg, Wolfhart, 52
paradox, xviii, 44, 123, 126, 127, 128, 152, 153, 170, 173;
   Christ as, 140, 186
Parker, Joseph, 73
Pascal, Blaise, 137n7
pastoral care, 111–20;
   and counseling, 116, 180;
   and house-calling ("futility in ringing doorbells"), xxxii, 111, 113, 120
Pax Romana, 122, 157
Peake, James, 73
Peale, Norman Vincent, 4
Pharisees, the, 6, 16, 126, 150n24, 169, 202, 206

philosophy, xxx, xxxiv, xliii, li, lviii, 41, 155, 168, 186, 195, 209
Pizarro, Francisco, 85
Plekhanov, Georgii Valentinovich, 53
politics, xv, lii, 64, 121, 122, 130, 156, 171, 174, 189;
"in the pulpit," 123
Pollock, Channing, 91
Porter, Cole, 146n10
prayer, liii–liv, 22–24, 36, 56–57, 67, 111, 118, 129–30, 152, 160, 164–65, 172, 174;
Prayer, liii–liv, 210;
private prayer, 129, 172
preaching (and sermons):
adjectives and adverbs, 101, 162–63;
Anglo-Saxon words, 101, 162;
as argument, lxii, 5, 32, 39, 46, 137, 175;
commentaries, 69–70;
and communication, 30, 43, 46, 133, 163;
delivery and voice, 103–5;
as dialogue, lxi, lxii, 163;
as drama, 29, 77, 81, 83, 92, 96, 100n5, 175;
as event (and eventful), 43–44;
expository, lxii, 60, 67, 96, and life-situation, 67;
as gospel (every sermon) 130, (cleaves to) 171;
and the hereafter (eschatology), 206–7;
and humor, 70, 78, 85, 91;
illustrations, 87–98, (biblical) 91–92, (autobiographical) 97;
introduction to, 78–80;
and the lectionary, 60, 61, 66, 81, 92, 94, 96, 115;
and manuscript (use of), 102–3;
during national crisis, 96;
new preaching, the, lx, lxii, 37–46;
outlining, 77–86;
and pastoral care, 111–120;
power of, 25–36;
preacher's thoughts, the, 68–69;
pulpit language, 162, 163, 175–76, 180;
purpose and object of, 26, 36;
sermon as "pudding-bowl, igloo, begin-with-an-explosion, airfield runway," xvi, 84;
sermon as "triptik," 38, 77;
sermons with left hand in the world, Bible in right hand, 55;
sermon writing, 99–101;
story-sermons, 96;
text and context, 59–66; true to, 63;
"tools" (various), 70ff;
"under the eyes of the Presence," 85;
worksheets, xl, 75, 79 *fig.*;
and worship, 118–19
Presbyterians:
Auburn Affirmation, 125n5, 210;
Board of Foreign Missions, liv.n115;
Louisville Pres. Theological Seminary, KY, xlvii.n93, lxi, 44n19, 46n23, 212;
Madison Ave. Pres. Ch., NYC, xxiii, xxvi, lv.n116, 60n4, 69n9, 76n43, 97n22, 102n10, 210;

Presbyterians (continued)
    Old First Pres. Ch., Buffalo, NY, xxx, xxxii;
    Pres. Peace Fellowship, liii;
    Second Pres. Ch., Amsterdam, NY, xliv;
    Union Pres. Seminary, xx, xxxiii.n39, lxiv.n145
Primitive Methodism, xxv, xxxi, xxxiii, 114n5, 207n42, 209
psychiatry, 17, 57, 116, 117, 146, 154, 164
purgatory, 203
Pusey, Nathan, lv–lvi

race and racism, xv, xxix, 9, 19, 41, 62, 78, 122, 135, 139, 145, 174, 181, 206;
    "white" and "black" homes, 65
Rain (Colton and Randolph), 181
Reader's Digest, The, 78, 89; *of Books*, 72
Reformation (Protestant), 122, 197n11
Reich, Charles, 53n13
reincarnation (Hindu), 45
Renaissance, the, 134
resurrection, 13–18, 193–207
Riley, James Whitcomb, 185n19
Roberts, Oral, 57
Robinson, John A.T., 61n9, 168n1
romanticism, lix; the new, 147
Roosevelt, President Franklin Delano (FDR), 114, 210
Roth, Philip, 53n12
Rougemont, Denis de, 149
Royce, Josiah, 69
Rubin Jerry, 43
Ruskin, John, 191
Russian revolution, 177

Sadducees, the, 6, 16, 169, 202, 206
Saint Augustine, 107, 127n10, 139, 142
Saint Francis of Assisi, 28, 29n7, 107
Saint Paul, xviii, xxxi, xliii, 19, 20, 21, 24, 25, 29, 34, 36, 38, 42, 51, 56, 104, 107, 108, 112, 119n13, 148, 157, 164, 188, 201
Saint Thomas (apostle), 138–39, 141
Salvation Army, 118
Sartre, Jean Paul, 168, 205
Scherer, Paul, 107
Schweitzer, Albert, xl–xli
science, xxxix, lvii, lix, 11, 16, 40, 87, 95, 118, 143–44, 147, 155, 156, 164, 168, 175, 177, 180, 186, 189, 191, 194, 195, 196;
    scientism, 143–44, 152, 180
Shakespeare, William, 35n31, 55n15, 59n1, 60n3, 66n28, 74–75, 99, 106n17, 175
Shaw, George Bernard, li, 4, 179, 182
sin, xlix, l, lii, liii, 7–12, **8 def.**, 179–84, 187, 188;
    national, xlix, l;
    original, 10, 183;
    sinlessness (of Jesus), 7;
    sinners, lii, 190, 194, 198n13, 199;
    sin-scarred, xxxviii; venial, xxvii
skepticism(s), xxxix, 16–17, 36, 61, 133–42;
    and the Bible, 137–38, 162
Smith, George Adam, 73

Index

Smylie, James H., xx
social gospel, 44, 121, 124, 150, 171
soul, 123–24;
 and body, 126;
 as self or personhood, 123, 151–52
Southern Baptist Theological Seminary, xlvii, lxi, 34n24, 44n19, 46n23, 212
Spengler, Oswald, 168
"spiritualist" cults, 189
Stevenson, Robert Lewis, 80
Stewart, George, 12nn28–29
Stewart, James, 41, 104
Stoics, the, 38
Sullivan, Harry Stack, 117

Tate, Allen, 183
technology, 144, 155, 189
Tennyson, Alfred Lord, 128n12, 130n17, 197n10, 207n44
Throckmorton, Burton H., 71
Tillich, Paul, xiv, 90–91, 107, 117, 200n20
Tittle, Ernest Fremont, 114
Toffler, Alvin and Heidi ("future shock"), 38, 53
Toynbee, Arnold, 211

underground church, 28, 52, 131
Underhill, Evelyn, 45n21
Union Theological Seminary (NYC), xlix, lx, 76n43, 91n7, 102nn10,12, 201n20, 210, 211
United Reformed Church (England and Wales), *Book of Services*, 131n18

Vahanian, Gabriel, 61n9
Vanderbilt Divinity School, lv.n120, lxi, 183n11, 211, 212
Vietnam War, xv, lii, 9n18, 10, 20, 30n12, 33, 43n15, 44, 89, 98n23, 111, 130, 144, 204
virgin birth, 45

war(s):
 all, 135, 136, 137, 144–45, 151, 162;
 Vietnam War, xv, lii, 9n18, 10, 20, 30n12, 33, 43n15, 44, 89, 98n23, 111, 130, 144, 204;
 World War I, xxxii–xxxv, 209;
 World War II, xlvii, xlix, lxiii, 32n19, 111n1, 181n7, 210
Warren, Robert Penn, 183
Warwick, Dionne, 45
Webster, Daniel, 104
Wesley, Charles, 34n25;
Wesley, John (and Wesleyan Methodism), xxix, xl, 34n25, 42, 69n6, 125n5, 161
Whitman, Walt, 180, 207n42
Wilder, Thomas, 176
Williams, Charles, 20, 118, 119n13
Williams, Tennessee, 75
Wittgenstein, Ludwig, 174–75
worship:
 and drama, 29;
 and gallows, 11;
 and pastoral care, 118–20;
 and preaching, 130–31;
 sterile, 147

Zealots, the, 6, 169